On The Action Of Examinations Considered As A Means Of Selection

Henry Latham

ON THE ACTION

OF

EXAMINATIONS

CONSIDERED AS A MEANS OF SELECTION

BY

HENRY LATHAM, M.A.

FELLOW AND TUTOR OF TRINITY HALL, CAMBRIDGE.

BOSTON

WILLARD SMALL

1886

PREFACE.

My chief object in writing this book has been to introduce some approach to method in the way of regarding the action of Examinations. This action is complex, and from want of analysis confusion has sometimes arisen, as I have pointed out at the beginning of Chapter v. I must warn the reader that this book is not intended as a manual of the art of examining, but as an enquiry as to what we want to effect by Examinations, and how far we can succeed. The *art* of examining has made great progress of late. Government as well as University Examinations are now conducted with great skill, and we owe to the former various valuable expedients in the way of marking, allowing alternative questions, and the like, to which I have referred in Chap. ix., on "Marking and Classing."

I should have spoken more particularly than I have done of the Examination for Selection for Indian Civil Service appointments, had not a change in the Regulations as to age been announced while this book was in progress, which will require a fresh plan of Examination.

The changes in the mode of setting and marking the papers which have been made from time to time have remedied many of the evils which existed when I began to write. Half of the Selected Candidates may be considered to take their stand on subjects which result in a practical power, like Classics or Mathematics, and if this power is attained there can be little fault to find with the teaching, wherever it be got.   With those, however, who only just succeed, and with the many who fail, the educational effects are still undesirable.   A weak man, under the paramount necessity of getting 1200 marks, must "take up" what yields an immediate return, though the diversity may be distracting to him, and his mental build may be such that he should beware of over-loading his memory.

Selection by competitive Examinations has many advantages, but it is open to one deep-lying objection. In the proper education of youth for active careers, such as is received at a good school, instruction and acquirement are much, but very far from all, while for a competitive Examination they are everything.   The boy, to obtain the full good out of a healthy school-life, besides getting knowledge, ought to grow in character, to gain the power "of doing the thing he would," and of "getting on" with other human beings in various relations.   No one expects Examinations to test this, but we look to find a fair share of these qualities in our candidates, in addition to the acquirements actually tested.   But the Examination may lead to a system of training which checks the growth of those qualities which we hoped our selected candidates would possess as largely as other people.   Boys taken out of school-life at fifteen, and stimulated by a morbid concentration of interest on one point, do not expand symmetrically—they have become learners and nothing else. Now we particularly want genial and harmoniously developed young men, and this we can only get by ensuring a genial education. The difficulties in England in the way of giving a preference to certain modes of education are great. The most practicable course which I see is, to adopt a system of *sifting* the candidates by distinctions which should have been previously gained in School, in Local Examinations, or in those of the First Year at a University: money is now wasted by parents on the preparation of youths whose case is hopeless. Certain shortcomings have been remarked in the Selected Candidates which are such as would arise from the cause just indicated, and it has been proposed to induce them to resort to a University after being selected. During this time they would be so engaged in their Oriental studies that they would be isolated from the rest of the University. They might possibly gain "social advantages," though if they felt themselves specially sent to look for them they would be less likely to find them. If at the age of 17 or 18 they could reside for a year at a University, aiming at the Class in the annual Examinations which should entitle them to compete for Selection, they would then become genuine partakers in University life, they would enter into the University spirit, and, if selected, after the two subsequent years of technical studies they might be enabled in proper course to take a University degree (see Appendix C).

I had to consider whether I should conceive myself as addressing professional readers only, in which case much explanation could be spared, or as addressing a wider circle. I have adopted the latter course, because society is now generally interested in Examinations, and it is desirable that their action and the value of their results should be properly understood. When too much value is attached to a place in an Examination list, candidates are rendered morbidly anxious by their fear of disappointing their friends, and teachers are forced, for their credit, to convey something that can be displayed in an Examination, even though, as is especially the case with young boys, the proper course of teaching must be interfered with to effect this object. On the other hand, when the verdict of Examinations is slighted, as has happened sometimes since the reaction against them began, young people harden themselves against the rightful punishment of their inattention by disparaging the instrument which reveals their deficiencies. The more just and discriminating public opinion becomes on these points, and the better it is understood what the decision of an Examination is worth, the less disturbing the action of Examinations will be.

This book has been long in hand, and owing to my College engagements it has been very interruptedly pursued; indeed a portion of it has been in print for some time. I fear that some repetition may occur from this cause, but I have now and then designedly repeated a remark rather than weary the reader with constant references. Besides, some readers may only want to refer to a single chapter. I have found it one of the difficulties in the way of putting this subject into shape, that many of the things that had to be said might be introduced equally well under several heads. The subject does not supply a natural order in the mode of dealing with it.

I had originally intended, instead of confining myself mainly to the action of Examinations as a means of Selection, to consider them also as appliances in Education, but I found that the book grew in size, and that circumstances made it desirable that it should appear at once: I hope however to pursue the subject hereafter. I have only touched slightly here on Pass Examinations, because they serve but little as tests. They affect education widely, and call for thorough consideration from this point of view.

The historical portion of my book is subservient to my main object. I have related the growth of our Mathematical Tripos at Cambridge in order to illustrate the working of the principles I wanted to make clear. I have acknowledged my obligations to my authorities, I believe, from time to time in my notes; but I must here mention specially the assistance I have derived from Dr. Whewell's books on Education, from Dr. Peacock's work on the Statutes of the University, from certain tracts on University matters in the works of Dr. Jebb, who was Tutor of St. Peter's College about a century ago, and, in my third Chapter especially, to Mr. Mullinger's *History of the University of Cambridge.* I find that I was misled in attributing the story of "Ego currit" passing for grammar among students of the middle ages — to Roger Bacon (p. 85). My friend Mr. Luard, the Registrary of the University of Cambridge, has pointed it out to me in the *Annals of Osney*, in the 4th Vol. of *Annales Monastici*, published by the Master of the Rolls.

Like most persons engaged in Education, I am under the deepest obligation to Dr. Carpenter for the instruction derived from his excellent work on Mental Physiology; and I am also much indebted to the Dean of Lincoln, to Mr. Henry Sidgwick, to Mr. Sayce, to Mr. Wilson of Rugby, as well as to various writers in the Quarterly Journal of Education, for valuable information and suggestions.

I have made large use of the Evidence given to the University Commissions of 1854–60, and I have thought it so desirable that the views of the Royal Commission on Scientific Instruction and the advancement of Science should be accessible to my readers, that I have given large extracts from their Third Report, issued in 1873, in the form of an Appendix.

TRINITY HALL, CAMBRIDGE,
August, 1877.

CONTENTS.

CHAPTER I.

INTRODUCTORY.

CHAPTER II.

GENERAL VIEW OF THE ACTION OF EXAMINATIONS.

CHAPTER III.

HISTORICAL NOTICES. DISPUTATIONS.

CHAPTER IV.

THE CAMBRIDGE MATHEMATICAL TRIPOS.

CHAPTER V.

THE FUNCTIONS OF EXAMINATIONS. SELECTION
(*on score of ability*).

CHAPTER VI.

EXAMINATIONS AS A TEST OF KNOWLEDGE.

CHAPTER VII.

PRIZE EMOLUMENTS IN EDUCATION.

CHAPTER VIII.

EXAMINATIONS FOR COLLEGE FELLOWSHIPS AND SCHOLARSHIPS.

CHAPTER IX.

ON MARKING AND CLASSING.

CHAPTER I.

INTRODUCTORY.

WITHIN the last thirty years the agency of Examinations has worked a revolution in the whole province of Education.

Examinations more or less competitive now stand at the entrance to many professions; they are the only means of access to Military, Naval or Civil Service appointments; and both at school and college valuable monetary help is to be acquired by success in the examination-room. The result is that a clever boy begins to earn his livelihood when he is about fourteen. To excel in examination is a profitable art; it may be called a Profession in itself, and parents and sons consider together as to the best training for this professional course and the best markets for attainments. Young people have often a keener perception in such matters than their fathers have, and thus one indirect effect of this system is to bring about what has been remarked as a feature of our time — the growing independence of parental authority on the part of the rising generation. Such independence in the case of an able youngster who is thus beginning to earn his own bread may not be injurious; he may be of too fine a nature to fail in filial respect or affection; but this independent spirit may spread to others so as to weaken authority in a way that we should lament. I have touched on this point, because it shews how Examinations make their influence felt in regions which seem out of their domain.

I shall hereafter shew how an Examination system is from its nature an encroaching power, how it influences the prevalent views of life and work among young men and how it affects parents, teachers, the writers of educational books, and the notions of the public about education. But before proceeding further, we have to draw some distinctions with a view of arriving at something like order in dealing with a very tangled subject. Examinations are used for many purposes, and many of the difficulties and evils connected with their use arise from the attempt of those who frame the Examinations, either to effect too many things by one instrument; as, for instance, to pick out the most proficient, to reject the dunces, and to give an impetus to a certain kind of study all by the same series of papers; or from their not having a clear view of what they are aiming at.

We may discriminate two kinds of action as being very distinct, and though most examinations will act more or less in both ways at once, yet we can consider the two kinds of action separately; and it will be serviceable to us, in this rough attempt to consider Examinations systematically, to lay down two heads of classification, according to the object for which they are especially used.

We shall have then:

(1) That in which the object is to select the most suitable persons for a certain purpose, or the men of most general ability.

(2) That in which the object is purely educational.

The view of Examinations which has led to their great extension of late is that which is placed under head (1). From the success at the Universities of Examinations as a means of awarding distinctions and emoluments with perfect impartiality, they were brought into use as a means of disposing of all kinds of appointments. It was not taken into consideration that this instrument, which on the whole seemed to decide so justly, was acting at the Universities under particular conditions ; that it dealt only with young men who were under similar circumstances, and had had nearly similar advantages, and that the branches of study to which it had been so successfully applied were those which resulted in the power of *doing* something, — that of translating a dead language for instance, or of working out problems and explaining physical phænomena ; and which in consequence could be readily tested; and that it had not been applied to a mass of young men prepared in very different ways, or to subjects, like history and literature, where the candidate gains information and general cultivation, but no power of *doing* anything which can be exercised in an examination, excepting that of transferring what he has read to the paper before him.

I shall hereafter have to speak further of this distinction between the studies which endow the pupil with a power of doing something he could not do before, and those which simply add to his knowledge. It will be found that the action of examinations is different when applied to subjects of one or the other of these classes.

Until within the last few years Examinations were entirely in the hands of educational bodies, and though they were used for purposes of classification, or selection, still they were mainly fashioned with a view to the object specified under head (2).

The mere saying of a lesson, or the week's repetition, is in fact the rudiment of the examination viewed educationally. The examination at the end of each school-time is a powerful instrument in the hands of the teacher; it concentrates attention, it forces the student to carry a whole book, or a whole subject in his head at once, and it acts as a powerful stimulant; it gives the boys an object to work for; they work to do well in the examination, they look no further than this, and there is no need that they should do so; but the teacher so arranges the subjects of study and the papers, that he who most steadily works with a view to success, shall get the most good, both in the way of knowledge and of intellectual training.

It will be of service to fix precisely the meanings in which the terms Liberal and Technical Education will be used. These two phrases are commonly employed so loosely as to be useless where precision is required. I propose then to use them in a rigorous sense; premising that most Liberal Educations are so far Technical that they enable a man to do something which he could not do before, and most Technical Educations are Liberal ones also in so far as they really improve the man, by disciplining his attention and forcing him to care and accuracy; moreover it has a good moral effect on a youth to feel that he has acquired a mastery over matter, or the power of doing something which is of service to other people.

I propose, however, to limit the terms as follows: —

An education is liberal so far as it concerns itself with the good and the cultivation of the pupil; valuing any accomplishment it may give him, for the new perceptions it opens out, for the new powers it confers, or for any other good it may do the man, and not regarding the work produced: Liberal Education would like to make a man an artist, that he may have a delightful occupation, and acquire an eye for beauty and for truth; she would like him to paint well, because this would shew the possession of such an eye and many other qualities as well, but she would not care much about the pictures themselves; she would not care a bit whether his pictures were valuable or not.

An education so far as it is technical is careful not for the workmen but for the work: Technical Education wants to get good pictures, and she only values any qualities of an artist so far as they conduce to this end. She aims at moulding the man into a perfect instrument for a particular purpose.

The general adoption of a system of competitive Examinations in the subjects which have usually been supposed to belong to a Liberal Education has tended to combine more completely in practice these two kinds of education, which were already to some extent combined by the nature of the case.

A young man has to present himself for an important examination on a certain day, a list of subjects is given him with the number of marks assigned to each, and the number required to ensure success is pretty well understood. His tutor has a limited time for preparation. The problem before him is therefore very different from that of simply doing what is best for the pupil. The tutor must consider not what studies or what kind of teaching will do him most good, but what studies will yield the highest aggregate in the given time, and he must teach his pupil each subject not with a view to call out his intelligence, but with a view to producing the greatest show on a stated day; for instance he must teach him a language

by some sort of Ollendorff process, which shall address itself to the ear and the memory, rather than by
a method which involves any grammatical analysis;
while in mathematics he must teach him such operations as can be performed by a sort of general *recipe*.
The tutor must turn the qualities of the pupil, such
as they may be, to the best account he can in point
of *marks*. He cannot try to remedy any mental defects, there is not time enough for any such undertaking to yield profit; he must make the most of such
qualities as the pupil has; in the case of one who is
tolerably quick but mentally self-indulgent and re-
pelled by the first serious difficulty, he must, instead
of forcing him to face the fancied giants in his path,
humor his weak points and make the most of his
strong ones, and he must direct him to take up several
subjects which require no further power than that of
carrying matter for a short time — a useful one indeed
in many callings, but which is sure to find all the exercise it wants; in short, the tutor in such a case has
to look to the work that can be turned out, more than
to the effect of the training on the producer; that is
to say, the spirit of technical teaching enters very
largely into the education given, though the subjects
may be those used for a liberal education.

Those who afford this kind of preparation are often
called crammers. Now so far as this term implies
any opprobrium it is unjustly applied; a market has
been opened for a particular kind of slight fabric, the
stouter and costlier stuffs are thereby rendered less
saleable, and the mill-owner must meet the popular
demand or close his mills. People are hardly aware how
thoroughly the educational world is governed by the
ordinary economical rules. While employing the mo-

tives of gain and advancement most profusely, the public seems to find fault with teachers and pupils for being influenced by these considerations,—they set young men to run a race, and then wonder that they run not to improve their *physique* but simply to win— they make learning a marketable commodity and then complain that it is grown for the market, and that few are now influenced by a pure devotion to science. All teachers would rather educate than cram. It is painful to them to say, " You must get off this list of authors and their works by heart. I know it will do you no good. I know that the words Drayton's *Poly- olbion* or Evelyn's *Sylva* convey to you no more mean- ing than if they were the names of Gasteropods, but they will probably be asked for to-morrow." Many of these men are fighting hard to retain their self- respect under the adverse circumstances in which they are placed; but to fight single-handed against a sys- tem enforced by official Examinations is to cease to be a tutor at all.

The words cram and crammer, as Mr. Todhunter observes,* are sometimes loosely used, and sometimes serve as a bugbear to raise a cry against some kind of teaching. This is frequently true when they are used by writers, but when used by a pupil or an under- graduate he means something very definite; he is the individual who wears the shoe, and such I have generally found can usually be trusted both when they tell you where it pinches, and where they find it best to cut a hole to make it easy. So when a youth says he has left a tutor's and gone to a "crammer's" in London to prepare for "his Army Exam.," he is sensible of a real difference; he does not mean any

* *The Conflict of Studies, and other Essays.* Macmillan and Co., 1873.

personal disrespect, but he looks on the latter person more as he would on a music master or a French master, as a person who has nothing to do with educating him as a moral or reasonable being, but whose business is to endow him with some one accomplishment; which in this case is that of being able to answer so many printed questions on a particular day.

The case just considered leads us to another point, which is very important in considering the operation of Examinations, and which especially affects the spirit in which the teacher works. It makes all the difference whether the teaching is subordinate to the Examination or the Examination to the teaching. One or the other is usually "given," to use the mathematical term, and the other has to be adapted to it. As long as Examinations were conducted only in schools and Universities, the educational effects were kept well in view, and the range of the Examinations was made to correspond with that of the work. The teachers of course would not be the actual examiners, but they would be part of the governing body who arranged the scheme of Examination, and would set themselves to put right any point in which the system acted injuriously on the course of reading. In these cases the Examination is subordinate — or rather was so, for, as I have said, its power is spreading far and wide — and its influence may be unexceptionable.

It is, however, essential for any public competitive Examination that it should be dissociated from any particular system of instruction, and that the particulars of it should be made known by timely notice. This notice determines the reading of the candidates all over the country, they will, if they can, obtain copies of the examination papers, — even if they were not published, imperfect copies would get abroad or particular information would be got from former candidates, so that publication is the fairest course — and having these papers and the notice, the pupil can determine on his own course of reading, and the tutor feels that he is no longer really directing his studies. Here then the Examination is supreme. If the tutor go ever so little beyond the prescribed subjects, the pupil will say, "That does not come in," and the tutor is hampered, and feels that he is no longer the educator. He becomes like a Professor in a French Lyceum, who is bound to prepare the students to pass in a certain "Cours" according to a detailed Programme, and who is apt to grow disgusted at the mechanical nature of his employment. This feeling has produced very disastrous effects in French education, and we should be careful not to break down the independence of the teacher; with it will go his love for his work and his faith in it.

How to adjust the balance so as to afford the teacher such independence as to let him give play to his individual turn, and claim a full share of attention for that study which he can throw his heart most into, without handing over a school or a class altogether to one master or one professor; how to provide by the examination just so much control over the teacher as shall prevent him from slurring over one part of a subject and unduly exaggerating the importance of another; or save him from sinking into negligence or indifference under the insidious temptation of having his work subject to no external test, — of being able to say, as a foreign professor did, contrasting his position with our Cambridge ways, "At . . . . . *I* am the Senate-House," — is a question which I shall treat of hereafter. I cannot promise a solution, but I may set people in the way of searching for one.

I have already spoken of Examinations as an encroaching power : the way in which their influence spreads is very remarkable.   Directly an examination is introduced into a school or college course in one subject, we find that the general interest is attracted so largely to that subject, that there is a danger of its starving the other subjects.   Hence subject after subject is brought under its range, and if Examinations leading to valuable prizes or privileges are introduced at all, it will soon be found necessary to comprise the whole work of the school or college in this range. Thus it is that Examinations, which originally gained their repute when applied to studies which resulted in a practical power, have been lately applied to subjects of mere information, where their operation is more uncertain, and their influence more questionable.

There may be subjects so ill adapted for the purposes of Examination, that it may not only be extremely difficult to test attainment in them, or to test ability by means of them, by questions on paper, but, though the subject may be of the highest value for purposes of mental cultivation, it may lose a great deal of this efficiency by being put into the *form* required to render it available for an examination ; for this new power is very tyrannical as to the shape in which it will have its aliment presented.   Take for instance English Literature.   It is very instructive for a small party to read a play of Shakespeare together, where each individual may be encouraged to dwell on any ideas suggested by the author; and where all feel at liberty to stray into critical discussion, and to use the Greek or French drama for illustration or comparison.   But if there is an Examination in prospect, and the subject has to be got up for the Indian or the Army Examination, no such easy or discursive treatment is possible. The pupils cannot afford time to stray beyond the limits of probable questions. No Greek or French can be fairly set in an English paper, where English is weighed against Greek and French as separate subjects. Especially there is no use in dwelling on any thought suggested by the author. "My thoughts," says the student, "are sure not to be set;" and so when he reads by himself he does not encourage himself to half close the book when a thought strikes him, and linger over it, and make a pencil note to arrest the idea—and yet this is the way in which half our mental wealth comes. What he has to do is to get up the Historical Introduction and the notes to the hard passages and perplexing allusions, and to know the context of familiar quotations, and the derivation of unusual terms. This sort of philo-logical study has its value no doubt; many students will take more interest in literature even so treated, than in many other kinds of work, but it is a different study from that which peoples a young man's mind with the creations of great writers.*

But we are in this dilemma: if we do not examine in English Literature it will be absolutely unknown; for an impending Examination is a jealous master—it absorbs all the intellectual energy of its servants. An anxious candidate would think it a piece of profligate dissipation to read a book requiring any close atten-tion that did not bear on his task. Young people now will not read Shakespeare, hardly even Byron or Walter Scott, in play-hours at school; and this is more espe-cially the case since these authors — who were our own

* Students who have been attending Lectures in English with interest, when the Ex-amination is at a distance, will say within three or four months of the struggle, that they can no longer afford to treat one subject so fully, and that they must get up their "Manual."

pleasant companions on winter evenings or summer afternoons—have been included in the lists of subjects for Examinations; they have thereby become lessons, and got to be regarded by the schoolboy as having gone over to the enemy altogether.

Here then we see that this system is like an irresistible power extending her dominion over provinces some of which are the better and some the worse for her sway, but for the latter, at present, no escape is apparent; and all that seems left is by careful adjustment and by getting an insight into the workings of this system and its effects immediate and remote to minimise the evils it brings with it.

There are many subsidiary influences which favor the spread of Examinations. We live in a time when we want to outdo one another and to have our doings known. Half the value of any kind of excellence consists in its being declared to the world, — the score of a cricketer, and the bag of a sportsman on the moors are duly recorded—and more is thought of outdoing a neighbor than of enjoying the pastime. The mischief of the athleticism now prevailing does not lie so much in the time given to active exertion, as in the undue importance attached to these matters by the public and the press. In the same way, the value of a high place in an Examination list comes from publicity;—it goes very easily into a newspaper, and though the exact amount of honor is not well understood, relatives make much of seeing a youngster's name high in a class list; the credit of a school is upheld by the distinction of its pupils in public Examinations, and pressure is thereby laid on the master to direct their studies with a view to such success. Further, a youth feels a stimulus in reading for Examinations, something akin to that aroused in a game; he is pitting his wits against those of his competitors—the darling spirit of combat so powerful in English lads is called to the help of the instructor ;—more than this, he feels also that he is struggling with his examiner—a much more questionable kind of contest—and he gets to pride himself on a faculty of divining, as he goes on, what is and is not likely to be set.

When once a young man thus gets habituated to have his work seasoned by this sense of being on the search for weapons which he is at once to bring to bear in an actual contest, he will find any study that lacks this condiment very insipid; he will be like the whist-player of a London club set down to play for penny points in a family rubber. He may try to force himself to his work, he may really wish to acquire the language or the professional study before him, but the comparative remoteness of the return will deaden his interest. He has been used to look for *points*, to regard every effective little bit of information, every new mathematical artifice or short method as something that was to give him an advantage in a passage of arms which he had in view, and when this is gone his work seems for a time to have neither savor nor salt. This feeling affects men in different degrees ; sometimes it soon passes away, as when a man goes into active life and interests of another kind are awakened ; in other cases, especially when there is no natural love of intellectual exertion, it gives a permanent distaste for study, — and as far as my observation goes, the later in life the Examination system is continued, and the more subjects are embraced in it, the more serious the effect is.

From this it follows that when once we begin to employ the stimulant of Examinations, we cannot do without it so long as the process of education lasts. Now this like all stimulants requires very careful handling, and the temptation to excessive use is great : judiciously applied it may carry on the student until the genuine interests of a professional career supply the requisite motives for exertion, and artificial aids may be given up.   Hence Examinations have a tendency to prolong the duration of their sway as well as to extend its bounds, and much injury may be done by subjecting men whose intellects are already mature — men who ought to give their minds free play and who might engage in original research — to the cramping effect of Examinations.

For young people, the advantages of Examinations outweigh the ills ; for full-grown men the balance inclines the other way.   A kind of Examination, it is said, should be found suitable to their case, and no doubt one kind may be less objectionable than another, but I know of none that is quite satisfactory : the spirit with which a man works whose object is display in an Examination, is different from that of a man who is engaged in doing good conscientious work, from devotion to a study of his own choosing.   A man of four or five and twenty is hampered by a sense of never-ending pupillage, if an Examination is hanging over him ; he longs to be doing his work for himself only.

It was something less than twenty years ago, about the time when the statutes of the Universities were being recast, that the world was so mightily taken with its new panacea of competitive Examinations. An attempt was made to introduce special Examinations apart from those of the University for the awarding of Fellowships to Graduates ; at Cambridge happily without much success.   It was seen that it was not good to keep a man in an expectant and unsettled state for some years after his degree, and that such a system favored those who had some private fortune, as compared with those who had to maintain themselves by tuition.

At that time most persons in public positions overlooked the important bearing of Examinations on education: they regarded them simply as a touchstone. It was thought that you could test "merit" by examining a man just as you might find his weight by putting him into the scales, and that one operation had no more effect on the constitution than the other. Besides, at that time it was argued that even if there were any educational effects they did not concern the selecting bodies. Our business, they said, is simply to get the best men we can: the education is your matter. They were like the oculist of the old school, who said, "There is a speck in your eye, and I must give you calomel till it is absorbed." "But about my liver?" said the patient. "That is not my business," replied the oculist. An oculist now would see that, to get the eye right, he must not lose sight of the general health of the patient. And in the same way, I trust that it is now understood that, merely with the view of securing for the state the best servants possible, we must not so frame our Examinations as to damage the general tone of the education of the country.

A reaction is already springing up with regard to Examinations, and we may have to guard against an equally unwise and indiscriminating disfavor. Now and then a novel and potent agent is brought forward in the medical world, and young practitioners will prescribe the fashionable drug or treatment in all kinds of cases. Eventually it is ascertained that this nostrum, when used habitually, ruins the constitution, and it is found that, besides its direct and recognized action, this specific has remote and indirect effects of a serious nature; these are not found out for some time, and in the meanwhile it is employed as if it were the safest thing in the world. But when disastrous effects have been brought home to it a reaction comes about, and the panacea falls into a discredit which it did not deserve; used by proper hands, in proper cases and proper doses, it might have been a very valuable therapeutic. Something like this is beginning to come about with regard to Examinations.

People cry out against the over-stimulation of the existing system, and they forget the complete stagnation of mind in which the ordinary British dunce spent his life after he had escaped from the hands of his schoolmaster. Some of us may recollect what the young men were who used to hang about "waiting for their commission;" or even what the Pass-men were formerly at the Universities in the long, undisturbed interval between "Little-go" and Degree. We may recollect, too, to turn to a higher class of men, that when the Indian Examinations were first introduced, and men were sent in to examination without any immediate preparation, those places of education which furnished lectures only without final examinations were unsuccessful, the work of candidates from such places was most usually *loosely* done; this drove these educating bodies to introduce special classes and examinations, which have been attended with results as good as they could have hoped for.

But the prevalence of Examinations affects the education not only of those who are going to be examined but also of those who are not. If there are at a tutor's

two sets of boys, one going to be examined shortly
and the other not so, the former will say to the latter,
"Why should you bother yourselves when you have
nothing to work for?" The notion of improvement
has disappeared with the former under the action of
the more cogent motive, and the others soon catch
the idea that they had better make the most of their
good fortune in not having, to use their own slang
phraseology — for Examinations have acquired a slang
of their own — "to grind for an Exam." And as the
former are eager for all the help the tutor can give
them, while the latter are indifferent, and as the tutor
feels that the welfare of the former and his own credit
rest on their success, while for the others there is no
immediate pressure, he can hardly help bestowing
more energy and thought, even though he distribute
his time equally, on those who are working with most
zeal and whose case is most urgent. The same influence is felt at schools, though in a less degree.

Hence, even if a youth be not intended for a career
for which an Examination is required, it may be
necessary to keep some such ordeal before him, that
he may not revel in the immunity, which is brought
into such strong light by contrast with the forced
labor of his companions. To have separate establishments for Examinees and non-Examinees would en-
tail still worse evils; you would have the plums in
one cake and the dough in another. It is easily seen
then from how many causes and in how many ways
the extension of a system of Examinations is ensured
when it has once taken a firm hold.

It remains for us to inquire why such a system
should have established itself, particularly in our own
time. It did not come about by the arbitrary act of

any person or of any educational body, it grew up ; but there must have been some reason for such an abnormal growth. A stray plant will not run over a whole country unless there be something in the soil or the climate which especially suits it. What elements, then, are there in the temper and in the condition of the times we live in, which have so fostered this new system ? What are the new needs which Examinations are found, or are thought, to fulfil ?

This inquiry will lead us to some general views on the nature of the agency which Examinations exert, and in the discussion of these we shall arrive at some sort of answer to the above queries.

CHAPTER II.

EXAMINATIONS do for young people what the contest of life does for men. It is the struggle of man with man for eminence or power or money that develops energy, and forces each individual to make the most of that which is in him. The struggle may seem to be for power or for gain, but it is not only for these, there is a charm for most natures in the struggle itself, man is "framed to battle with his kind." Many persons would feel that an interest would be taken out of their lives if by any means they dropt at once into a position which they were in the way to win by a fair fight. Some no doubt exhaust themselves by overstriving, and they tax circumstances, or the high pressure of the times, with the mischief consequent on what they call overwork, but which more frequently is overworry, and is more due to their own habits of mind than to anything external. On the whole however the struggle of each man towards the front is as good for him as it is for society at large; it keeps him vigorously exercising his powers, and from such exertion he gets a fuller sense of life. What is true of the great conflict is also true of the minor contests in which young people learn their relative strength.

With the young and healthy there is a redundancy of this combative spirit; the pleasure of all sports and games comes from the gratification of it, and Education must take it into account if she would fit herself to the nature of those she teaches. A few boys out of a thousand will have a turn of mind so abstract, that they will find all the contest they want in a struggle with a hard problem or an intricate passage; but the great body of young people require concrete antagonists. We know how hard it is to put any life into a young man's work if he is being educated by himself and does not look forward to any struggle. We sometimes hear people grieve that youths are urged on by a spirit of outdoing one another and not by a love of improvement; this spirit no doubt should be kept within bounds, it should be kept healthy and chivalrous, by the tone inspired by the teacher and by such arrangements of the Examinations and prizes as may best exclude sordid considerations and personal antagonism. But before we expect young men in general to do steady work without the stimulus of emulation or the prospect of reward, we ought to ask ourselves whether we find that their seniors usually labor in professions without being influenced in some degree by similar motives. No doubt men must love their work more or less in order to do it thoroughly, just as no youth will do well in any study unless he have some genuine interest in it, but this love and this interest do not come all at once, and meanwhile a motive is wanted. Moreover, without ambition or the need of making a livelihood few men will endure the routine which enters into all professional courses. Many might indeed do amateur work of some kind just as many young men would engage in some desultory study, passing lightly over what is distasteful; but few will either work or study in a thoroughly business-like way without some inducement beyond the satisfaction of the work itself. Do statesmen or barristers or physicians pursue their courses without any stimulus either from the love of triumph or of distinction or of gain? Out of the thousands of men in England who by their wealth are freed from the need of professional toil there are a certain number who devote themselves to some noble end, to philanthropic or scientific or literary work, but these answer to those few boys who delight in the abstract triumph over difficulties and the acquisition of learning for its own sake: while the majority of men do not engage in either work or study, but are content with the occupations that fall in their way; — how then can we look to boys to do what men will not do?

We must consider this matter a little further. In education we commonly aim at effecting two things, we want in some sort to discipline the mind and also to fit it up. By fitting it up, I do not mean the merely storing it with dead matter, with information, but also the furnishing it with machinery which it can set to work at pleasure. The power of speaking a new language, of seeing in the mind the way in which forces are acting in any case of motion, of referring at sight a bird or a plant to its proper order, these are mental capabilities which are analogous to practical accomplishments, such as swimming and skating, which once acquired remain by us for life.

Some branches of study are especially valuable for the first of these purposes, for training the mind and giving a man the use of his brains, while others are chiefly important for the accomplishments in which they result, and some combine both sorts of advantage. Now many boys will see the value of the studies which yield them new capabilities, and will pursue these with some good will for their own sake, but very few will devote themselves of their own accord to subjects which do not result in such capabilities, however valuable they may be for mental discipline; they will usually say that such subjects are of no use. Now, in fact, method and good mental habits are more valuable than particular acquirements, because they are part of the individual's self, while the others are only perishable apparel, and also because a person who possesses them, who can apply his mind and get hold of a question by its right end, and fix his attention on one set of circumstances at a time, can with the greater readiness acquire any particular accomplishment which he may want. But the studies which are best calculated for imparting these valuable habits are, as we have seen, those which young people are the least likely to learn of their own will. A youth is often desirous of being able to speak French just as he is of being able to play the flute, and he will want to pick it up as quickly as he can; he never thinks of getting education out of the process of learning, and it is in general better that he should not do so, for self-consciousness might spoil the process; but, unless he is a mathematical genius, he does not want to learn geometry, although it may do him ten times the good that the learning of French will, especially if the language be picked up, as it most readily is picked up by a boy, by some reiterative method depending mainly on ear. The teacher then must look for some external inducements to lead youths to these important studies; his main resources should be drawn from the moral region, from the pupil's faith in the teacher's guidance, and from his sense of the duty of getting that done which is given him to do; but the teacher has as auxiliaries the spirit of emulation, the hope of reward, and the dread of censure or of failure; these auxiliaries are coming more and more to the front, they are getting to be more thoroughly organized and are now perhaps the most effective of the teacher's forces.

Possibly the tendency of the time, and of the tone of opinion which young people gather from newspapers or what they hear at home, may be to diminish this faith and reverence for authority among certain classes, and certainly there has been a growing disposition both among old and young to look for positive measurable results. Parents want something to shew for education; a place in an Examination list seems to gauge the advantage which they have paid for, and besides it frequently has a positive market value as opening the door to some emolument or profession. From these causes, and also from a political one which we shall notice presently, has arisen that growth of Examinations alluded to at the end of the last chapter; the emulative or combative spirit is brought to bear in Competitive Examinations, and we shall find presently that the place of censure or coercion is taken by Qualifying Examinations, the former urge forward those who are in the front, the latter oblige those who hang in the rear to keep up to a certain pace.

It will be seen that the use of Examinations as educational stimulants or for coercion, implies that young people need to be stimulated or compelled to work, that is to say, it assumes the existence of human imperfection, and undertakes to deal with certain forms of it. We shall see later that we may by Examinations modify the ways in which this imperfection shews itself, but it will not disappear. The human element of education, that is the action of the wise man on the weak one, may indeed remove the evil altogether, but the mechanism of education of which Examinations are a part, can only dilute or transform it. It may indeed be said, that by our stimulants and palliatives, we are really encouraging the disease, and we may no doubt use these agencies so injudiciously, as to give truth to the charge. We may employ the motive of gain so excessively, as to thrust into the background that faith in the teacher and regard for a kind word of approval, which ought to serve us as our main-spring, and this danger must be kept in view.

There are some who think it possible to engage the interest of young people in their own mental culture, as much as in the acquisition of accomplishments — these say, "You should impress on your pupil the need of training and strengthening his faculties, you should induce him to mark his mental defects, and take the formation of his character into his own hands." This is very often attempted, it is rather a popular course; some young men like to be taken into partnership as it were with their teacher, and to discuss their own mental peculiarities. So fashionable practitioners find it answer their purpose to discuss the patient's case with him and let him indulge in his own hypotheses, and suggest the mode of treatment.

In the great majority of cases, however, entreaties to a youth to take earnestly to a study, in order to expand his mind, are pretty well thrown away. A boy is firmly persuaded that his mind is very well as it is — he cannot for the life of him understand what is meant by its being expanded — when you begin to talk about studies doing good to his mind, he takes it to shew that you have nothing better to say in their favor, and that in reality they are "of no good." You will do more with him usually, by calling on him to work in pure faith as a matter of duty, telling him, that at that time he cannot be made to see the good of these studies, but that he must work, taking it on trust that there is a good, and that you know what it is, and would not worry him with lessons for lessons' sake.

Sometimes a persuasive teacher will lead a few boys in the upper classes in a school to fancy that they are interested in the training of their minds. The result too often is, that they are made self-conscious prigs. They will tell you that they are studying this and that to give them method, or accuracy, or a command of language. They are frequently discovering peculiarities in their own mental structure; they will consult their tutor on the way to remedy certain defects of which they are conscious — which defects, by the way, are mostly of that kind which they in their hearts believe to be only excellences transformed — and so they get positively injured, either by the habit of introspection in reality, or by the affectation of watching the action of their minds, and by boundless talking about themselves.

We have come then to these conclusions. A very large proportion of our young men require to be stimulated to study in the same way as men in active life require inducements to keep them to work; Competitive Examinations answer to the struggle for advancement in life; Qualifying Examinations to the necessity for competent ability — a necessity which is becoming daily more imperative: — and lastly the subjects which are the most repulsive, or which yield the smallest immediate return in the way of a practical acquirement, are the most in need of this adventitious encouragement.

It should always be recollected that there are two ways in which the miniature struggle in Examinations

is preparatory to the real encounter of life : it is so
not only because it leads men to lay up weapons
in the way of acquirements, or to strengthen the
sinews of the brain by exercise, but also because it
calls out the moral qualities needful for success in life
— it requires teachableness, concentration, and above
all the power of " enduring hardness," of working when
one would rather not work, and setting one's self to
master thoroughly what may be distasteful.   I believe
myself that *one great effort* in the way of a heavy Examination is a very valuable piece of mental discipline;
it calls out the courage and the resources that there
are in a man, and merely to have made this effort conscientiously, and have done his best, gives a moral
elevation to the character, even if he fail in winning
any very marked success.   It gives a man confidence
and self-respect through life, to have performed something like an achievement — some result of steady
self-denial — at the outset of his carreer.

   No doubt there are some persons too feeble to make
any considerable effort.   There is, I fear, an increasing
proportion of our young men who are so weakly that
the machine can only just be kept going — it cannot
be made to do work.   An effort might indeed be
dangerous to these persons, and it might be slightly
hurtful to those who are only a few degrees stronger,
but there is little fear that such persons will ever venture on an effort too great for them.   As our wishes
are said to be the fore-feeling of our capacities, so our
languor or timidity is the forerunner which keeps
incapacity from the danger of over-exertion.   But
while some parents are eagerly pitting their sons
against each other for scholarships at school or college, others have a terrible fear of overworking the

brain, and seem to hold that the proper state of that organ is one of complete repose. Persons engaged in education will agree that cases are now not infrequent in which both mind and body are in danger of being coddled into flaccidity, from the fear which fond relations entertain, of their darlings' energies being overstrained. We cannot afford to let all severity pass out of education, for the world is no easier for men, though indulgent parents may make it so for boys.

I have said *one* great effort;—of course this one effort will involve many preparatory rehearsals; but these should be all subsidiary to the great struggle; these trials will not affect the unity of the end which the candidate sets before him; in this unity part of the wholesomeness of the effort lies. Singleness of aim is a most important lesson. I am not, be it observed, supposing here that the Examination is of any particular kind, or limited to one subject; only it should be such that it may readily be conceived as a whole. If the subjects of Examination are very multifarious, the student loses this singleness of purpose; he is always balancing the comparative advantages of investing his time in this branch of study or the other. Hence comes doubt, and doubt often leads to inaction—an inaction, by the way, which is anything but rest; for though the man may not stir, he is being pulled by conflicting claims in two or three ways at once.

I do not say that two such efforts would do absolute harm; but the second would not bring a like amount of the moral good that we have spoken of; it might however, have good intellectual results in the way of carrying the student through a fresh range of subjects. More than two such efforts would usually impair the elasticity of the mind, and a series of them would cramp and enfeeble it. A succession of *small efforts*, such as a series of trials for scholarships or appointments, has a decidedly injurious effect; there is in them none of the discipline of a grand effort; no gathering up of energies and concentration of them on a single purpose. The constant canvassing of the number of vacancies and of probable competitors, the talk about marks and money value, is far from elevating, and the constant getting up of subjects and letting them go again, leaves the mind like an india-rubber band which has been too often stretched. It has been already said that Examinations should not be carried far on into life : when it is time for the real contest to begin the mimic ones should be given up. I should put the age of twenty-four or twenty-five as the extreme limit within which any Examination is advisable (beyond a qualifying professional Examination), and I should prefer that a young man should have done with Examinations by the time he is twenty-three.

I referred just now to one cause for the spread of Examinations, which was of a political nature. It has been the policy of our Government to free themselves from the burden of patronage, by throwing appointments open to competition. This use of Examinations as a means of dispensing Government patronage withdraws them from the province of purely educational science. In a purely educational treatise we might say, under certain circumstances, they ought not to be employed at all. Just as medical men might say that no man should engage in some unhealthy handicraft — the making of needles for instance ;—but the world must have needles and the

Government must dispose of its patronage, and all that medical or educational bodies can do is to bring the mischief to a minimum. In this, as in many other matters, it is the business of our own time to weigh, and to adjust, and to correct,—to make measurements, to estimate comparative magnitude, and to strike the balance between opposing tendencies.

I think that *a priori* it is not to be expected that we can remove by any ingenious mechanism all possible ill effects from such competitive Examinations. The reason is that the necessity for these Examinations arises from some social and moral evils which belong to another region altogether. Such evils will bring about practical inconveniences. They have a way of asserting that they are evils in a very unmistakeable manner, and you can no more do away with moral evils or with their effects by any agency that is not moral in its nature than you could change by ingenuity of construction the amount of laboring force transmitted by an engine. Now Examinations may, no doubt, when taken as part of a course of education, help to call out moral qualities ; but they have little or no moral bearing when they are used simply as sifting apparatus, and are not connected with any course of teaching.

Our mode of government requires a system of Examinations as a means of dispensing patronage so as to avoid solicitation and the suspicion of favor. Now a system may be found which shall answer the above purpose well, and which may nevertheless give rise to a bad mode of study. Here the difficulty arises from using an educational agent for a purpose which is not educational. The Examination, in order to give a fair chance to all comers, must be equally adapted to all kinds of education. I believe that no such general adaptation can really be effected, but we shall see that the attempt to effect it is the cause of much mischief. Education does not undertake to provide a machine which shall sort out men according to *merit*. Education would at once ask you what is meant by merit, — whether there is not one kind of merit for soldiers and another for civilians, — and would indeed put so many unpleasant and Socratic questions that she would be sent about her business. She would insist upon it that the only thorough remedy for an openness to the suspicion of shewing favor on the part of the governors — or for a suspicious temper of mind on the part of the governed — or for the corrupting influence of solicitation, was to improve the tone of public opinion. She would say, perhaps, that she has been trying to do this in her own way, and to raise teachers and learning in public estimation as a step in this direction, but that to make information an article that a youngster only wants to run to market with and get the best price for, is not the way to promote this. Statesmanship would thereupon reply that a mechanism was wanted at once to meet an urgent need, and that the matter could not stand over till the world grew wiser; and Education, like a sensible body, would allow that, in our complicated state of things, no one department can look for a clear stage all to itself, but must make the most of what room it can get and be ready to lend a helping hand, when wanted, for the general good.

I have said in the last chapter that Examinations have two leading functions; they may serve for selection, and they may assist education; but an arrangement suitable for one purpose may be bad for the other; so we may arrive at a kind of *antagonism.* This is the source of many of our difficulties; and it will frequently present itself as we proceed with the subject.

The case before us is of such importance that it must be considered at some length. No doubt in a perfect state of things, those who have to give appointments would be incapable of partiality, and the public would not dream of suspecting them; but we have to deal with imperfections which we cannot remove, and all we can do is to mitigate the mischief which results from them; it will still exist, but we may make it take another form. Instead of solicitation and corruption on the part of the electoral body, we shall have a certain amount of demoralization in the educational world; tutors and pupils will occasionally conspire for the simulation of knowledge, and a mercenary view of the object of instruction may be spread among parents: the nuisance will have been transferred from the electoral to the educational arena, but then the educational interest will get some very decided advantages by way of a set-off.

The evils of the competitive system admit of being very forcibly depicted, and it is thus easy to create a strong feeling against it; but we shall find that, in many departments, more good than harm has resulted from it; only the disadvantages of the present system are before our eyes, and those of the system it has displaced are coming to be forgotten. It is surely better for clerkships to be awarded by competition than for young men to be content to remain dunces, as they used to do, because the borough member had promised to do something for them.

With regard to the lower class of appointments

such as the clerkships in some of the larger government departments, the balance in favor of the present plan, considered educationally, is very considerable. The Examinations have caused a large body of young men to get an education which, though not all we could wish, is better than the "schooling" which used to be obtained at the "Classical and Commercial Academy" of twenty years back. The class of persons who obtain the appointments is probably not much changed by the system. Some improvement will have been effected in their arithmetic, and in their power of expressing themselves; this will be permanent, because these accomplishments will be in daily use; moreover, the selected candidates must have shewn an acquaintance with the leading facts of history and geography; but this knowledge is often transitory. What the performance of the candidate really represents is the power of carrying a certain amount of matter in the mind for a time. This power is a useful one as far as it goes; but the great good that has been effected by the system is, that a better class of middle schools has been called into existence. This no doubt is partly due to the University Local Examinations, but the success of these examinations themselves would have been much less decided if parents had not been aroused by prudential motives to the necessity of training their sons to encounter such ordeals.

With regard to the higher class of appointments such as those for the Indian Civil Service, I am of opinion that the system works injuriously for the higher education, and I cannot but think that the department itself does not obtain such effective public servants as it might command. I need not insist on the main defect of the plan, because it is generally allowed. I mean that the essential requisites for an Indian Civil Servant are that he should have a vigorous will and be self-helpful in emergencies, qualities which an Examination does not pretend to test. I am now concerned mainly with the good of the candidates themselves in an educational point of view. In regard to this, the evils have mainly arisen from the want of foreseeing the effects of so wide an Examination, backed by such vast prizes, on modes of education. The present system was framed mainly with a view to selection and to giving fair play to different kinds of knowledge. It was intended to fashion the Examination so as to give full recognition to all branches of learning without favoring any particular kind of education; but it was not perceived that when a system of Examinations like that for the Indian Civil Service is put forward, this contains implicitly a scheme of education in itself. There must be some special course of study and mode of instruction more adapted than others to ensure success; what this most effectual method is can be made out from the published papers and the tables of marks, with the help of a little experience; and after a time this method will be usually adopted by candidates. Few parents can venture to consider anything else than how to secure an appointment; they have to look not for sound education, but for "successful preparation." The consequence is, that what the framers expressly intended to avoid has come about, and a particular sort of education is pressed upon the candidates for these appointments; either they must get it at a special trainer's, or in a particular class in a school which is put into the hands of a particular master who has studied the working of the system. If the education thus practically enforced has injurious tendencies, then we are compelling a very important class, in whose sound cultivation we are greatly interested, to adopt a mode of learning which is not satisfactory.

I will, for example's sake, name one or two of the influences of this kind of training which have come under my own observation. I have remarked that damage is done to energy and concentration of mind by the encouragement which this system gives to the "getting up" of a great diversity of subjects at the same time. The feebler the youth, the less way he can penetrate into any subject, — for the resistance may be said to vary as the square of the distance from the surface — and therefore the more subjects he must take in to give him a chance of the needful "marks." He gets to crave the stimulus of constant change of study, and the attempt to carry many subjects in his head at once produces a distraction which is physically injurious; it results in languor and a contempt for learning.

Again, the trainer must pick out the subjects to be taken in according to the marks they are likely to yield, not according to the good they are likely to do the candidates. A youth who is averse to a certain study often requires particularly the discipline of that study; a muddle-headed youth needs geometry; an inobservant one, botany or the like; but the trainer must keep each youth to the subjects in which he can do best; and if any new subjects are to be taken, those must be chosen in which, by some mnemonical process, a fair show can be made in a short time. I have frequently had to prepare candidates for the Indian Civil Service Examinations. At first, before the range of the Examination had been taken by the special trainers, the course for it ran along side by side with that which would be followed for educational purposes, and the work was satisfactory enough ; but of late a particular kind of preparation has been thought necessary. I have also frequently had as my pupils in College those who had just failed in getting an appointment — these are not likely to be very different in their mental character from those who had just succeeded — and I have found very generally indeed, that those who had gone through a series of such trials, had the same kind of mental defect. They were usually, for a long time, incapable of giving their minds steadily to any subject requiring close attention.

We see, then, with regard to competitive Examinations, that evils arise from their employment which represent as it were the moral defect which rendered them necessary, and we shall find something analagous in the case of compulsory qualifying Examinations : on these I must now make a few remarks.

Just as some persons are urged to put out all their capacities in battling for pre-eminence, so there are many people in the world who are saved from torpor of mind or body by having to win their bread. "Must," says the proverb, "is a hard master." So when young people are rehearsing under education their parts for life, something must stand for this stern but salutary necessity of doing one's daily work. Thus coercion steps in where competition fails.

There are many youths who have little aptitude for anything that is intellectual ; their attainments will never have any market value, but they themselves may be improved in a very great degree: their brains will grow and harden under steady exercise. The youth who, if left to hang about home, becomes densely stupid and good for nothing, might have become a useful person with average practical sense, if he had been properly handled at the important time when the brains take their shape.

Dull youths require strong motives to make them use their minds; people will tell you that some subject could be found which would interest them, and if you may include field-sports or games in this word "subject," the observation is true; if not, it is not borne out by my experience as a general proposition, though it holds good in particular cases. The aversion of idle boys is to brain-work as brain-work; and in the majority of cases their dislike to it depends less on the kind of work than on the intensity of it. As they get older, and the business of life comes in sight, they will often take a genuine interest in what bears on their future career.

Some motive, however, must be supplied meanwhile to spur them to the salutary exercise of their minds; we should be glad to find such motives as sense of duty, confidence in teachers, and kindly encouragement sufficient for the occasion. Happily in many instances they are so, but they often require to be supplemented by some kind of coercion, and the form in which this is most conveniently administered in our days is that of a qualifying Examination; or, what acts much more effectively, a course of Examinations so arranged as to supply constant and appropriate mental exercise. The necessity, then, for compulsory Examinations arises from the wide-spread human failing of laziness, and we shall see that the increased call for them arises in part from the growing disinclination to exercise authority or to oblige any one by *direct* compulsion to do what is disagreeable to him.

It makes all personal relations much smoother to shift the duty of exacting work off the teacher's shoulders and put it on a relentless piece of mechanism. The pupil may then be brought to look on the teacher as an ally and a guide, and an indulgent parent may even consent to the exercise of some pressure on the master's part, rather than have his son devoured by the pitiless monster "pluck." In this way such Examinations help the master to regain some of his waning authority, but the spirit of the instruction is affected; the boy allows that the master's duty is "to keep him up to work," not because it is wicked for him to be idle, but because the master is bound to get him through, and unless the teacher be preserved by high personal qualities, there is a danger of his coming to be regarded as a skilled confederate in a game.

Two causes of the extension of the demand for compulsory examinations call for especial mention.

One of these is the increased need of requiring a certain standard of ability and acquirement as a qualification for various positions in life; and the second is the growing aversion to the exercise of authority, either parental or scholastic, which has been already spoken of, and the anxiety to find a stimulus which shall take its place.

The first named cause comes partly from the increasing severity of the struggle for existence and partly from the extension of the province of scientific knowledge. Formerly there were three "learned professions"—now the army and navy would claim to be added to the list—and many kinds of business require a special knowledge which, to be effective, should be based on something like a liberal education.   In all these callings men are wanted who have a certain amount of brains and have learned the use of them; this use they do not get without education.   Examinations are in consequence instituted to test this education; and it was at first taken for granted that by the examining process, the quality of the education or the ability of the man could be tested as accurately as a gauger could estimate the amount of alcohol in a sample of spirits.

But the examiner does not test qualities of mind directly, he only infers them from the answers to questions: for these answers he gives "marks," and by these marks the result is determined.   No doubt in looking over papers, a practised examiner does see a good way into the character of a man's mind, he gets an impression over and above his marks; but of his marking he must, in the case of many government appointments, be prepared to give an account — he is told to note every word or figure that is wrong, and an impression is not a thing easy to justify, so he assigns his marks strictly according to the correctness of each answer as it stands.   He may have some notion that one man has got his knowledge in a way that will have done him good, and another in a way that will not, but this must not affect his appraisement.

We here come to one of the great difficulties of the Examination system.   A teacher is educating a pupil *by means* of geometry or *by means* of the analysis of sentences in a foreign tongue, but the education given is not proportional to the geometry or the linguistic knowledge acquired in the process.   Two boys of equal ability may be taken in hand by different teachers, and at the end of a certain time one will be able to write out fifty propositions, while another can only write out twenty, but the latter may have got much the most education of the two; for every proposition may have been made the basis of a discussion which has forced him to use not only his memory but his mind. Again, one may have learned five books of an author with a translation, and knows no more of the language than when he began; and another has done one book without such help, and has learned how to unravel a passage by himself. Speaking more generally, one man has learned to apply his mind and to work with method, while another can only learn bits given him by a tutor, and yet the score of the two may be the same. The result is that a student may be trained to get marks, without possessing the qualities which the marks are supposed to indicate. The weight of so many yards of cotton cloth was supposed to be proportioned to its substance, but a way has been discovered of communicating weight by the sizing. Something of this kind we may fear takes place now and then in getting up an article for the examination market, and the demoralization thus produced is the more grievous because the article in question happens to be a young human being.

We used to hear it said, " How does it matter in what way the knowledge has been got so that it is there ?" Now we know better. It does make all the difference *how* a man has learned, and still more *how* a boy has learned; he may get the use of his brains in learning, or he may have got the results of some kind of learning by some process which wants no use of brains. He may have got a smattering of a modern language by some of the processes which are advertised as ensuring a power of talking French in three months to "persons of the lowest capacity." Besides, there is knowledge and knowledge; there is that which has soaked in and saturated the system, and that which has been poured in quickly and runs out as fast. I set very little value on the verdict of a single Examination in given subjects. I should think far more of the fact that a youth had gone creditably through a school with an able master, and had been a year in the 6th form, than that he should have obtained a pocket full of certificates for Examinations in specific subjects away from his school. The value of Examinations, excepting those of the highest kind, is far greater as an engine in the hands of the teacher to keep the pupil to definite work than as a criterion. What they chiefly shew is a power of carrying matter in the memory; and as this power cannot have been obtained without work, we may infer, indeed, that the pupil has some steadiness of purpose — but the value of this work again depends on circumstances, for it may have been done under pressure, when the boy was under the master's eye, and could not escape; or on the other hand, it may have been done when the youth was in the midst of temptations to amuse himself, and when he steadily exercised a mastery over himself. The distinction in moral value between work done freely and work enforced by close supervision is one that must be kept well in view. The superior value of work done at the University over that done at school as a guarantee of moral power rests very much on this distinction, and many of the disappointments arising from the failure at college of boys who have got scholarships from school arise from the want of this moral power.

I have spoken of the growing aversion to exercise

authority as another cause which has operated to increase the demand for Examinations. Children at the
present time are treated with much more indulgence
than they formerly were; they are no longer kept at
a distance either by their fathers or their schoolmasters, they are encouraged to think that their pleasures and amusements demand great consideration,
and a much more friendly and confidential relation is
established between them and their elders. So long
as this is effected without any loss of authority on
the part of the parents it is an unmixed good. But
there are many circumstances in the present day
which are unfavorable to the maintenance of this
authority. There has been much wealth recently
acquired by persons of little cultivation, and their
sons soon see that their education has given them an
advantage over their parents. Again, many fathers
who are hard at work and have little opportunity for
spending money upon themselves, delight in heaping
indulgences on their children, and will smile compla-
cently at the easy way in which young master assumes
that the world about him is to be fashioned for his
convenience.

Moreover, I am not sure whether the current
philosophies of the day have not had an effect in this
direction. Viewed cursorily, they leave many young
people with the impression that they are to look
solely to getting all the enjoyment out of existence
they can. Now, if enjoyment is to be the object of
life, the time spent in hard study by an unwilling
boy is a great sacrifice for an uncertain good; while
in order to become a good shot, a good horseman, or
a good cricketer, he need only follow his favorite pursuits, and he gets an accomplishment which will be a

resource to him through life. Hence great value is
set on practical accomplishments, and the authority
of the parent does not always act on the side of the
tutors, who are beginning to see ill effects from the
worship of athletic sports. For all but highly educated parents think in their hearts pretty much as
the boys do about the worthlessness of those studies
which do not yield some accomplishment to shew.
Mr. Brown is represented as saying to himself in *Tom
Brown's School Days*, "I might tell him to work hard
and mind his Latin and Greek, but he knows I don't
care a pin about them."

Thus the authority of the parents, so far from supporting that of the schoolmaster, often runs counter
to it; they will keep their sons at home when the
holidays are over, or beg for them to be let to leave
school for a day or two on very slight grounds, perhaps merely to take part in some amusement; for
there never was a time, as one of our leading statesmen has told us, when the wealthier classes in England thought so much of amusement. Now, even if
all boys had fortunes waiting for them, and were free
from all pecuniary necessity for "bothering themselves
about learning," as they express it, yet the schoolmaster cannot see minds running to waste without
grief. Moreover, idleness involves disorder in a
school, and will probably lead to vice, and yet the
master finds himself too weak to enforce diligence; he
experiences a great difficulty in making a boy do what
he does not like; he invents new kinds of study, in
hopes that boys may dislike them less than the rigorous "old-fashioned classics and mathematics;" but
these "modern studies" too often turn out to be

neither study nor play.* The idle boy sees his advantage in taking to a study where he has only to look at experiments or to listen to what is told him, and where the subject cannot be put definitely in the shape of a lesson. Finally, the master is driven either to take up with the idea that with half the boys intellectual cultivation is hopeless, and that he must content himself with keeping them out of harm's way, or he casts about him for some kind of compulsion. He then finds that there is hardly any kind of punishment to the infliction of which there is not a grave objection on some score, and at last he turns to Examinations to provide him with the stimulus which schoolmasters used to provide for themselves, and these Examinations are required quite as much to keep parents alive to their duty as to keep boys up to their work. When the Local Examinations were first set on foot, a schoolmaster observed to me, "I cannot afford to punish; parents tell us that we are to use moral suasion, which means that we should go down on our knees to the boys, and beg them to learn their lessons, but we get tired of this posture, after a time, and so we are very grateful to you for giving us these Examinations to set before the boys."

Hence tutors and schoolmasters have urged the Universities to set up various kinds of Examinations

---

* I cannot forbear quoting the following passage from the Autobiography of Mr. John Stuart Mill: — "Much must be done, and much must be learnt, by children, for which rigid discipline, and known liability to punishment, are indispensable as means. It is, no doubt, a very laudable effort, in modern teaching, to render as much as possible of what the young are required to learn, easy and interesting to them. But when this principle is pushed to the length of not requiring them to learn anything *but* what has been made easy and interesting, one of the chief objects of education is sacrificed. I rejoice in the decline of the old brutal and tyrannical system of teaching, which, however, did succeed in enforcing habits of application; but the new, as it seems to me, is training up a race of men who will be incapable of doing anything which is disagreeable to them."

which shall act upon the mass of boys. The Examination of an entire school in the whole of the school-work is a most wholesome and effective proceeding: it leaves the master free to direct the studies as he thinks fit: it gives a sanction to the course of work he has marked out, and it keeps him and his assistants on the alert. Unfortunately, however, an Examination cannot now be floated, even in school, on mere authority or from the love of distinction. Boys will not work merely for the approbation of masters; there must be something to be got by it; the consequence is, that some kind of Certificate has to be given, and some market value must be attached to the Certificate; this being done, it will be said to be unfair to confine the advantage attached to this Certificate to those who are at certain schools. Hence it becomes necessary to open the Examination to all comers, and the position then becomes altogether changed — for instead of the Examination giving a sanction to a particular kind of teaching, and being subordinated to it, as is the case in the Examination of a school, it becomes simply a challenge held up to the world; boys will be sent to certain trainers not to be educated but to be got through; with these trainers the teaching has to be subordinated to the given Examination, the old struggle of "crammer" and "examiner" is renewed, and the tone of the tuition as well as the authority of the teacher with his pupil suffers accordingly.

It may be asked whether Qualifying Examinations are found necessary in other countries in order to strengthen the hands of the schoolmaster.

The answer must be, that in France the higher education is directed to certain qualifying Examinations, namely those for the *brevet* of Bachelier ès

Lettres, and Bachelier ès Sciences; these bar the way to the professions and to most departments of the public service. It should also be observed that the Lyceums which prepare lads for these Examinations are under government control, and in these establishments, although corporal punishment is forbidden, other inflictions are very frequent, and such as few English parents would allow their sons to be subjected to. The withdrawal of a certain portion of the daily food, never too ample in a Lyceum, is the form of punishment mostly in vogue. My impression is, that parents in France have lost their authority over their children more than they have in England, and I doubt whether the interference of the state through its Lyceums and its Maisons Paternelles, which latter are positive prisons for unruly boys, may not really weaken parental authority by leading both parents and boys to look to something external to, and more stringent than, domestic government. Neither do French parents, as a rule, value learning for its own sake more than we do in England. I have seen *brochures* on Education which represent French parents as regarding the state Examinations with terror and hatred.

The result of the French system has been unsatisfactory, but that of Germany may be considered successful. Parents are there far more on the side of learning than they are in England or in France; but, so far from doing without coercion for the idle, we shall find it supplied in a very stringent shape.

Education in Germany is much more in the hands of the state than it is with us, or than the temper of the English people at present would allow it to be. A boy is pretty much taken out of the hands of his parents. In order for a boy in Prussia to qualify himself for a profession or for the principal branches of the public service, he must go regularly through the classes of a Gymnasium. Hence some of our great difficulties do not there present themselves, or do so in a much less degree. There are few irregularly educated youths; there are none answering to those who come, at the age of 16 and 17, from Australia or New Zealand, very moderately prepared, and who need to be got ready for the Universities or for some Examination which stands at the entrance of a profession in a very short time; neither does the state feel called upon to avoid giving an advantage to those who have been educated in a particular way; a necessity which with us causes one of the main difficulties in the Examination for the Indian Civil Service appointments. The Examinations in Prussia have all reference to an established course of instruction, and in many cases the place of a youth in the classes of the Gymnasium, and the report of his general work, are taken into account together with the results of the Examination itself.

As regards coercion, the schoolmaster is supplied with a more powerful engine to enforce industry than has ever been placed in the hands of any other scholastic body. This is furnished by the compulsory military service. Unless a youth can pass an Examination to qualify him for the highest class but one in the school, and unless he continue in that class, conducting himself with diligence for a year, he cannot obtain the privilege awarded to educated persons of serving in the army for a single year instead of three, and that in the town where he may be living — but he must serve for three years in a barrack as a common soldier. This is a great terror, and it keeps dull youths working at school in perfect obedience, long after the time when they would have left school in England. The masters complain that 75 per cent. of the boys leave directly the desired exemption is obtained.

The fact that the German system has been on the whole successful, while that of France has proved a failure, illustrates the working of a very important principle, to which I have frequently alluded. In Prussia, the examination is subordinate to the teaching, while in France the teaching is subordinate to the Examination. The Examinations in a German Gymnasium are conducted by the teachers themselves, though in the presence and under the control of a Government official. Thus the independence of the teacher, his self-respect and sense of responsibility, are maintained, while sufficient external supervision is introduced to prevent laxity or collusion. In France, on the other hand, a minute programme is put forth by the Government, and the business of a Professor at the Lyceum is simply to prepare pupils to pass in an Examination in the subjects thus definitely marked out. In the conduct of this Examination the Professors have no part, neither can they readily make themselves heard, if they desire any modification of the prescribed course. "We are not the educating body," say the Professors, "the State constructs the machine of education, and it only gives us a handle to turn." In all systematic education there must be indeed a mechanical organisation, but the vital element is free human action, — the main good which the pupil gets is from contact with a superior mind. If the teacher can give no play to the bent of his own intellect, if he have only to drill the pupil in a prescribed course, if his own thoughts or views can find no place in the Examination, he will not care to occupy his pupil with them, and the pupil will not attend to them if he does ; so after a time the teacher will keep his thoughts to himself, or possibly he may cease to think ; at any rate the pupil will only come into contact with the husk of the man, and not with the real human being himself.

It is one of the drawbacks to the use of Examinations in general that they tend to crush spontaneity both in the pupil and the teacher ; and this tendency is far greater when the Examination is supreme and external to the teaching, than when the teaching and examining bodies are one, or when in some way each can influence the other.

The French have exaggerated and perfectionated the mechanical element in education ; the minister of Public Instruction can boast that he can tell at any moment what lesson every boy in France is learning, but in so doing they have destroyed the human element, and they are beginning to find that it is only men that can make men, and that a system of machinery worked by wires from a centre, however ingenuously it may be constructed, turns out but poor imitations of humanity. How fully the Athenians grasped the truth on which I have just dwelt, is seen from their word for attendance on a great man's teaching, it is συνουσία — it was the improvement to be got from *his company*, which was the first thing they thought of.

We find then that Examinations are means by which the motive powers of competition and of the need of working to win bread, are brought to bear upon young people. The Examinations, it must be recollected, are not motive powers themselves, but only instruments by which some other power is brought into play. As I have already said, boys ask, "What is to be got by the Examinations?" They want some distinction or some exemption or some professional advantage, something in fact to shew for their labor, and there are many parents who view these matters much as their sons do. Some young men, indeed, will be actuated in the pursuit of learning by ambition, some by a sense of duty, some by a genuine desire of improvement. Where the study results immediately in professional skill, or in some other capability of which the young man sees the advantage, it may pretty well be left to take care of itself: with such studies I am here but little concerned, as I confine myself to considering the case of a liberal education.

But when we come to consider the inducement towards obtaining a high general cultivation, we shall find there will be little prospect of this falling to the lot of any considerable class in this country, or indeed in any country, unless some outlay is incurred to recompense persons for obtaining it. In England this want is met by the rewards and endowments of the Universities, as it is in Germany by the large number of Professorships and other emoluments open to persons of high cultivation. In the German empire alone there are near 1000 salaried Professors in Universities. In Austria and Switzerland there are also many. A chapter will be given to the subject of Fellowships and Scholarships, and I shall perhaps have occasion hereafter to contrast the inducements to study held out in England and in Germany.*

* It will be sufficient here, in order to shew that if you are to have a larger cultivated class, you must make it worth people's while to obtain cultivation — to call attention

It is often asked, "Why should you pay a man for doing what is for his own good?" and the answer is that the country benefits by the existence of a considerable class of highly educated persons, and that you would not have this class if you did not pay for it ; for a liberal education certainly does not bring a sure return in the way of "getting on." A millionaire has often made his way without a high education, and probably would not have made more money if he had had this advantage. Again, the extent of every branch of study is increasing ; time, labor, and money must be invested freely in order to acquire high attainments, and young men, or rather parents, will not engage in such an investment without a good prospect of its securing some palpable advantages. A father will say, "I should be glad for my son to be an accomplished scholar for his own sake, just as I should like my

to the length of the list of candidates for honors at those Universities where there are emoluments, and to contrast it with the scanty roll at those where there are none. It may be said, also, that of the few candidates for honors at the scantily endowed Universities, a large proportion are buoyed up by the hope of obtaining a reward subsequently at Oxford or Cambridge; thus the capital, so to say, of these two Universities helps to work all the others in Great Britain.

In Germany, where public life and professional careers offer poorer prospects than with us, a larger number of young men of ability adopt learning as a profession: but the number of persons who have high attainments in a branch of science or literature, without looking to this as their profession, would, I think, be found to be less than with us in England. This has been observed to me in Germany, both by natives and English residents, and I see the same stated in the evidence given by Dr. Perry, who was for many years at Bonn, before the Select Committee on University Education in the year 1867 (pp. 266, 7). Statesmen in Germany do not write on Greek literature, or on the astronomy of the ancients, or translate Homer into verse. In no other country than England are there persons of so high an order of cultivation writing for the public press and for periodicals. The advantage of this to the public is incalculable; it nationalizes the results of our educational foundations in an effective way.

A German once observed to me, on taking up an English magazine which I had with me, I think it was the *Cornhill*,—" We have nothing like this, and we have no class of persons suited to write anything of the sort. We have endless scientific journals; they are written by men of learning for men of learning, but we have not the class of cultivated gentlemen who will put good criticism or the results of science into an attractive form, and the fertility of you Englishmen in works of fiction, and well-written books of travel, is to us surprising."

daughter to play the harp, but I cannot afford it as a luxury. Shew me that my money will be spent as an investment, and I will consider it. I shall be ready to make some personal sacrifice on account of the pleasure I shall find in my son's profit and distinction; but in educating my son I must first see my way to his getting his bread." The question of the *proper proportions* of the funds to be spent on *rewards* and on the other functions which college endowments fulfil will be dealt with in another chapter.

A political element also enters into the question, for if it were not for such endowments high general cultivation must become nearly the monopoly of the wealthy class. Now such cultivation makes itself more felt perhaps in a political career than in any other, especially in the higher part of the career; a self-educated man, though he may have great force of character and much power of seizing on salient points, usually fails in certain particulars — fails in the power of amalgamation with others, for instance, or in that of looking readily at a great whole from different points of view, and these deficiencies are most apparent in the highest positions. Hence if our statesmen are not to come in an undue proportion from the upper strata, we must let down shafts by which the material which is below can come to the surface — such shafts our University endowments supply. The political feeling of the present day brings very forcibly to men's minds the need of such shafts or ladders; public attention is much directed to the machinery by which they are worked, and consequently it is especially directed to Examinations, which are the most important engines employed.

It will be worth while to turn aside for a moment

to the economical aspect of the question ; for although
the matter will be fully discussed later on, it will be
well to have some clear ideas on this point to carry
with us in the historical notices which will be given
in the next chapter.

I will take as an illustration an apparently incongruous thing — a cattle-show. We have heard lately
that a short-horned cow has been sold for £5000.
She represents £5000 worth of thought, risk, and
outlay, but her milk and her calves will never bring
£5000 to her owner. How then is it worth any one's
while to call her into existence ? It is so because she
can win this money and more in prizes at agricultural
shows.   Now, these prizes are subscribed for by persons interested in agriculture because they think they
get a return for their money by improving the breed
of cattle; by calling into being a race of animals
which will carry much flesh or give much milk on
cheap food, or fulfil some other conditions highly
valued by the grazier. What then we have to shew
for the money contributed is not only this cow or her
progeny, but a large number of cows very nearly as
good, which have been bred in the hope that one of
them might turn out a first-rate animal: the existence
of these materially improves the cattle and increases
the wealth of the country. So when asked what we
have to shew for fellowships and scholarships, we
point not only to the fortunate competitors, but to
the general high standard of attainment caused by
the competition itself; we point not only to the honor
lists above-named, but to the sixth forms of the various schools: these would be smaller, and the subjects
taught less advanced, if there were, so to say, no
market for high attainments: we might further point

to the many cultivated persons who, some in their professions and some by writing for the press, are keeping up an elevated tone in English social life. These advantages result from the prizes of learning, just as the improvement in the breed of cattle is effected by the money subscribed as prizes in the shows.

We may further consider how this money is distributed : it does not really all go to the fortunate competitor, for he may have had to spend a larger sum in getting his education than he otherwise would, so that part of it goes to the tutors and to the schoolmasters in the higher schools. Moreover, this is one of those cases into which, like mining speculations, the gambling spirit enters, so that far more money is spent in reading for Fellowships and Indian Civil Service appointments than is received from them ; and thus the educational profession benefits immensely by the impulse caused by these emoluments. Indeed, we may say, that the special tutors for the Indian Service are in part paid by the Government, for a parent anxious to get an appointment for his son has to invest £300 more in his son's education than he otherwise would, and he looks to the amount of the salary, and to the prospects in India, to repay the outlay and the risk, so that if the stipend had been originally merely what a man would do the work for, the Government would have had to raise it, when they introduced the system of Competitive Examination.

It appears, from comparing the published marks of the successful candidates for some years past, that the attainments of those who succeed are gradually declining : the cause of this may be the increasing

cost of the special preparation.   Parents can find
something better for a clever boy at less outlay.

There is one danger which meets us in Examinations, although it is not confined to them, which I
must point out here, as we shall frequently have to
guard against it.   Whenever acquirements are to be
turned to account in a particular way, either by being
displayed in an Examination or otherwise, the form
which these acquirements will take will be affected
by the mode in which they are to find their reward..
In old times the glory of scholars was to maintain a
thesis in a disputation ; they went on disputing in
schools all their lives, and we see that all their learning was cast into a dialectic form ; they sought not so
much to attain truth as to be irrefragable : this spirit
may be traced in much of the literature of the middle
ages.   So in our time there is a danger that some of
our studies may be thrown into a conventional form
by the influence of Examinations.

We might study a subject in one way if we wanted
to keep it by us as a possession, and in a very different way if we wanted only to answer questions on it,
or work problems in it on paper, and that in a given
and very limited time.   Again, a subject taken on
one side may be much less adapted for Examination
than when taken on another ; one part of it or one
way of treating it may yield examples or illustrations,
or be made the means of shewing that the student
has really assimilated it.   This side of the subject will
be the favorite field of Examiners, and the attention
of the student will therefore be turned in this direction,
and other parts of the subject, which may be no less
important, but which may yield no principles which
can be readily applied, and be in other respects ill

suited for Examination, will be comparatively neglected.   The writing of an essay under Examination
would seem to be a capital means of finding what
there is in a man's mind, and if none of the candidates had been trained for such an Examination,
their productions might afford some criterion of their
mental fertility and powers of expression, but my experience on this point quite brings me to agree with Mr.
Mark Pattison* in his mistrust of essays produced in
Examinations when young men are trained to write
them.   Such training, he observes, is apt to lead to
the ready appropriation of the results of "modern
thought" without going through the process of thinking : he shews that the effect of this is enervating,
and says that the teaching of the Honour Schools at
Oxford (in 1868) seems directed to fit men to write
pointed but shallow leading articles.

Considered even as a test of capacity of writing,
the production of a dissertation under Examination is
not quite satisfactory; by forcing a man to write on
the spur of the moment without authorities to which
he may refer, we are trying him under very exceptional conditions, and we are therefore calling into existence a special and particular art : whereas our object
should be to see what the man could produce if he sat
down to write an essay under no extraordinary circumstances, but with the usual opportunities for reference
and revision.   If these could be allowed, an essay
might be made an excellent test of certain qualities
of mind.   To this point I shall have to recur.

* *Suggestions on Academical Organisation*, Mark Pattison, B. D.   Edinburgh,
Edmonston and Douglass, pp. 294-5.

CHAPTER III.

HISTORICAL NOTICES. DISPUTATIONS.

FROM the History of Universities we may gather much that will be of use to us in pursuing our subject. It would carry me beyond my limits to enter upon a connected account of the growth of Examinations; I can only deal with a few stages of their progress, and I must take those which will serve best to "point a moral," or to bring out some of the more general principles which govern their working.

We have already seen enough to shew what we might have expected beforehand, that as soon as by means of an Examination or any equivalent contrivance intellectual acquirements may be turned into honor or profit — as soon, that is, as learning through such instrumentality acquires a directly exchangeable value — then its production and distribution will be governed by certain laws.

In the beginning of the 11th century we find among the south-western nations of Christendom all the tokens of renewed youth. The spirit of that time stands in strong contrast with the listless despondency which had prevailed a century or two before.

The successive deluges of semi-barbarian hordes had then ceased; people could look on their country as their own — probably, too, the mixture of races which had ensued from these invasions had improved the physical vigor and the energy of the populations.

Lastly, there was a cause in operation to which some writers attach much importance. Christendom was recovering from the scare of the impending destruction of the world; the terrible thousandth year had passed away without any threatenings of universal conflagration. So long as people were looking to the extinction of all things utter prostration naturally prevailed, it was of no use to cultivate the land, still less to educate the young, if the world were on the brink of destruction.

From this there came a great rebound. The world woke out of its hideous nightmare with a belief that a great future was in store for it. It had not been spared for nothing. The failure of the expectation threw no doubt or discredit on religion. The world, it was said, had had its existence renewed to be a scene for the triumph of the Faith. Happily a healthy tone was, in this way, given to religious sentiment. To believe that the world was spared for great things under God's guidance, and that the men of that day were given the duty of setting these great things afoot, could not but have an invigorating and elevating effect.

Great enterprises were undertaken, monasteries were founded or restored, vast cathedrals were planned and commenced, and institutions which were to mould the manners of future generations, feudalism, chivalry, and universities, sprang up. The last-named were not perfected by founders and laid down according to a design made out beforehand — they did not embody the ideas of one man or of a set of men — they grew up, because a need had made itself felt among people who had energy enough to set about meeting it in a way that should serve both their own time, and time to come.

A boy plans his career, and in his own mind he is to be young all through, only bigger, and all about him is to be always the same as it is then. The generation I am speaking of worked in a spirit not unlike this, and it argued youth and strong vitality in the race. They never doubted but that the great things which they set going would last, and grow, and be of the same service to posterity which they were to them. This confidence lay so deep in them, that it was free from all self-consciousness; it could not have come from a want of familiarity with violence or danger, for men then went with their lives in their hands. There were wars and calamities constantly about them, but these only troubled the surface of things, and the foundation of what we call "society" rested in the depths. Doubt was then unknown, or at least hidden; religious belief was unquestioned and supreme, and this lay at the foundation of all their structures. Districts might change their masters, and individuals were subject to sudden changes of fortune and laid their account to meeting with them, but it was taken for granted that the orders of chivalry, the monasteries, and the universities were part of the necessary order of things. Men will always invest their interest and their energy in what gives promise of lasting, and what will enable them to carry their views *forward*, and so they threw their whole hearts in those days into the corporate existence in which they were bound up; they could conceive that as going on in the way they had known it, after they and their children should have perished. So too contrariwise, when individuals can live in assured comfort, but institutions are threatened, the temptation is not to care about the latter overmuch, but to concentrate interest on personal or family well-being.

Early in the 11th century, security and prosperity were in some degree restored to Italy; property increased, and the need of law to regulate transactions was soon felt; people bethought them of the codes, and of the works of the jurists which had formed the great boast of Imperial Rome. They had been forgotten, but a company of students at Bologna devoted themselves to the revival of this study, much as a body of persons might now form a club or a society for the cultivation of some science or art.

After a time (A. D. 1158) this school of Law obtained a charter of incorporation from the Emperor Frederic I., which emancipated the students from the municipal jurisdiction and gave them courts of their own. Students resorting from all quarters to Bologna formed a society which had nothing in common with the people of the town in which they happened to be residing, and by whom they were probably looked on as a prey. This made them seek special privileges, and in those times it was quite usual for the jurisdiction under which a man lived to be dependent on personal and not local considerations. Hence arose that Studenten-Recht, and immunity of the student from municipal courts which we still find in Germany, though it is disappearing in England. I may here notice that *universitas* is simply the Latin word for a corporation, meaning "the whole regarded as one," and that it has nothing whatever to do with the object of the corporation — it might be applied to a civic guild — it has obtained its special meaning from the circumstance that incorporated bodies of learned men were the most dignified corporation,— the corporation

par excellence — in early times. I should hardly have
mentioned this fact, now very generally known, but
we occasionally still find writers who fancy that the
name university implies universality in the range of
subjects taught. Bologna, we see, was a *universitas*
while as yet only a school of law; theology and medicine were introduced later. We get glimpses of the
questioning of students in these early days, and even
centuries before, in schools of grammar and rhetoric,
but as we cannot find that anything excepting praise
or punishment resulted from it, we may conclude that
examining was then nothing more than catechetical
teaching.

As Bologna had set afoot an isolated school of law,
so at Paris shortly after a school of "artes" arose;
to this was soon added one of Theology which became
the leading faculty.

All the Universities of northern Europe were
framed after that of Paris. The similarity of usages,
and the general use of the Latin tongue, tended to
bring about a freemasonry of learned men, which had
influences to which I can only direct attention as I
pass by. A student from Oxford or Cambridge might
enter the schools of Paris, or Prague, or Cracow, and
find disputations carried on in the form with which he
was familiar, and the same authorities cited as settling
a question. A Doctor at one university was a Doctor
everywhere. The authority for granting the diploma
was supposed to emanate from the Pope and thus to
hold good through Christendom. Our Lambeth degrees represent this Papal power inherited by our
Primate. Even now, a Doctor is created at Bonn and
elsewhere in Germany with the same ceremonies, the
presenting with the book and the ring, the placing the

cap on the head, and the *accolade*, and in the very same form of words with which Doctors were created at Cambridge twenty years ago.

The fact that Paris began with arts, and Bologna with law, which comes to this, that the school at Paris was framed originally with a view to a liberal education, and that of Bologna to a technical one, had a consequence of which we still trace the effects.

A student in law would generally be older than a student in arts ; besides this he had a stronger inducement to learn, he wanted to qualify himself for practice; every maxim of law or interpretation that he could pick up might be turned to account in his career; he might therefore be left to himself, no discipline was required in order to enforce diligence in his case; but the student in arts, besides being younger, did not usually mean to make his bread by any branch of the Trivium or Quadrivium, and so, in his case, the stimulus which the student of law found in looking to professional practice had to be supplied by discipline and emulation. Discipline requires something like domestic supervision, and thus it is to Paris that we owe the domestic element — the college system in our English universities. Colleges existed for many centuries at Paris, and were only destroyed from political causes.

The technical sense of the word "arts" bears on a point which is important for my subject, and I must digress from the course of the history to make some remarks about it. The branches of study comprised in the faculty of arts were divided into two courses: the Trivium, embracing grammar, logic, and rhetoric; and the Quadrivium, which included geometry, arithmetic, astronomy, and music; of these, the Trivium was much more followed than the Quadrivium. The point to which I would call attention, is this — all these studies resulted in acquirements which could be put into practice. They did not merely furnish the student with the knowledge of physical facts or of what other men had said or done, but they undertook to equip him and train him to perform certain functions or operations which required skill. Grammar gave the faculty of reading and writing Latin. Logic and rhetoric furnished the power of arranging arguments dexterously in syllogisms, and of writing an effective thesis.

" Bene disserere est finis Logices "

was the received adage.

Of the studies of the Quadrivium, the first three were directed to practical astronomy, the calculating of "ascensiouns" by the astrolabe and the "chilindre," and, possibly, the casting of nativities. From these studies, being classed with a purely practical accomplishment, *music*, we see in what light they were regarded. A man who had possessed himself of these arts could *do* a number of things which other people could not. The complete world of knowledge contained, besides arts, science and humanities—science, comprising facts and theories which did not at once give a man any new department of action, though acquaintance with them might be of great service to him — and humanities, which comprehended the works of the great Latin writers. The latter improved a man by putting his mind in communication with the minds of great men, and bringing out what was most distinctly human in him, but they did not put him in possession of a fresh "art," in its technical sense.

Early in the first chapter I observed that there

were two classes of subjects, one of which was more suitable for Examination purposes than the other. There are studies which aim at endowing the student with a power which he can be called on to put in practice, and others which store and cultivate the mind, but convey no new power that can be exercised —these classes of subjects we find, then, nearly coincide with the old division of the realm of knowledge into arts and sciences. "Humanities," which answers to Latin literature, forms a middle term. The possession of a new language comes under the head of arts, but the information and wisdom obtained from studying Latin authors, falls under that of "humanity," and all knowledge of facts or systems under that of "science." Considered with a view to Examinations, these two kinds of subjects present a broad distinction. The one — the *arts* class — admits of *direct* measurement. In these we try the student's acquirements by seeing how far he can do that which his study expressly aims at enabling him to do. He can be called upon, if a "grammarian," to shew his scholarship by writing a piece of Latin; if a logician, to detect the flaw in some vicious reasoning, by throwing the argument into syllogistic form; if an astronomer, to find the hour of the day from certain observations.

But in the class of what were then called "sciences" we cannot *directly* test the advantages derived from the study. These may be very great; they may be wisdom or insight into human modes of judging, or cultivated taste, elements which are, with our present apparatus, not to be exactly weighed in an Examination: we can only infer their presence in greater or less degree by the amount we discover of certain concomitants, which usually accompany these precious but imponderable elements more or less, but in no fixed proportion that we can determine. For instance, a student of history may have got great benefit by reading slowly, and encouraging the suggestive power of his own mind, with the help of a good teacher, who will keep him on the alert. But we cannot accurately gauge this benefit by questioning him : we cannot examine him in *wisdom*. We may indeed ask for his "views" and he will give them, but they will most often be a "parrotting of other people's notions."* Men who are just come to the "thinking" stage of life fall foul of their own education because they were not made to think sooner, and try to set their pupils thinking in their own sense of the word ; but with young people, there is a learning stage, and a reasoning stage, which precede that of generalizing or of "original thought." Teachers sometimes form a man's *opinions* by giving him their own ready made, and then take to themselves credit for having formed his *mind*. They have in fact done just the reverse. They have paralyzed his mind, and given him something to prevent his feeling the want of a mind. Many young men of ability who have looked to public life have suffered from having fallen into the hands, either of a clique over-mastered by an elaborately wrought out theory, or of a Mentor ready to supply on every point an original opinion spiced with that dash of paradox which the palate of the clever young man requires.

But what our process really discovers is, that the pupil has read and recollected certain histories, or literary works, and we *infer* that he has gained the desired benefit. Now the prospect of this very Ex-

* J. S. Mill, *Autobiography.*

amination may have prevented his so doing; it may have lead him to read, not in order to judge, but solely to recollect. He may hold the knowledge for a time and yet rather lose than gain in point of mental qualifications.

History, however, with a due proportion of its attendant sciences, affords a completion of the higher education admirably suited for many young men; and so, things being as they are, such a course of study must be made to lead to its share of the advantages to be got by Examinations. I believe that some kind of Examination (not solely depending on papers to be answered in a given time) may be applied to these subjects with advantage even as regards education; but the Examination must harmonize with a definite system of instruction, and the Examiners must have studied their profession scientifically.

Where history and literature form an item in diversified Examinations of a lower order, they are very difficult to deal with satisfactorily. Examiners are often driven to give up as hopeless the attempt to test directly the real good got by the study — the quality of the kernel itself — but they try to judge of it by scrutinizing the husk — they ask questions of facts and dates, they ask for genealogies and "short summaries"— but these are just what the man who profits most cannot give them, and what the man who has "got up" the subject by means of an analysis, has at his fingers' ends.

Moreover, the husk is perishable. A student trained for such Examinations has called into being the particular kind of memory he wants, just as an animal develops in course of time the kind of leg or wing which his habits of life require; and by means of an

Examination memory, which is a variety of the school-boy memory, he will rapidly acquire a certain quantity, hold it for three days and then forget it for ever.

It is this class of subjects which constitutes our great difficulty; if we do not examine in them, in the present state of things no one will pursue them; but even as treated in qualifying Examinations they are of too much value to be let drop, and must therefore be included. This leads to their being cultivated in a particular way, with a view to the test applied. Any quality which is prized in the *husk* will certainly be developed, but the kernel may be overlooked.

Just as popular taste determines the shape in which a commodity must be brought to market, so Examinations impose a conventional form in the results of study, and this is especially the case as regards this last-named class of subjects. There are subjects, like English literature, of the highest value, which, unless the Examination be subordinate to the teaching, may lose their beneficial effects by being studied with a view to answering questions after a given pattern.

The disputation system had the like effects, as we shall see on returning to the period at which we left our history.

The arts of Logic and Rhetoric were then cultivated not in order to train the mind, but for practical use; they were the weapons wanted for controversy, and success in public disputations led to advancement. No doubt young men got their wits exercised in acquiring this logic, just as a man gets a quick eye and a nimble hand in learning to fence, and we should now recommend logic as a study or fencing as an exercise chiefly for the faculties they cultivate; but both the one and the other were required for actual self-defence in those days, and the slighter advantages of the training they supplied were lost sight of as compared with their actual utility. The student really believed that he possessed in logic an instrument which would lead him to new truths from old data, merely by a process of ratiocination; he hoped to widen the range of human knowledge, and to resolve the perplexities that beset existence, by skill in the manipulation of logical forms.

It would appear that when students first drew together into Universities, the only teaching they got was from a sort of mutual instruction; a student who had gained repute among his fellows gathered a little body of pupils around him, and thus supported himself for a few years until something better offered. It is characteristic of Universities in general that the *teaching*, I mean teaching as distinguished from Professorial Lecturing, has always been very much in the hands of young men.

As the Universities grew in importance, it became necessary to insist on some proof of the competency of the teacher, and there was no better means of ascertaining this competency than by seeing how the teacher himself could do what he professed to enable his pupils to do. In his school he taught them to dispute syllogistically one with another, and so it was reasonable that he should be called on to hold such disputations himself in the presence of qualified judges. Here we have arrived at the first instance of any proof or evidence of qualification in the way of learning carrying advantages with it. Students, no doubt, had always been catechised in their schools, and might have gained credit and commendation from their way of answering; but now we come upon a

recognized position and title obtained by the display
of attainments.

This is a very important point in our subject, the
value of acquirements, instead of being *mediate*, becomes *immediate;* they are no longer esteemed only
for the improvement or increased capacities they
bring to the individual; a mint is opened, so to say,
to which this knowledge can be brought and assayed
and cast into a form which shall itself carry a current
value. The result, we shall see, was, that a great
stimulus was given to intellectual effort in the first
instance, a stimulus which we must own was beneficial, but that eventually mental activity was cramped
and rendered morbid by being forced to expend itself
in that way in which alone it produced a marketable
commodity. I would not have it supposed that persons, in seeking the distinctions which were to be got
by learning, were mostly actuated by what we should
call mercenary views; some sought no doubt for gain,
but many also for renown; many were not sure
whether they really had grasped what they had been
studying, and had got the power of bringing it out,
or whether they really had the ability which partial
friends ascribed to them, and these gladly took the
opportunity of submitting to a recognized test, more
especially as this test rendered them that service of
which young men of talent so often feel the need — it
concentrated their energies in a definite channel, it
marked out the work they had to do.

But the appointed criterion in those days was not
got over all at once, it was not contained in a single
process, it was the result of a course of disputations
and determinations* which lasted over several years;

* A student at a point of his course analogous to our B.A. was called on to preside
over disputations, to reject inadmissible questions, to allow or disallow authorities, to
sum up the case and give his judgment. He was then said *quæstionem determinare.*

the result of this was that the student, at the end of
his course had become, not always a sound theologian
or jurist, but at any rate a practised debater; he had
acquired some skill in logical fence and in the resolution of tangled questions; he had acquired readiness
of tongue and acuteness in drawing distinctions and
catching points, but he had at the same time so
shaped his mind to a certain groove that it could not
move in any other. Students we are told were ever-
lastingly disputing, even at meals, and in their walks,
and what was more, they forced all kinds of studies
into the form of disputation, however ill-suited they
were for it; even grammar, it is said, was treated in
this way. So we now find that all branches of learning, however little adapted for such treatment, must
be made the subjects of Examination, or they run great
risk of being lost sight of altogether.

The old Academical course took shape little by
little, and at last received sanction from the government of the country in which the University lay, and
also from the Pope. The old statutes in the Universities seem to have been tolerably pliable. The course
they laid down extended over six or seven years. The
student sometimes opposed a proposition, bringing
objections in a syllogistic form, thus; If *A* is *B*, then
cadit questio; but *A* is *B*, as he would shew by argument or authority, *ergo cadit questio*, to which the
respondent would reply *nego consequentiam*, and a
fresh issue would arise. Sometimes the student would
appear as a respondent, he then wrote a Latin Essay,
or *Thesis*, as it was called, in which he maintained a
proposition; and also towards the close of his student
course he acted as *determinator*, the meaning of which
term has been explained already. Those who had

proved their competency in such a course, and had, besides, attended certain Lectures, and submitted to the questionings of the other Doctors in the faculty, were admitted Doctors or Masters in this faculty. These titles implied a *right to teach;* it was in this that their essence lay. They were not meant for mere marks of having received a general liberal education, no one probably sought for them who did not mean to teach. Indeed the graduate was generally bound by an oath to act as a Regent, for a certain period, at Cambridge, originally for one year, then for three, and under the Elizabethan Statutes for five years; and a Regent in early days was a tutor, having youths perhaps living with him, but certainly under his teaching and authority, and receiving fees. Every teacher was a Regent, whatever his standing, and the Regentes formed originally, at least in great measure, the governing body. In later days at Cambridge, Masters of Arts of less than five years standing, and Doctors of less than two, were called Regentes, but only a few vestiges remained of the original meaning of the word.

The introduction of Degrees carrying titles and authority to teach gave a new aspect to the Universities, it raised them from being mere societies for promoting education and learning into institutions, which formed an important part of the fabric of society, and which had a life of their own.

The profession of teaching became dignified by its connection with the Universities. Doctors and Professors acquired much respect and an amount of emolument which, though probably moderate, was relative wealth when compared with the pittance of the schoolmaster.

But these disputations and degrees had an attraction

far beyond what could be accounted for by the profit
or the dignity they conferred. They afforded to a
young man of ability a means of bringing himself into
notice; they offered him a fair field where he could
try his strength against others. They fulfilled in this
respect the function which our University Honors do
now, and, like them, afforded in their own age a
powerful and on the whole a beneficial impetus to
University life.

There was one ladder open to the lowly born in
those days, it was the Church. The young clerk might
rise to be, not only a bishop, but a judge, an ambas-
sador, or a high officer of state, but if he were without
interest he must find some means of singling himself
out from his fellows. The public disputations in the
schools of the Universities supplied what he wanted.
Hitherto, the Universities had only offered learning,
now they could offer fame. Moreover these exercises
fell in with the strong combative spirit of the age.*
They grew up in the days of the tournaments. They
afforded an attraction to stirring and active spirits,
who not only wanted the fruit of the struggle, but who
enjoyed the struggle itself. These were men of different metal from the quiet students who only wished
to learn and to teach in peace.

Many a humble lad who looked on at the brilliant
tournament, and sighed to think that he could neither
break lances nor win chaplets, brightened up at the
thought that there was something yet open to men
like him, a place where strong will and active brains
would make their mark, — a tournament of wits —
and he fancied himself going from University to Uni-

* We find frequent complaints of the distraction caused to students at Cambridge
from "jousts and tournaments," held in the neighborhood.

versity, just as the knight went from lists to lists, maintaining his *thesis* against all comers, pronouncing his "determination" in masterly style, and winning, amid the ringing applause of the students, high encomiums from the most learned doctors of the day.

The new institution took firm hold, and grew rapidly. The scholars formed a fraternity, and a student life sprang up with marked features and usages of its own. People always feel a sort of tenderness for the generation which is to be, as a French writer says, "the world of to-morrow," and these gatherings of young men and their competitions in argument were soon regarded with interest by the public at large.

The statutes, which required certain exercises for degrees, might require the sanction of the Pope or of some external authority, but practically they emanated from the academical body, and so they met wants as they arose, and expressed the wishes of the teachers. Moreover the University seems to have had the power of dispensing with certain of these requirements, and this appears to have been very liberally exercised.

Thus the ancient Universities developed their system for themselves, and arrived by degrees at a state of very complex organization. We can easily understand that the vitality of an institution following this natural law of development should be superior to that of a highly organized creation which, though fashioned, like a Frankenstein, with great study, is made and set going all at once.

The fact that before the Reformation only a small proportion of the students proceeded to degrees helped to keep the disputation system in repute. Those only engaged in the disputations who were competent to acquit themselves with credit, and these were thoroughly in earnest in their endeavors to maintain their point. In Germany, where the disputation system is still retained, although supplemented by Examinations, these contests are only engaged in by the more distinguished young men. Not one-fifth of the students at a German University take a degree at all, the rest are content, as they used to be in the Scotch Universities, with obtaining a certificate of having attended Lectures, this certificate being sufficient to enable them to enter on their professional course.

It may be as well here to give some few particulars as to the number of students and of degrees at the University of Cambridge, in early times.

Wonderful stories have been told of the number of students at Oxford and Cambridge in the 13th and 14th centuries. They rest mainly on the statements of a monk in a controversial sermon, which were made with a particular object. Recent historical research has shewn that these statements are unfounded. Probably there never were nearly so many students proceeding to the English Universities as there are now. In 1873 near 700 students were admitted at Cambridge, and about as many at Oxford. M. Thurot, in his work, *De l'Organisation de l'Enseignement*, quoted by Mr. Mullinger, *Hist. of the University of Cambridge*, p. 362, says that there never were 1500 students at Paris in the best of times, and Paris was more famous than the English Universities. In A. D. 1312 there were at Cambridge 575 persons liable to *tallage* (householders) (see Cooper's *Annals*, Vol. I.). In A. D. 1376, a poll-tax of 4*d.* upon every lay person, male or female, above the age of 14, was granted to the king, and the number of persons charged to this tax in the town was 1722. The scholars and their servants were, possibly, exempted, but we cannot suppose that the scholars outnumbered the adult inhabitants of the town.

It must be recollected that at this time the customary duration of residence was much longer than it now is. Students entered between the ages of 14 and 16, and remained six or seven years at college, instead of about half that time; thus the proportion of the whole body of students to the number annually arriving was twice what it is at present.

If we suppose that the whole number of actual students at Cambridge in the 15th century was 1500, which seems to me reasonable, judging from such notices as we have, and from the accommodation which the town and colleges could supply, this, taking six years as the time of residence, would give 250 freshmen in a year. We find from our records that, roughly speaking, about 50 in a year at that epoch proceeded to degrees, or one-fifth of the whole annual number of freshmen. At present, one-half of the students at Cambridge take their degrees in Honors, so that the disputants would answer to the first two-fifths of those who obtain University distinctions. As long as the disputations were confined to persons of this calibre, they continued to be realities.

After the time of Elizabeth it grew to be the practice that every student should endeavor to take the B. A. degree; the mere attendance at Lectures conferred no professional advantage, and, although a University degree conferred but trifling privileges, yet it had a social value, and every student endeavored to obtain it, while a certain discredit was attached to leaving the University without a degree. The consequence was that these disputations were carried on by those who knew little Latin and less Logic; they became a burden, instead of being a coveted opportunity for display. Some students tried to do the least that was needed in order to escape the terrible "Descendas, Domine" of the presiding authority, which answered to the modern "plucking." The fact is that disputations were never meant for any but willing and *bonâ fide* students, and when others were forced to engage in them, they became a farce, and perished. That the candidates for degrees were not numerous is, indeed, implied in the whole of the proceedings formerly required for a degree, which were long and complex.

But these Acts* and Opponencies had an indirect influence, which extended beyond those who engaged in them. The common subjects of debate, which would seem dry enough to us, were taken from what were in their own time the questions of the day, and the abstract character of the proceeding was relieved by personal interest in the disputant, and the excitement of a genuine contest. Books were scarce in those days, and persons were accustomed to learn by their ears as we are by our eyes; sermons and disputations stood them in the place of current literature, and the power of attending to what is delivered orally was much more commonly possessed than it is now. This power has indeed almost disappeared in our time among the cultivated class, at least with the male sex. If you want an audience for a formal lecture you must look to ladies or to working-men.

Whatever the causes, we have evidence that a crowd of students were ready to listen eagerly to de-

---

* He who maintained a thesis was said " to keep an Act."

bates in Latin on the points in dispute between Nominalists and Realists, and this shews that a considerable amount of intellectual activity had been called forth. Even in those outside the University an interest was awakened in philosophical discussion. It is surprising in those times to find how well, considering that there were no newspapers and no regular means of communication, people were acquainted with what was going on elsewhere. University news spread by travellers. Students and doctors went to and fro on their way, making short stages on horseback. The traveller found shelter in the Hall or in the Monastery, and his news was eagerly sought. The account of a great dispute between well-known doctors would have all the interest which an important trial would now attract, and thus some tincture of philosophy permeated the society of that day.

The writers even of the lighter literature of the middle ages take it for granted that their readers are familiar with the technical terms of philosophy, and have an interest in the perplexing problems with which it dealt. To take one ready instance. None of Chaucer's tales was more likely to be widely read than the Nonne Prestes tale, the popular story of the Cock and the Fox. Yet there we meet with the following passage : —

> Whether that Goddis worthy forwetyng
> Streigneth me needely for to do a thing,
> (Needely clepe I simple necessité);
> Or elles if fre choys be graunted me
> To do that same thing, or to do it nought,
> Though God forwot it, er that it was wrought;
> Or of his wityng streyneth never a deel,
> But by necessité condicionel.

The system of scholastic disputations, then, was happily suited to the circumstances of its time, and its immediate effects were no doubt beneficial. We might say much the same of the system of University Examinations, which succeeded it, and which, though it grew up gradually, came first to be well known and understood by the public early in the present century. The more remote effects of both systems are of a mixed nature, and require careful tracing.

The effective point of both these systems, as regards their action in stimulating study, is the same.

In each case a mart was opened, at which certain kinds of learning could obtain immediate consideration. The harvest of knowledge is long to wait for, and much may befall the crop before it is reaped and winnowed, and stored in the granary : only the patient and trustful will sow for it ; but when a factor comes and offers to buy the crop *as it stands*, green and in blossom, then the case changes its aspect : at once a great breadth of land is sown, and care and capital are bestowed on the husbandry ; only there is this to be observed—the grower's interest is thereby turned to having a fine plant at *blossoming time*, it is no longer his business to trouble himself about the hardening of the grain.

At the end of the last chapter I have alluded to one of the indirect actions of this system, an action which worked unseen, but which powerfully affected the turn which the intellects of that age took. I mean that it cast all learning into a dialectic form.

We have seen that, as far as logic and rhetoric went, this system fulfilled one of the requisites for a sound Examination — it measured them by their own natural fruits. A student applied himself to one of these branches in order to learn to argue and to put his points forcibly, and this form of Examination called on him to put these accomplishments in practice; but when we consider the subject-matter of the disputation, which might be theology or philosophy or jurisprudence, the case was different. Whether a man *was* a theologian, or philosopher, or jurist, no one could positively say, but he was pronounced so in the schools because he could *argue about* theology or philosophy or jurisprudence. This we see would concentrate attention on one aspect of each of these subjects, and that would not be the side on which new truth was likely to be found. Attention would be turned to those points which offered grounds for controversy, and a field for the display of subtilty in framing artificial distinctions, and of dexterity in syllogistic fencing.

The schoolmen took up some of the interminable problems which beset human existence, and though they might not even pretend to have solved them, yet one would insist on a particular way of viewing a question, and another would just as plausibly insist on another. Here was room for endless discussion, and men were led to expatiate in this unproductive region, because it afforded an exercise ground which just suited their weapons and their evolutions.

No doubt there were great men in the middle ages, like Anselm and others, whose genius proved superior to all adverse influences. The great men who have grown up under a system are often cited as proofs of its value; but great men, of all others, are those who are least affected by any system. Their native vigor overcomes the strength of systems, and asserts its own law of growth. A system must be tested by its effect on the many — on those whose innate force is but moderate as compared with the external pressure — and, applying this to the case before us, we find that the shape which thought and learning were made to take under the influence of scholastic disputations, was such as to check free expansion and variety of individual growth. If a great man met with a philosophical theorem he would not be easy till he had sifted out the truth of the matter; but when a thesis came in the way of an ordinary man, the point with him would be, not "Is this true?" but, "How is this to be maintained or impugned?" He would frame his arguments with *nego consequentiam* always sounding in his ears, and he would especially look to see how in the last resort his position could be reduced to statements which were supported by some received authority. A proposition which could not be made to rest ultimately on such support would not be suited for the display of his skill. This consideration narrowed his interest in intellectual questions.

A disputant, too, could never afford to acknowledge his own ignorance in the face of an adversary, and so he got out of the habit of allowing it to himself. Now, until a man owns his ignorance, the way is not cleared for any advance to knowledge, and the man is not in the right temper to set out in quest of it. The learned in the middle ages were in this condition: they had framed theories — flimsy structures, spun out of their own heads, with the smallest possible quantity of anything material to rest upon, — in order to fill up the gaps in their knowledge; and this they did because in a disputation they were obliged to maintain that what they held was part of a complete system. If there was any point of their line undefended, the position was untenable. From this necessity of pretending to know everything, they were driven to construct hypotheses resting on *a priori* grounds: a mode of

proceeding which prevented their learning anything
rightly, and, what most of all disqualified them for advance in true science, they lost the feeling of the sa-
credness of truth; they studied not in order to convince
themselves, but to silence an opponent.

People in those times did not understand such a
phrase as "an open question." When they came to
hear a debate, they expected the point at issue to be
cleared up by the "determinator"—at any rate they
wanted one side or the other to *win* in the dispute—
and they did not need to go to the bottom of every
question, for before going very far they were met
by some authority by whose verdict they were content
to abide.

The disputant brought with him into the schools
his Bible, his Decretals, or other ecclesiastical authorities bearing on his point, or else his Aristotle, or his
Corpus Juris, according to his subject. Besides this
he had a little store of *dicta* of the schoolmen which
were held absolute on points of logic; and when he
had brought any position under a head on which his
authority spoke clearly, then it was *valet quæstio* or
cadit quæstio et argumentum, as the case might be.

Hence the practice of disputations kept *authority*
before men's minds as being—not perhaps the basis
of all truth—but as being the firmest ground that
they, practically, could reach: and thereby it encouraged a proneness of that age which was already too
strong.

This tendency to cling to authority is one of the characteristics of infancy, and the intellect of Europe was in
its boyhood at the time I speak of. Now a boy *will* have
a right and a wrong on every point. If you tell him
that a passage may be taken, either this way or the

other way — he says "Yes, but which is the *right* way?" and is ready to take your answer as decisive. Such trust indeed is necessary for a child up to a certain point, but he should be weaned from it in due time. The men of the middle ages remained too long in this state of pupillage, they had succeeded to certain fragments of a great inheritance, which, as they believed, embraced all human wisdom and knowledge, and they confined themselves to treasuring up what they could find of this; they never dreamed, with one or two exceptions, of looking for new sources of truth. In Chaucer's time people were beginning to be inclined to break loose a little, and yet he never ventures to lay down a moral precept or a general maxim without sheltering himself under the authority of Cicero or "Boece," or "Daun Caton." Hence the system of scholastic disputations cramped men's minds by forcing them to cast all their knowledge into a particular shape, — to prepare it, as it were, for a particular market — and it kept them too long in leading-strings, accepting the dictates of authority and disparaging the exercise of their own reason. We may take a lesson from this when we come to consider Examinations. There is further this point to be noted. The evil would have been much less if these disputations had been confined to youths and viewed solely as means of education. Young people must up to a certain time, be drilled methodically, and must accept something on trust. But these disputations were not confined to youths; learned doctors carried them on all through their career, they formed their business and their glory.

Now this is just as if our great scholars or men of science were to make it the occupation of their lives to go about from University to University and compete with one another in Examinations. Not only would these men be lost to literature and true science, but they would help to create an artificial science, and to inaugorate a deplorable worship of puzzles and of *tours de force.* From the time when a complete system of scholastic exercises was established throughout the Universities of Christendom down to the time when Examinations began to supersede them, there was little change in the form in which acquirements had to be presented in order to reap their reward. The subjects taught varied indeed considerably, and the spirit of the teaching much more as time rolled on; but as these changes did not, unless very remotely, arise from the form of the process by which learning and ability were exhibited, they only come into consideration here so far as regards certain tendencies which helped to bring about the change from disputations to Examinations.

The system of Scholastic disputations may be looked on as a vase which had been fashioned to hold and to display human knowledge in the 12th and 13th centuries; the flowers of learning, so to say, were for a long time grown and trimmed with a view to how they would fit the vase, and how they would look in it. But in time there came new methods of cultivation and a new spirit in the cultivators; printing was discovered, and the great intellectual movement of the Reformation came. Experiments were introduced on the basis of science, a new kind of produce arose, of luxuriant growth and divers forms, and the old vase answered its purpose no more. Its dimensions were confined to certain limits, and its shape was thought to be so much of the essence of the thing, that no one tried to fit it to altered circumstances. No new kind of disputation was introduced; the exercises established by the Statutes of Elizabeth were of the same kind as those that had been in use before. The system was never patched, but in England it wore out, while in Germany disputations were till lately held in the old form. We see here, as we may a hundred times every day, what permanency there is in external forms, how they lay hold of men, and may survive their use and meaning.

But besides the general effect which any intellectual movement must have in causing human knowledge to outgrow a receptacle of fixed dimensions, there are one or two kinds of action peculiar to this case which it will be worth while to trace.

I have remarked how in the days when the system of disputations grew up, all knowledge was regarded as resting on authority, and how this view was embodied in the rules of practice according to which these contests were carried on. Now the very essence of the spirit of the Reformation was one of revolt against accepted authorities, and hence disputations ceased to be in complete accord with the spirit of the age. But this incompatibility was not found out all at once. People broke, indeed, with Duns Scotus and scholastic philosophy, but Aristotle was held in as much veneration as ever, and no one dreamt of giving up the syllogistic form of argument.

The spirit of the Reformation, no doubt, was one of intellectual freedom; people had come to the conclusion that they ought to think and act for themselves; but they did not, with the exception of a few fanatics, revolt against authority as authority; they asserted their liberty by choosing the authorities they would adopt; they put the Bible in place of the Church, and Aristotle in place of the schoolmen; and thus the disputations went on the same in point of form as ever. But this could only be for a while; the spirit that had been awakened was sure to question eventually the credentials of the authorities that were for the time accepted, and a form of discussion which necessitated a constant appeal to authority was not fitted for the investigation of the questions which were beginning to stir mankind.

The printing press came more and more to take the place of public lectures and discussions, as a vehicle for spreading opinion. The questions at issue were no longer such as only interested scholars, as the disputes of the Nominalists and Realists had been—they came home to every man, and they were discussed by a wider public. The Universities ceased to be the sole foci of intellectual action; in England indeed they were for a time almost deserted—the bulk of the students had looked to the Church for their prospects, and the path of clerical advancement was much narrowed; moreover the courtiers having swallowed the lands of the monasteries, had turned their eyes on those of the Colleges; these were however saved, partly by the intercession of Catherine Parr, but a feeling of insecurity remained. Many of the teachers left, and parents hesitated to send their sons to enter on a career of which the rewards were so precarious.

The Universities revived in the time of Elizabeth, but as we shall see, they performed a different function in the national life. Academical exercises now became an ancient institution, retained by statutable provision, instead of being the natural outgrowth of academical needs. In spite of all the strict injunctions about disputations in the Elizabethan Statutes, the impossibility of dispensing with them and the preposterous time* bestowed upon them, they never, after the Reformation, were what they had been in the ages in which they sprang up—they belonged henceforth to the category of University ceremonies and traditions.

There were two causes which very palpably brought about the discredit of Disputations in later times; one was that already mentioned, namely that they were engaged in by incompetent persons, and the other was that the Reformation did away with the general familiarity with Latin. Before this period, every educated man knew something of the language in which he said his prayers. Moreover before the Reformation, Latin was to some degree a living language. Barbarous words were used, it is true, and Roger Bacon says, that "ego currit" was let pass for grammar: still youths seem to have picked up more Latin than they do now, for when they came to the University they were capable of reading, writing, and speaking that language, if not with correctness yet with tolerable ease,—so much so that in the Statutes of Trinity College it was directed that the Latin Grammar should not be taught except to the choristers: the College was not to do the work of a Grammar School. At the present time a youth from the fifth form of a school, even of the best repute, might be much puzzled by a plain bit of Latin if he had not previously got it up with a "crib."

Something of this difference may be attributed to the greater strictness of ancient education: but much must be set down to the fact that Latin was in great part taught orally. Boys heard it spoken at church and in school, and on certain occasions they were not

---

* An Act was to go on "*per trium horarum spatium.*"

let to talk anything else; besides, Latin was not in those times one of the things which a boy would think useless; there were then many foreigners in England, ecclesiastics especially, and Latin was the means of communicating with them. Latin phrases and Latin proverbs were frequent in ordinary conversation—witness the Canterbury Tales—and the lad would know that he could do nothing without Latin at the University.

Now the Reformation destroyed the oral teaching of Latin; it made it a dead language instead of a living one, and in England it destroyed its use as a universal language of the educated world by introducing a barbarous pronunciation, which we are only just beginning to throw aside. The general familiarity with Latin appears to have declined rather rapidly after the Restoration. French took its place as the language of the "polite world," and it was in the general laxity of that period that University discipline, and with it the reality of the Academical exercises, began to fall off. As soon as the Acts and Opponencies came to be kept by youths who were alike ignorant of the subject on which they were talking and of the language in which the discussion was carried on, the display became so discreditable that the authorities were glad to convert the proceedings, as far as the pass-men were concerned, into a mere form.

Another point calls for notice. In the 17th century, physical science began to attract attention. During the whole of the 17th century, physical conceptions were working themselves clear. Physical Philosophy was passing through the controversial stage; it was mixed up to a certain extent with theological notions; the propounders of new views came every now and then to some great difficulty, and fell back on theological considerations. A science in this state of transition afforded admirable scope for disputations, and it took the place of the Scholastic Philosophy to a very great degree at Cambridge. From the renown of Newton and some of his contemporaries and successors, Natural Philosophy established itself there as the dominant study of the place; and we find in the 18th century, that two of the three questions which a candidate for Honors had to maintain would usually be taken from the works of Newton.

As long as the Newtonian Philosophy was struggling with the older systems, there would be life and reality in these contests, but when it had finally triumphed, astronomy and mechanics ceased to furnish open questions for discussion; there was a certainty on one side or the other, and a disputation on such subjects became only a sham fight — it might be made a field for shewing ingenuity or mathematical knowledge, but there could be little spirit in a contest when men were disputing about a matter which both knew to have been long settled. We shall see further on that as mathematical science became more fixed, it proved less fit to be employed as the *sole* instrument of education: we want to call on young men to judge of probabilities as well as to understand what is proved.

Eventually, then, even among the candidates for Honors, these contests ceased to be real; the point in dispute had a foregone conclusion, and soon all interest in the matter died out; few cared to go and listen to the Latin discussion, and the students no longer contended for victory. The opponents met overnight and arranged the course of argument, and the authorities, feeling that the process was a mere monument of the past, were unwilling, and wisely so, to give it an artificial value by making it of importance in the obtaining a degree.

In the next chapter we shall see how the Mathematical Tripos grew out of the exercises required for the B. A. degree. These Acts and Opponencies, as I have already said, became a mere form with regard to the ordinary degrees, and finally they lost their importance in the case of degrees in Honors, so that, in 1837, the University, by a stretch of its powers, wisely abolished them altogether in the Faculty of Arts.

They continued, however, to be carried on in the Faculties of Divinity, Law, and Physic, until they were legally abolished by the statutes of 1858; and a vestige of them is still retained in an essay which candidates for the Doctorate deliver to the Professor, and which is made the basis of a *vivâ voce* Examination.

CHAPTER IV.

HISTORICAL NOTICES. THE MATHEMATICAL TRIPOS.

In treating of the growth and decline of the system of scholastic disputations, I have confined myself mainly to its general effects, purposely avoiding historical detail. It is not my purpose to write a history of learning or of University education, but simply to trace out the influences of the different modes of providing an immediate acknowledgment for the results of instruction; neither do I intend to give a descriptive catalogue of the various sorts of Examinations that have been employed at different times and places. Unless a process of examination have some specific operation, I am not particularly concerned with it. It will however be serviceable to take one existing system of Examination for close consideration, to observe how it grew up, what those who framed it wanted to do by it, what were its immediate and what its remote consequences, what difficulties arose and what mischiefs threatened, what warnings were uttered and what remedies applied. I propose to take the Mathematical Tripos at Cambridge as my typical specimen; I do this, partly because I am familiar with its working, but also from one or two peculiarities which render it suitable for dissection and study.

In the first place it has a history; it has been long enough in existence for its remote and indirect effects to have become apparent, and for the action of the remedies which were applied to be observed. It has grown up much as an organism may be supposed to be developed in the course of ages ; we shall find that one member dropped off when it ceased to be wanted, and that another was thrown out when occasion required. These changes were in part due to the changes in the external conditions which had to be fulfilled ; but besides this, they were in part due to the effects of the public opinion of a highly educated body of teachers, who were quick to mark unhealthy tendencies. If the scheme of the Mathematical Tripos had been laid down once for all on paper, like that of the Examination for the Indian Civil Service, it would have been less suitable for my purpose ; it would then have been not a growth but a construction, and we could have learnt nothing as to any laws of development it might obey.

Moreover this Examination acquired quite early in the present century a high reputation for the integrity and ability with which it was conducted. Lord Macaulay repeatedly pointed out the correspondence of its verdicts with successes subsequently gained in life, and his remarks have attracted much attention. In awarding Fellowships, the result of the Mathematical Tripos has been allowed great weight, and no complaints have been heard as to the fairness of the selection.

In consequence, when a difficulty arose about the bestowal of Government patronage, the public caught from the Mathematical Tripos the idea of introducing competitive Examinations. The word "competitive" has become a technical term, and must be rigorously defined. I would say that an Examination is strictly competitive when one candidate is depressed or excluded by the superiority of another. The Mathematical Tripos is competitive in point of depressing, not of excluding. The *place* of a candidate in a class is affected by the number of those who do better, but his *class* is not affected by the number of competitors; there may be any number of Wranglers, Senior Optimes, and Junior Optimes, provided sufficient candidates reach the respective standards, which are approximately fixed by tradition. The Examination for the Indian Civil Service is competitive in both ways. The names are placed in order of merit, certain advantages arise from position, and a candidate, however well qualified *absolutely*, is unsuccessful if fifty candidates obtain a greater total of marks. The Oxford Examinations are not competitive in the limited sense in which I mean to employ the term. The names in each class are placed in alphabetical order. We hear, indeed, now and then, that a person is the "best first-class of his year," but this rests only on rumor. As, however, a closer discrimination is required in order to award Fellowships, the public Examinations at Oxford have to be supplemented by subsequent College Examinations, which are in the strictest sense competitive.

It was owing to its historical origin that the names in the Mathematical Tripos came to be arranged in order of merit, for the "Tripos," as we shall see, arose out of an order of seniority which had to be established among the Bachelors of a year in order to determine precedency and priority of claim to certain University offices. We shall find that the order of seniority came more and more to depend on merit, and thereby greater credit was attached to a position. Such a list was found of service in estimating the merits of candi-

dates for Fellowships. There were times in which
the elections to college emoluments were not only
affected by crown influence, but were as much exposed
to the action of jobbery and party spirit as government or local patronage has been since. Those who
had it at heart to raise the moral tone of the University in this respect pointed to the "Tripos list," as it
was called, as furnishing a criterion of relative merit
unaffected by personal predilections, and exposed to
the healthy influence of publicity. The more the
"Tripos list" came to be used for this purpose, the
more carefully it was framed, and the more it was
freed from a certain element of favor which it had
contained. Thus the growing interest in the Tripos
betokens a certain honesty of purpose existing in
Cambridge amid the general laxity of principle of the
first half of the eighteenth century, and, again, the
habit of respecting the Tripos fostered this love of
fairness and right.

The drawing up of a satisfactory list in order of
merit was much facilitated by two circumstances
which did not exist at Oxford.

Firstly, the subjects of Examination were all of one
kind; for though Moral and Mental Philosophy entered into the course of education, they were overpowered in the Examination by the weight attached
to Mathematics and Natural Philosophy.

Secondly, these are subjects which admit of very
definite answers to questions; not only must a solution be either right or wrong, but it is easy to see up
to what point the mode of proceeding is correct, and
thus the comparative merits of the answers can be
estimated: the more settled and scientific Natural
Philosophy becomes, the more this is the case. In

the moral sciences it is otherwise: a question may be answered in ways altogether different, and every answer may have its merits; candidates also will differ as to *how fully* they suppose the Examiner wants them to answer his questions. This can hardly happen in Mathematics and Natural Philosophy; neither do they afford much room for variety of taste. Examiners may differ a little in opinion as to the style of the solution of a problem, but not nearly so much as they often do in regard to the merits of a copy of Latin verse. Again, it was due to the two circumstances above stated that the system of "marks" became applicable. This is an important point, because it was to the definiteness of result which the "mark" system affords, and to the attractiveness of the discovery that selection could be reduced to arithmetic, and all the responsibility of choice put off upon a relentless addition of figures, that the Examinations owe a great part of their popularity.

If the Examinations had embraced widely different subjects, it would soon have been found that the taking of "totals" gave wrong results, and if the subjects had been classics or philosophy, the difficulty of assigning proper values to the answers — though not insurmountable if approximate results only be required, — would have been such as to prevent the *origination* of such a system, though it may not be such as to hinder the partial *adoption* of it, when it has once been originated.

I will begin my account of the Mathematical Tripos by relating the circumstances from which it takes its name. I should hardly have done so, had I not found it stated* that the name is taken from the three

* Report of the French Commissioners, 1870.

classes into which the Honor Lists at Cambridge are usually divided. It is really derived from the tripos or stool on which stood the "Bachelor of the Stool" on two occasions, when the names of the new bachelors were arranged in order of seniority. The days on which this took place were called Tripos days, because this Bachelor, who held a kind of mock disputation, and made the fun of the proceeding, was the important character of the day. The Bachelor was himself called "Tripos," from occupying the stool. Ash-Wednesday and the Thursday before Mid-Lent Sunday were respectively called the first and second "Tripos days."

The following is taken from Dr. Peacock's * work on the Statutes of the University (Appendix A, p. ix.). It is an extract from an account of the ceremonies on Ash-Wednesday, given by Matthew Stockys, who was Esquire Bedell in 1557: "Then shall the Proctours apoynt them (the new Bachelors) their Senioritie[1];" which done, they proceed "so orderlye unto the Philosophie Schole" (the Arts' Schools) "and when every man is placed, the Senior Proctour shall with some oration shortly move the Father to begyn, who after his exhortation unto his children shall call fourthe his eldest sone" (his seniority having just been determined, so that he answered to our senior wrangler) "and animate hym to dispute with an old Bachilour[2], which shall sit upon a stoole before Mr. Proctours, unto whome the sone shall propounde two Questions."

Dr. Peacock's notes are as follows:

1) "This seniority of the commencing bachelors or determiners, which was formerly made at the pleasure of the proctors on Ash-Wednesday, constituted

---

* Dr. Peacock, tutor of Trinity College, was made Dean of Ely in 1839.

the first Tripos List, which has since become so celebrated : it is probable that the list formed by the posers or examiners, which was headed by the most distinguished of the questionists, generally guided the proctors in their selection, though they frequently placed at the head of it some one or more of their personal friends or favorites."

(2) "He was called the bachelor of the stool, or tripos, which gave the name to the day : he was generally selected for his skill and readiness in disputation, and was allowed, like the *prævaricator* at the *majora comitia*, and the *terræ filius* * at Oxford, considerable license of language, a privilege which was not unfrequently abused."

In another account of similar proceedings in 1665, by the Esquire Bedell of that day, John Buck, we find "the Sen. Proctor calleth up the Tripos and exhorteth him to be witty but modest withall."

It was not till the second Tripos-day, that the Proctor declared all those whose seniority had been reserved, either on the first or second Tripos-days, to have finally performed their determination, and to be actually "Bachelors in Arts."

Although no change was formally sanctioned by the University, the mode of proceeding gradually

---

" *Terra filius.*" This was a title which invested the speaker with a sort of impersonality. I think that this name had, in the days of Elizabeth and James, got into current use among young men as a slang term emanating from the Universities; it expressed the independence and *camaraderie* of student life, and possibly it conveyed the idea of a certain tinge of the " Bohemian " character which was then rather the mode. In Ben Jonson (*Alchemist*, Act IV. Sc. 2) we find a play on this expression. Subtle addresses Kastril, the young squire, as follows:

" Come near, my worshipful boy, my *terræ fili*,
    That is my lad of land; make thy approaches."

Compare also *Hamlet*, Act II. Sc. 2, line 221 :

" HAM. My excellent good friends! How dost thou Guildenstern!
    Ah, Rosencrantz! Good lads, how do you both?

Ros.   As the indifferent children of the earth."

became shortened, and the disputations were carried on with less spirit. We have pretty full accounts of the state of things at the University early in the 18th century, owing to the disputes relative to the proceedings of the celebrated Dr. Bentley, who was master of Trinity College. The aspect of affairs at that time was dreary enough.

There was however one redeeming influence, one spark of vitality kept alive in Cambridge; this was the pursuit of Physical Science. "The problems of Aristotle," says Professor Peacock, "were replaced in the schools by questions on Moral and Natural Philosophy, and the system of the University continued to verge more and more to the nearly exclusive pursuit of Mathematics and Natural Philosophy. But the course of study which thus sprang up as it were spontaneously, was sanctioned by no academical legislation; and during the first seventy years of the eighteenth century we cannot discover a single byelaw or grace in the statute-book which either regulates or authorizes the new system which had thus arisen. The examinations of the questionists, which in ancient times had been considered as subordinate in importance to the series of scholastic exercises which were required for the complete degree of bachelor of arts, appeared gradually to have acquired a well-organized form, though still disturbed by the somewhat irregular though statutable intrusion of regent masters of arts." The regent masters had a right to question any one who was admitted of their faculty. This right they exercised freely, some in the character of "Fathers of Colleges," and some merely for their own satisfaction. This interference continued till near 1790, after which the conducting of the Examination was left to the Moderators.

"Towards the middle of the century," continues Dr. Peacock, "the Tripos lists, which had formerly attracted no great degree of attention, as not being unequivocal testimonies of proficiency" (for seniority was in some cases granted by the Proctors as a piece of patronage), "began to assume a prominent character in consequence of the total abandonment of the quadragesimal * and other statutable exercises, and the consequent expediency of making the selections from those candidates who had most distinguished themselves in the only regular and systematic trial to which the questionists were subjected, and the public attention which was thus attracted to those authorized certificates of honor, and the spirit of emulation which they began to excite amongst the whole body of the students, determined the character of the studies of the University."

The earliest Tripos list which appears in the Cambridge Calendar is that of 1748; no distinction is made between the Wranglers and Senior Optimes. They are included under the head of "Baccalaurei quibus sua reservatur senioritas comitiis prioribus" (i. e. the first Tripos-day). 24 names are given in 1748, and there are 15 Junior Optimes "quibus sua reservatur senioritas comitiis posterioribus" (i. e. the second Tripos-day). In 1753 and subsequent years, the Senior Optimes were divided from the Wranglers.

Cambridge shews a few respectable names during this period, but the number of students seems to have fallen very low. We find a writer speaking of the University who talks of "400 young men living together," and from the number of matriculations in the Registrary's books it would appear that the number

* These were disputations during Lent.

of undergraduates was not more than four or five
hundred, or about one-fifth of what it is now.

We pass on to the year 1774, when we get a full
account of the proceedings for degrees given us by
Dr. Jebb, Fellow and Tutor of St. Peter's College,
who was the first person who stirred up the University
to take steps for repressing the idleness that prevailed.
He and those who acted with him never doubted but
that by means of Examinations they might effect the
improvement they had at heart, and a great balance
of good I believe was effected by the measures which,
though his proposals were rejected, resulted from his
agitation. His schemes however principally affected
College Examinations and those for the Ordinary
Degree, and I am now only concerned with his narrative of the course of proceeding for the Mathematical
Tripos.

Of this I shall here give an abridgment. The candidates for the B. A. degree send in their names to
the two "moderators"; these are two functionaries
who preside at the disputations. Each candidate appears on the appointed day, in order to "keep his
act." He brings three propositions, which he is to
maintain against three students of his own standing.
These are his "opponents." The following is a specimen of the Question Paper:—

Q. S. (Quæstiones Sunt).

Planetæ primarii retinentur in orbitis suis vi gravitatis et motu projectili.
Iridis primariæ et secundariæ phænomena solvi possunt ex principiis
    opticis.
Non licet magistratui civem morti tradere nisi ob crimen homicidii.

Resp. Jan. 10th.

These questions are approved by the moderator a
fortnight before the day of the act.

The candidate appears before the moderator, and reads from a rostrum a Latin thesis on one question. The first opponent is then called by the moderator. He mounts a rostrum opposite the candidate, and brings eight arguments against his position; each argument is supported by three or four syllogisms. The other opponents follow in turn.

"The exercise," says Dr. Jebb, "after being carried on some time according to the strict rules, insensibly slides into free debate; the moderator restraining the parties from wandering from the subject, and frequently giving his own determination."

"These exercises," he adds, "are improving, are generally well attended, and consequently are often performed with great spirit." It appears that some of the authorities were even then offended at the badness of the Latin, and advised that the exercises should be held in English. No such change was, however, made. To resume the narrative:

"The moderator dismisses the disputants with a compliment, and sets marks to their names, indicating their relative merits. When all the candidates have kept their acts, the moderators form the students into divisions of six, eight, or ten, according to their marks above-mentioned. Each of these sets is examined separately, for an hour or an hour and a half at a time, and the Examination extends over three days."

"The students sat round a table, with pens, ink, and paper, and the moderator gave out questions, beginning with Euclid, trigonometry, and algebra, and going on to the 'four branches of philosophy,' viz. mechanics, hydrostatics, apparent astronomy, and optics, as explained in the works of Maclaurin, Cotes,

Helsham, Hamilton, Rutherforth, Keill, Long, Ferguson, and Smith."

Some "proceed to the higher parts of Natural Philosophy, viz. the theory of pulses propagated through elastic media; and the stupendous fabric of the world."

"The moderator," we read, "sometimes asks a few questions on 'Locke's Essay on the Human Understanding,' 'Butler's Analogy,' or 'Clarke's Attributes.' But as the highest academical distinctions are invariably given to the best proficients in Mathematics and Natural Philosophy, a very superficial knowledge in Morality and Metaphysics will suffice."

"Problems are proposed to the higher divisions, with which the student retires to a distant part of the Senate House, and returns, with his solutions on paper, to the moderator, who compares it with the solutions of other students."

While the moderator was occupied in examining one division, the "Fathers of Colleges," that is to say, the college officers who had charge of the candidates in the respective colleges, "zealous," we are told, "for the credit of their societies," were busy with the rest; each Father examining, sometimes for an hour and a half at a time, those candidates from other colleges, "who were most likely to contest the palm of glory with their sons." All the members of the Faculty of Arts were considered to be interested in ascertaining the qualifications of those who were admitted into it, and if the moderators wished for the assistance of any well-known mathematician, he would feel it his duty to render his services. The smallness of the remuneration originally given to Examiners at Cambridge is perhaps in part to be attributed to the idea that every Master of Arts had a duty to his Faculty.

To proceed with Dr. Jebb's account: The Father of one college would take aside a student from another college, and examine him, *vivâ voce*, in all that he professed to have read. He reported his impression to the moderators, to all the other Fathers, and to any other M. A. who might have examined. The moderators and others then met, discussed the comparative merits of the candidates, and eventually picked out the four and twenty who seemed most deserving. The names of these were printed in two divisions: the first called "Wranglers," or disputants, *par excellence;* the second, "Senior Optimes," probably from the form of the Moderator's compliment,— "Optime quidem disputasti, Domine."

On the day after Ash-Wednesday (the first Tripos-day), at a Congregation of the University, these names were read over publicly in order. When the name of the Senior Wrangler was pronounced, the Proctor said, "Nos reservamus ei Senioritatem suam"; and he went on saying, "et ei," "et ei," after each name as it was read by the Bedell.

On the second Tripos-day the same process was gone through with twelve more names. These were the Junior Optimes. The Wranglers and Senior Optimes were said to be "in the first Tripos."

These lists were printed on the back of papers containing copies of Latin verses, in part satirical or facetious, written by a student appointed by the Proctor. These papers were called Tripos papers, and were distributed among those who were present. This custom is still continued, and is the only remaining vestige of the old institution of the "Bachelor of the Stool."

Of all this course of proceeding the disputations

alone were required by statute.   There were no University regulations as to the mode of examining, or as to the degree of importance to be attached to each of the very incongruous sorts of *data* from which the moderators framed their list of Seniority.   This list had in old days merely been known within the University, and was only regarded as furnishing an order of precedency ; but during the 18th century, it came, as I have said, into notice, as a register of the comparative merits of the Bachelors of Arts.

The advantages of seniority of degree had been too trifling to attract much interest, but as soon as to take a good place in this register became equivalent to securing a College Fellowship, the "Tripos List" acquired much importance.   The Proctor's privilege of granting Seniority was dropped, the order was strictly regulated by merit, the ambition of the abler students was awakened, and fresh life was thrown into academical work.

I have already said that to induce parents to spend their own money and their sons' time in obtaining a high liberal education, and also to lead the young men themselves to work steadily at a definite course of advanced study, some more cogent motive is usually required than intellectual advantage, or the mere emulation of youth.   This motive the Fellowships at Cambridge supplied.   The stipend of a Fellow a century ago was small, but he got a creditable position, prospects of preferment, and he made sure of a maintenance in the College, which became his home.   This leisure for application offered great attractions to studious young men, and education prospered by the presence of a body of persons who were ready to teach or to examine for little or no remuneration.   The

Fellowships have now, as will be shown, a different action altogether, but if we had had no Fellowships at Cambridge we should have had no Tripos: our lists of Honors would have been hardly ampler than those of Edinburgh or London are now. The solid advantages which high Academical distinctions carried with them drew able men to Cambridge, and led them to work with energy and in a thorough manner; some few, no doubt, would have occupied themselves with Mathematics and Natural Philosophy without such inducement, but they would have been liable to the besetting sin of all amateurs — that of avoiding drudgery, and hurrying over the dry parts of the subject, in order to expatiate in its pleasanter regions.

The competition that was thus called out set the standard of merit high; it soon was found that those who had been at the top of the List of Honors took the lead in life and in the professions; the mysterious appellation of "Senior Wrangler" was everywhere regarded as signifying something stupendous; even to "have taken Honors" carried with it considerable credit. When once a high standard had been attained, and a fair proportion of the students were engaged in reading for Honors, many would be drawn into the competition from the desire to do their part and to take their place among their fellows. When a body of men are pressing earnestly in one direction, a number of others are always drawn on in their train. The larger the mass, the greater is its attraction; and the more numerous the competitors, the more spirit is thrown into the contest. A small class-list conveys the impression of a neglected study, and there is no criterion of distinction so readily understood by the public as that of having beaten a large number of others.

From what we can see of the feeling ot a century ago, University distinctions, apart from prospects of gain, went for more in the world than they do now. In our time the attention of the parents and of some of the students is pretty closely directed to the question of profit.   This arises partly from the increasing severity of the struggle to "get on," partly from the fact that a much larger proportion of our students is now drawn from a class used to take "business" views of matters than was formerly the case, and more than all, from the competition for scholarships, when at school, having brought pecuniary rewards much under the notice of young people.

The course of proceedings for the B. A. degree, which has just been related, had gradually grown up, and the regulations rested on a traditional but well-understood practice.   Dr. Jebb's proposed changes attracted the attention of the University to the state of the Examinations, and in 1779 a code of regulations was drawn up.   The general purport of this code was to warrant by legislation what had hitherto rested on custom, and the mode of procedure continued to be, in the main, very similar to that which has been described; but one or two points call for notice.

Prior to 1779, it had been found that many candidates for Honors had hurried forward to the more advanced subjects, without being thoroughly acquainted with the lower ones.   Tutors had been asked to warn their pupils that the moderators would not allow credit for answers to questions in the more abstruse parts of subjects to those who had shewn ignorance in the lower parts.   This warning was embodied in a Grace in 1779.   A candidate who is deficient in his Euclid and elementary Natural Philosophy is to be given to understand — "altiora mathesios nequicquam se assecutum."

This complaint of the neglect of the lower subjects, as we shall find, frequently recurs; this evil may no doubt be encouraged by certain forms of Examination, but it is not one with which the Examination system is to be specially charged. It is brought to light, indeed, by Examinations, but it exists in systems of education into which Examinations do not enter. A remedy for this evil was afterwards found in a lengthened preliminary Examination in the lower subjects.

According to this "Grace" of 1779, the candidates are to be broken up into classes for examination by the moderators, according to the estimate they have formed of them from the "Act." A day was to be given to questions in Natural Religion, Moral Philosophy, and Locke *On the Human Understanding.* The words of the Grace "Quum Philosophia Moralis in Examinatione plerisque nimium neglecta videatur," point to a neglect of this branch. The candidates were divided into six previous classes, which were to be examined in different subjects, according to their reading. The questions from books were given out *vivâ voce;* the problem papers were printed, if not so early as 1779, at least within a few years afterwards. The morning problems were given to all the classes in the Senate House: no writing-tables were provided, but the candidates usually knelt down and wrote in the window seat; or sometimes on the flat board of the college cap, the tassel having been torn out. The evening problems were only given to the higher classes who went to the moderators' rooms.

Only two classes were to be examined in book-work at a time by the moderators. The reason given for this is a curious one: "Quo cautum sit ne Quæstionistæ ab Examinatoribus nimium occupati aliorum Regentium et Non-Regentium Examinationi minus vacare possent." This shews that the body of Masters of Arts still exercised their privilege of examining — of course gratuitously, and were tenacious of it. In fact, the whole residing body of the Senate regarded themselves as engaged in education, as well as in supervision.

At the end of the Examination, the moderators and Examiners (for the moderators of the preceding year were to act as Examiners) were to put out a list of names "in classes quam minimas," that is to say, a rough classification took place. These classes were called "Brackets." If all those whose names were included in a Bracket were content to abide by what they had done, the Examination was at an end; but if any one wished for an additional Examination, some well-known Examiner was called in for this purpose. After this the moderators, taking counsel with all those who had assisted in the Examination, drew up a final list in order of merit: this was the "finalis Honorum designatio."

We observe in this Grace of 1779 that, though the Examination was more than heretofore viewed as a means of ascertaining relative superiority, yet that its educational bearing was kept distinctly in view. An effort was made, we see, to give effect to the Moral Philosophy, and the co-operation of the Prælectors, who were then persons engaged in college tuition, brought the working of the Examination under the notice of the teaching body. We shall see, as we proceed, that without the supervision of those who are interested in education, an Examination may become absolutely injurious to the cultivation of the young.

After this, the length of the Examination was increased from time to time, but the general plan of it remained the same until 1828, when the number of the previous classes was reduced to four, and the Examiners were permitted to give the same Examination to all if they thought fit. They availed themselves of this permission to some extent. The Moral Philosophy seems by this time again to have become inoperative. In order to enforce attention to the lower subjects it was directed that on the first day of the Examination the Differential Calculus should not be used. But the change which had the most practical effect was, that the whole of the questions — those from books and not only the problems as hitherto—were ordered to be printed, and they were published in the *Cambridge Calendar*. This brought the course for Mathematical Honors clearly before the public; and it very soon shewed its effect in an increase of the number of candidates. It spread the influence of the Examination over the whole country, and the *direct* and *immediate* effect of this was salutary, as that of Examinations generally has been. The *remote* effects require a fuller analysis than can be given in this narrative, and I shall speak of them hereafter.

The course which the successive changes took shews that the Examination, which at first had been only an incident in an academical education, came gradually to be so important, that the younger part of the body might well fancy that the final cause of University teaching was to train students to take high

degrees.   We shall see as we go on, that those who
clung to the old-fashioned educational view, viz. that
the object of University teaching was to do the most
mental good to the students, and that the distinctions
were subsidiary to this end, resisted this tendency,
and, as the legislative power was largely in the hands
of these persons, their opposition moderated many of
the evil influences which they saw growing up.   But
we observe that everything that impeded accurate
discrimination between the candidates was gradually
swept away, and so far as we have gone it cannot be
said that education suffered much from the loss, although the old provisions had been introduced on
educational grounds.

   We shall find that when an Examination is left in
the hands of the Examiners, and is not controlled by
those who are interested in education, discrimination
is more thought of than anything else : for Examiners
consider that classification is their *raison d'être*.   This
is a positive law which we may see exemplified in the
history of all Examinations, and the operation of
which I shall often have to note.   The subject of
Moral Philosophy destroyed the homogeneity of the
Tripos, and was thereby an obstacle to exact classification.   This was looked on coldly by the Examiners,
in consequence, and it eventually disappeared.   The
interference of the Fathers of Colleges was another
element of confusion.   It hindered the Examiners in
arriving at an exact result, and it was got rid of
accordingly.

   Again, a difficulty arose from the practice of giving
different questions to the different classes.   The
marks allotted to the paper given to the first class
might be twice as many as those of that given to the

third ; but if the paper was more than twice as difficult, it would answer the student's purpose better to get placed in the third of the previous classes than in the first. It seems that this practice did actually lead to some "jockey-ship" of the kind, and it was in consequence entirely abandoned in 1839. It was certainly a clumsy contrivance, but it aimed at providing that each candidate should be thoroughly examined in what he had read. If all were given the same papers, there would either be so little within the reach of the weaker men that they would learn on speculation some scraps of subjects beyond their legitimate range, or the questions from the lower subjects would have to be so unduly numerous as to load the papers and embarrass those who had read the full course. This evil became sensible soon after the change was made, and was remedied in 1848 by the preliminary Examination which I have already mentioned, and of which an account will be given further on.

The code of regulations sanctioned in 1837, which came into operation in 1839, completed the series of changes which converted the course of academical exercises for a degree in Honors at Cambridge into a competitive Examination in Mathematics and Natural Philosophy. By a stretch of the powers of the University, the series of Disputations in the Arts' Faculty, which had for years become so mere a form as not even to furnish satisfactory grounds for dividing the candidates into previous classes for Examination, was now utterly swept away, and the whole system laid down by the Statutes of Elizabeth was replaced by a continuous Examination, lasting for six days, in which all candidates had the same questions proposed on paper.

We may observe here that the mechanism of Ex-

amination became gradually simpler. This was necessitated by the increasing number of the candidates,
as well as by the more refined accuracy of discrimination which was now expected. We shall find a similar
tendency to simplification in the history of other systems of Examination. Those who frame the schemes
in the first instance usually have their attention drawn
to the cases of various classes of possible candidates ;
and the educational bearing of this or that regulation
is sure to be commented on by tutors or schoolmasters.
Hence adaptations and corrections are introduced, and
the machine is made somewhat complex, in order that
it may perform many functions at once. But when the
scheme has been launched, it falls into the hands of the
Examiners, and the changes they make or get made are
apt to run in one direction. These modifications are
almost sure to remove one after another the checks
or the options which had been introduced, as well as
to economize the Examiner's pains. The ideal of all
Examinations, in the eyes of some of those who are
taken up with conducting them, would seem to be, a
machine capable of discriminating "merit" with the
utmost nicety, at the least cost of labor and time.

Regarded from this point of view, the Tripos in 1839
had nearly arrived at perfection ; the questions were
most carefully chosen, the simplicity of form it had
attained made it readily understood by tutors through
the country, and the number of candidates for Mathematical Honors steadily increased.

Cambridge was proud of the institution she had
perfected, and she might well be so. She had invented
a method of estimating merit, which was extremely
definite, and which as long as it was confined to the
Mathematical Sciences, was singularly correct. The

credit of the Tripos rests on the order it lays down being confirmed by the judgment of the principal Tutors. A Tutor who has marked the way in which different men take in matter and make it their own, must be able to rate their powers more nicely than an Examiner can, who only sees what they produce on paper in a limited time; and if the teachers go steadily against the Examiners, and say "you have put the wrong man first," the public — at least the University public — will be inclined to side with their opinion. But as a matter of fact, the verdict of the Examiners usually accorded very remarkably with the views of the Tutors.

The Mathematical Tripos had certainly accomplished one immense good; it had, in its own sphere, exterminated "jobbery" and the influence of personal interest. This may not seem much to us, living in a time when so much publicity is given to all transactions that people must "assume a virtue if they have it not;" but in the days when the Tripos grew into existence things went almost everywhere by favor, and it took a long time to persuade those of the former generation that it was not at Cambridge as elsewhere.

The system of numerical marks helped to foster the integrity of the Examinations. The numbers furnished by the different Examiners *in subjects of the same kind* were added up, and the resulting figures determined the order. It was not like voting that one or more individuals should get a prize, or be placed in a first class. We may conceive that in this case, particularly if discussions were allowed, a person might be unconsciously swayed by some unacknowledged influences, or he might bend to a stronger and more self-asserting colleague, but no one could falsify figures as he was marking separate questions, without being really a dishonest man.

We may now think, since a Fellow of a College became in most cases one of the governing body of a place of education, that certain personal considerations, such as temper and good breeding, might have been properly taken into account; but such was the horror of falling into a system of patronage — of becoming, as it used to be said, "just like Deans and Chapters," bodies which were altogether different 40 years ago from what they now are — that Colleges adhered to the verdict of the Tripos to an extent which may sometimes have been a little prudish.* A belief in the sanctity of Examinations thus became an article of every Cambridge man's creed, and a charge of favor or of neglect would have been most damaging to an Examiner.

We have now reached a point where disputation had sunk altogether out of sight, and people were stretching hopefully away to that region of Examinations in which we are now dwelling; and here I must observe one or two instances of contrast between the old "Cambridge Tripos" and the new "Mathematical Tripos." The difference of names half tells the story of the change. In the last half of the eighteenth century, when a young man of ability came to the University and was desirous of gaining distinction, it was not his primary object to become a mathematician, or that of his Tutor to make him one. He wanted to be the first man in the "Cambridge Tripos." This meant, the list of the ablest of her sons which the University put out when they had completed her

* Excepting where there was a distinct Examination for the Fellowships, as was the case at Trinity College.

course of study. It happened that Mathematics and
Natural Philosophy were most prominent in this
course, because they were thought most valuable as
instruments of a liberal education; but some knowledge of Latin and Logic was taken for granted, and
Moral Philosophy was upheld by the authorities, as
we have seen, after it had lost favor in the opinion
of the younger members of the Senate.

The authorities did not think of producing professional mathematicians; what they wanted to do was
to turn out able men, and this they did. The difficulties that beset the reading man at that time hindered his progress, no doubt, but were excellent discipline for the struggle of life. Students in those
days were not allowed private tutors during their last
year, and rarely had recourse to them at other times;
neither had they text-books adapted to examination,
with the subject cut up into detached propositions.
They did not find the knowledge they wanted in sec-
tions numbered off for reference and put into the
form in which it was to be written out; they had to
cast it into this shape themselves, with the help of
directions given in the College Lectures. They read
works written by men of science for men of science,
such as those of Newton and others enumerated by
Dr. Jebb in a passage quoted above. These books
contained some echoes of past controversies on the
principles of mechanics, which still made their rum-
blings heard in notes and in prefaces; and sometimes
an ingenious disputant in his Act would wake into
momentary life some old crotchet, which had gone
to take its place in the "History of Human Error."
These discussions relieved science of its purely abstract character; they brought up recollections of

great intellects in conflict, and they served to keep
alive the human sympathies of the students of physics.
When the youngster now skims over the chapter on
elementary principles in his manual, and gives it
scanty attention in his eagerness to get forward, he
little thinks how hardly those same primary truths
were come by.

The Cambridge manuals of five-and-thirty years
ago were taken from the manuscripts used in the
College Lectures, and in consequence they were little
more than a Syllabus containing the demonstrations
of theorems; the explanatory matter was to be given
by the Lecturer off-hand. It was owing to this that
such books were rather assemblages of propositions
than complete treatises, and this original accident of
form has injuriously affected Cambridge manuals
until very lately.

It was no doubt good for the abler young men to
make their way through books which were not written for Students or for Examinations. They read not
as schoolboys learning lessons, but as those would
who wanted to know the secrets of physics. They
were brought into contact with great minds, and this
had an elevating effect; it made men of them. But
on the other hand, they got over much less ground
than those of like ability do now; they knew fewer
branches of science, though they got a greater amount
of educational advantage from what they did know.
The feebler ones however, came off badly; the exertion of hewing from the quarry, which braced the
sinews of the vigorous, paralyzed or exhausted them.
The stronger men very soon made their way to the
front. Any little advantage in point of previous preparation was soon lost by the weaker man. The stiff-

ness of the course brought out power and steadfastness of resolve. The weaker ones suffered in two ways; they were disheartened by the demand on them for energy and resolute work, to which they were not equal, and also by seeing how easily the men of greater vigor passed them by. We see here, as we so often do, how unfavorable the condition of things was to the feebler ones in old times. The theory of that day, not only in University matters, but in school life and domestic life as well, was that people were to be made hardy and vigorous. The "survival of the fittest" produced perhaps a generation of more sustained energy than our own; but we cannot reconcile ourselves to the extinction of the less fit which this state of things involved. We now hold it our duty to do the best we can for all, and to give to all our material, good and bad alike, the highest polish it will take. This duty complicates the problems we have before us.

At the time which I have reached in my narrative (1839), Cambridge had as yet no doubt about her system, she was exulting in the distinctions of men who had been trained in a course more conducive to thoroughness and self-reliance than that which was then actually in operation, and the Tripos took credit for Lord Lyndhurst, Mr. Justice Maule, Sir Frederick Pollock, Baron Alderson, and others who had been reared in the rough school I have been speaking of.

We hear people who have not looked much into the matter speak as if Senior Wranglers had degenerated. This, I believe, if we reckon by ability or even vigor of mind, will be found to be untrue. But it is a fact that the type of man is changed. The highest mathematical education of Cambridge is no longer simply a liberal education, training the powers of the man for active life, but it is for the highest men also a technical education in mathematical physics. A high wrangler formerly was a man of highly-developed general mental power. Now he is also an accomplished mathematician, qualified for immediately undertaking a scientific post, and such posts exist in sufficient abundance to provide for the highest men at an early age.

For many years no Senior Wrangler went to the Bar; on the other hand there was not a Professor of Mathematics or Natural Philosophy in Great Britain that had not been a high wrangler. A Professorship offered a young man an immediate competence for work which was congenial to him, and this he took in preference to entering on an apprenticeship to a new study. It is true, however, that, at the present moment, Professorships seem to be rather less coveted. These posts bring in stipends, so moderate as hardly to answer the expectations which young men of ability now entertain, and they in consequence are turning their eyes to the more brilliant but uncertain prospects of active life. It may seem humiliating, but it will be found to be true, that the results of the higher education are, on the whole, influenced by supply and demand, very much as those of manufacturing industry are. We may find a few cases of men who have a strong bent for some kind of learning or some profession, and who will make sacrifices to pursue it, just as we find now and then a porcelain manufacturer who spends a fortune in improving art; but as we should not reckon on finding such enthusiasts, in our transactions in trade, so in all schemes of education which are left, as those of the English Universities are, to the sole operation of supply and demand, we must suppose that the great mass of people will be actuated by considering the return, in the way of profit, or position, or means of enjoyment, which their children will obtain for the pains and money spent on their education.

We must not claim for the Cambridge Tripos too large a share in the credit of producing the great men I have named. The education they got was indeed admirably calculated to give them firmness of mental grasp; but what Cambridge especially did for them was, that it brought them early to the front. Great men will usually get somehow or other cultivation for themselves, but they may be buried so far down that they only struggle above ground too late to come to perfection. The main credit due to Cambridge in these cases was that of right discrimination. The man who had been at the head of the Tripos came to be the head of his profession. It must, however, be recollected, that in the beginning of the century the competitors at the Bar were fewer in proportion to the business than they now are, and they were more restricted to particular classes.

A young man proceeding to the Bar with a good degree carried with him in those days a strong prestige; and this, besides its external advantages, helped him on. He felt that much was expected of him, and he looked to doing over again in the world, what he had done in the University. It may have made him conceited, but it was no petty vanity; it was a conceit which made him think that he might try for any prize or position in life, and I wish that our young men had more of it. His early success had pitched his life in a high key, and given him confidence in his strength and eventual success, so that he would be encouraged to pass by small temporary advantages which might otherwise have lured him from playing the grand game.

While the Tripos was becoming more and more an exclusively Mathematical Examination, and at the same time was being regarded very generally as an avenue to Fellowships, those who followed other branches of learning began to complain. There had always been at Cambridge a small but distinguished body of classical scholars. The Chancellor's Medals, the University Scholarships, and the Fellowship Examinations at Trinity College, had supplied prizes for the ablest men, but there was little or no encouragement for any short of the ablest. I have before observed that all through the time that we have been considering there may be marked a growing desire to do the best not only for the first-rate men, but for those of different degrees of ability as well; and as it is only in a general class list that second rate men can hope to see their names in a place of credit, a movement was set on foot to establish what, from the analogy of the old name, was called a Classical Tripos. Still the Mathematical Tripos represented the old Cambridge course, it alone gave the degree, and it was made necessary that in order to compete for Classical Honors a person should have attained at least the position of a Junior Optime. This provision added a new function to the Mathematical Tripos, it was no longer purely an Examination for those who were competing for distinction in Mathematics; for a certain number of the candidates it became a pass Examination.

The Mathematical Tripos, for some years after 1838, appeared an unqualified success; it called out a great amount of energy both in teaching and in learning, and in the eyes of the younger people it came to be regarded not as the means of education, but as being itself the end to which all education was directed; thus it became an idol just as idol-worship has come about in other cases. People found at last that, from having been a servant of University education, this Examination had become the lord and arbiter of all: instead of the Examination giving a sanction to a mode of teaching, the Examination called into existence that kind of teaching which was most suited to ensure success for the competitor. It was quite agreeable to the ordinary economical laws that this should be so : but it was not then understood that these laws extended to educational matters.

When a certain kind of Examination is set up, when by success in this, advantages are to be obtained which are desired by many, and especially when the whole range of the Examination is before the public, so that the conditions for gaining the greatest success with the least labor can be made out, then it is just as certain that a kind of teaching adapted to the purpose will appear and supersede other teaching, as it is that if a new fabric come into fashion, a loom specially adapted for producing it will be brought into general use. The public teaching of the University consisted of Professorial lectures which had fallen into disuse, and the lectures given in the Colleges. There had always been a few private tutors. These now became so much resorted to that the teaching seemed to have passed out of the hands of the University. But the University could still have exerted her supremacy if she only began at the right end. If the fashion was calling into existence a flimsy fabric and bad work, it only lay with her to alter the fashion. It was her Examinations that created the demand for the article, and if they brought a bad article into the market, it was sufficient ground for altering them. The Examinations had, as I have said, by degrees been made into an excellent instrument for selection, but they were also used as the main guide for education, and this purpose had of late been lost sight of in framing them; in part however they brought into light shortcomings in the public teaching.

Pupils found that to do well in an Examination they must not only have what they ought to know set before them, which the College Lecturers had done, but that they must also have some one to see that they knew this, and could produce it. They had to be shewn how to put their knowledge on paper: for this they needed Examination Papers in portions of their work, which should be looked over with them; such assistance was only supplied by the Colleges in the last Term, when the Prælectors, according to old custom, examined the Questionists to ascertain their fitness for entering the schools.

Private tutors afforded the assistance required, they made it their business to see that the pupil learnt, and the system of private tuition so spread as to threaten, as some of those who raised the alarm said, to overwhelm all other teaching. This new system had the advantage of supplying the pupil with a continuous guide who knew his mental constitution, and could advise him as to his course of reading accordingly, while in college he passed from one lecturer to another, and his communication with his College Tutor, whose function it is to supply this element of continuity, was not always close or constant enough to answer the purpose.

It happened at the time I am speaking of, that Cambridge was very fortunate in the person who obtained the greatest eminence as a private tutor, Mr. William Hopkins (for some time President of the Geological Society). He occupied in fact at Cambridge the position which a Professor Extraordinary holds in Germany; he taught his pupils in well assorted classes of from four to eight, and this is probably the most perfect mode of teaching the higher mathematics; thus the ablest men of the different Colleges were brought together; and, being a very high-minded man, thoroughly earnest in his devotion both to science and education, he gave his pupils an elevated view of their work. He banished from his Lecture-room all reference to the Examination; the keenest pursuer of the main chance never ventured to ask him, if this or that "would pay in the Senate House." He taught his class Mathematics and Natural Philosophy in the best form. They must, he would say, learn in the faith that what was most for their profit would bring them their due credit.

There can be no healthy teaching which does not rest for its working on this sort of confidence between the teacher and pupil. It may require the sanction of some advantage in prospect to induce the pupil to embark on the higher course of study, but when he is embarked, the Examination and the rewards should pass out of his sight; he should not be constantly stimulated by being shown the profit which this or that bit of knowledge may bring. The kindly feeling between pupil and teacher should make the cordial approval of the latter sufficient encouragement for what the pupil wants on the way, and he must trust the teacher to take him along the right road. The teacher, moreover, to do his work satisfactorily, must feel confident that the questioning in the Examination will justify the course he has taken in adopting a liberal and intelligent kind of instruction : he must trust the Examination, and the pupil must trust him.

Here we come to the truth on which we must rest. If we can frame an Examination in which that which will enable the candidate to do the best is that which it is best for him to learn, and to learn in the best way, then we shall have constructed a perfect educational instrument. In the case of mathematics we may, I think, hope to arrive at what we want, approximately, in this essential point, provided that we keep our main object closely in view, and do not expect our system to do too many things at once.

All tutors were not like Mr. Hopkins, and an idea got abroad that private tutors directed their teaching more immediately to success in the Senate House than was the case with the College Lectures, or than was always desirable or even politic in the end. The Lecturers indeed always maintained high ground in this respect. Mr. Blakesley, Tutor of Trinity College, now Dean of Lincoln, who tried to bring the private tutors into connection with the college system, repudiates all notion of working up to the Examination. He says :* "College Lectures should be most religiously kept free from any other object than that of putting the subject lectured on in the clearest light and on the most philosophical basis."

The objection to private tuition, which was most strongly taken up by the public, was grounded on the expense of the system and of the advantage thus given to the richer men. The expense has been

---

* *Where does the Evil lie?* A pamphlet by Rev. J. W. Blakesley, 1845.

much reduced, and practically, if an able man could not afford to pay for this assistance himself, the College or College Tutor would supply the means. The richer men have no doubt advantages in being able to purchase any books they want, and in other ways, but these are counterbalanced by their having less strong inducements to industry. An objection that lies deeper, is the tendency to *overhelping* inherent in a system of private tuition. Young men, as Dr. Whewell says*, ran to their tutor for the solution of a difficulty before they could clearly say where their difficulty was, and there were tutors whose special art lay in storing a pupil's memory with little artifices and convenient formulæ, to the starving of his mind. I conceive the temptation both to overhelp and to the overcharging with formulæ may be obviated to a very great extent by a thoroughly scientific system of Examination : this view is taken by Dr. Merivale, the present Dean of Ely, in his evidence given to the University Commission in 1852. Indeed, taking the Examination as it is, it is found that students of fair ability do better in the Senate House when they have been made to depend a good deal on themselves, and are not overloaded with formulæ and "short methods." It is a great advantage in the Tripos that the course for it extends over so long a time that the fruit not only of instruction but of good habits of mind inculcated has time to come to light. Thus a tutor may hope to see the good of having formed his pupil's mind, and not only that of having filled it to meet the occasion. This is the great point of difference between preparing a pupil for a University de-

---

* Whewell, *Of a Liberal Education*, 1848. This book gives a full history of the Tripos, and I have been much indebted to it.

gree, for which he has three years' time or more, and "coaching him up" for some competitive Examination which is to take place in a few months. In the latter case a little training of memory of course takes place, but there is no time to form good habits or remove bad ones.

Another objection rested on the effects of the system, not on the pupils, but on the tutors themselves. Every young man who had taken a high degree soon got as many pupils as he cared to have. He was naturally tempted to increase his income in this way, instead of employing the "trusted leisure" which his Fellowship afforded, for research or for high cultivation. These young men had no experience and little authority, they were therefore likely to direct their teaching to the points which the pupils most valued. The pupils who resorted to them would usually be of the weaker sort, for the College Tutor would take care that the abler men had the help of one who had made teaching a profession, and these feebler men would force their tutor to give them more help than was good for them. Weak men have a craving for help, and they set much value on short methods and compendious formulæ, and advice immediately relative to the Examination, so that a tutor anxious for pupils would be under temptation to teach in a narrow spirit. These evils were forcibly exposed by Dr. Whewell in the work already quoted, and also by Mr. Blakesley. Dr. Peacock, in the work of which I have made free use above, proposed the reintroduction of the old restriction on private tuition, but no proposal to this effect came before the Senate. Such a step would, I think, have been nugatory. It would have been like prohibiting the use of a certain kind of advantageous mechanism in a manufacture.

Private tuition has now become a regular profession; it has its recognized place in the teaching of the University, and some of the ablest mathematicians in Cambridge are engaged in preparing pupils for the Tripos. Many of these are also College Lecturers. Private tuition was indeed called into existence not by what was bad in the Examination system, but by what was its most undeniable good, by the necessity it imposed on a man of bringing his knowledge into a clear and definite form. Examiners have no mercy on the man who shews that he only half understands a matter. Now the knowledge carried away from a lecture which is not strictly catechetical, that is to say, which does not in a degree partake of the character of private tuition, is almost sure to be misty, or at least to have bits of cloud hanging about it. The special art of a good teacher lies in being able to bring to the too easily contented pupil the consciousness that he has only half apprehended some points and wholly misconceived others. This costs labor and requires skill, and the pupil must be in close communication with the teacher and in earnest to learn. Examinations supplied the motive, and the requisite sort of teaching came into existence when wanted. It might have been supplied to some extent by the Colleges, and it now is so to a considerable degree, but part of the good of the system lay in its being one of perfectly free trade, and the combination of free trade with Universitiy superintendence required more organic changes than could have been carried out at the time I am speaking of (1841–45).

A movement had taken place in mathematical science between 1800 and 1820, to which I must now refer, inasmuch as its effects influenced the form of the Examinations. The works of several French mathematicians, Lacroix, Lagrange and others, had been translated at Cambridge, and came into general use. They presented a method of mathematical investigation, which was technically called the Analytical method, as opposed to that used by Newton and his followers, which is called Synthetical. In the former the use of algebraical symbols greatly predominated, while in the latter geometrical constructions were chiefly employed. Hence we find the terms Analytical and Synthetical often used as though they were synonymous with Algebraical and Geometrical respectively, which is by no means the case*. The Analytical methods were more powerful, more easy to handle, and led more readily to results. By means of them new fields of mathematical investigation were laid open, and some of these were especially fertile in attractive problems. This highly recommended these methods to the Examiner, because an Examiner finds it much easier to rate a man's knowledge by making him apply it than by seeing him produce what he has learnt. He will therefore always have a leaning to that side of a subject which yields applications and examples — that side, in fact, of the science which results in an "Art," using the word in its old sense. The teachers also rejoiced in a method which furnished an abundance of useful and interesting examples, and which, indeed, created one subject, Analytical Geometry, which offers countless problems. It is one of the results of publishing the Examination

---

* I cannot here give a criticism of these methods, or an adequate comparison of their values, in education. I must refer to the evidence of Prof. Stokes, Mr. Leslie Ellis, nnd others, in the *Report of the Commission in 1852*, and to the *Report of the French Commissioners in 1870*. The latter agree with Prof. Stokes, that for the full comprehension of a subject, the pupil should for a while carry on both processes side by side.

Papers, that all practicable problems get used up, and Examiners are driven to invent puzzles, — for it is a point of honor not to set what has been given before. Hence an Examiner seizes with avidity on a newly-discovered vein of science which is said to be rich in problems*. Teachers and Examiners both, therefore, hailed the new methods, and we may add pupils as well, for much hard headwork was hereby saved, and many subjects were opened to the feebler men which they could not have dealt with by the old methods. Those who were interested in scientific investigation would, of course, use the new processes exclusively; they had been developed in France in order to meet the needs of original investigators, and without their help, the progress of science must have been much restricted.

Hence pupils, teachers, Examiners, and *savants*, concurred in advocating the use of Analytical methods, and the old Geometrical methods went out of use altogether.

But in 1845 Dr. Whewell, though he had himself taken part in early life in introducing the new methods, advocated the restoration of the old methods for elementary teaching on purely educational grounds.

---

* I have said in the last chapter that the old disputations forced all knowledge into a dialectical form; so, in a slighter degree, our Examinations have induced those occupied with them, to view scientific subjects as matter for problems, and to invest the sciences, as it were, with difficulties beyond those which they naturally offer, that they may serve as exercises for determining the relative power and ingenuity of the competitors. The longer a kind of Examination has been in existence, the more apparent this tendency becomes. Our Examination Papers are growing more abstrusely scientific than science herself. The French Commissioners, M. Demogeot and M. Montucci, complain, and with much truth, that our papers will train men *à opérer plutot qu'à réfléchir*. They, however, had had no experience of the exigencies of a long-established series of examinations mainly directed to discrimination. In Classics, Theology, English Literature, and other subjects, the same tendency may be observed, and that not at Cambridge only. Examination papers are everywhere becoming more and more a repertory of the difficulties which the subjects can be made to present.

It was argued that by following the old method the student saw at every step what he was doing; that in the new one, after he had written down certain equations, whether the subject were mechanics or geometry, he lost sight of the distinctive character of the matter, and arrived at the result by performing certain algebraical processes. This it was said, and truly, detracted much from the educational value of the study. The pupil was like a spectator who sees linen rags put into a receptacle at one end of a paper-mill, is told to put one piece after another of machinery in motion, and is then taken to see these same rags passing out from under a roller at the other end of the mill in the form of a smooth breadth of paper. It was admitted that many of the weaker men, — and the compulsion laid on the classical scholars had loaded the Tripos with such men—performed operations in some branches of mathematics by following a sort of *recipe*, and that they hurried over their lower subjects in hopes to be able to answer a few questions in subjects which they had better never have touched.

This controversy, raised by Dr. Whewell, happily forced the University to consider the question, "What is it that we are teaching the undergraduates mathematics and physics for?" It appears that the case is different for the higher and for the lower men. The good of our education, and indeed of all education, is twofold, it is made up of the value of the acquirements and of the intellectual benefit obtained in the process of acquiring: with the abler men the first, with the inferior ones the second preponderates. A high wrangler has acquired a mastery over the language and the conceptions of science, he is in a position to apply himself to the higher teaching or to embark in research. Thus the attainments he has acquired have a great positive value, while in point of mental training the University has done no more for him than for those whose acquirements are much smaller, indeed possibly less; because men of great ability usually train their own minds for themselves almost unconsciously. A considerable body of those who take mathematical honors obtain knowledge, inferior indeed to that of the gifted few, but still well worth the having; it may be hard to say whether these profit most by the knowledge they attain or by the improvement of their faculties. But there will remain a large number who, though they may keep in mind such elementary laws of Mechanics, or Optics, or Astronomy as are exemplified by what constantly passes before their eyes, and may find greater interest in nature in consequence, must yet set down nineteen-twentieths of the profit derived from their course of study to its having hardened their brains, and given them a more perfect use of their own powers. The minds of the ablest men are well disciplined before coming to the University. They have got their attention, their memory, and other faculties well under command. The weaker men need the training of a system, and the good they get from it is frequently very marked. The improvement in the *man* is often striking, while that in *his knowledge* is only moderate. Thus the benefit which accrues to the candidate for honors is made up of two elements, training and acquirement. With the Senior Wrangler nine-tenths may be set down to the acquirements obtained, with a low Junior Optime nine-tenths to the training.

This suggests that different modes of treatment may be desirable for those who are to draw such different kinds of benefit from their studies. Dr. Whewell accordingly proposed to divide the Examination into two parts, one framed particularly with a view to mental training, and the other to test high acquirements. Many of his recommendations were carried out in a new code of regulations for the Mathematical Tripos, which came into operation in 1848. It did not however introduce any *viva voce* Examination, though on this Dr. Whewell had laid great stress. The educational interest had rallied in great force under Dr. Whewell; but still, with the majority of the Senate, the paramount object was to secure perfect fairness of *selection;* and as in a *viva voce* Examination different candidates would be asked different questions, this, it was said, would derogate from that " equality for all " which was the pride of Cambridge. Moreover, there were two objections to a *viva voce* Examination for the Tripos which were weighty because they were practical. To examine orally in mathematics with good effect, demands a special insight into the working of the learner's mind, and a happy knack of hitting on his strong and weak points. Many excellent mathematicians, whose services might in other ways be most valuable, would never obtain these faculties : just as there are many excellent lawyers who have no gift for cross-examining witnesses. If, then, the oral part of the Examination were to be thoroughly well performed — and if it were not, it would become only an appendage to the paper work — this rare faculty would be regarded as essential, and the choice of Examiners would be restricted to the happy few who possessed it. Hereby, it was said, the advantage arising from the frequent introduction of fresh minds would be lost : the questions would run in grooves, and the candidates would find it more remunerative to study the papers of past years than to read in a liberal way.

The other objection applies to all *viva voce* Examinations, and will limit their use to cases in which the number of candidates is moderate. It turns on the costliness of the process in time and in labor. Two Examiners at least must be present to conduct the Examination; the same Examiners should question all the candidates, and the examination of each candidate should last twenty minutes. Hence the time requisite for examining a number of candidates is very considerable, and cannot always be afforded.

On the other hand, all those who have treated of Examinations have perceived that a *viva voce* Examination supplied a good corrective for the narrowing effect of a paper Examination, and had other advantages. Questions put orally are not recorded in the published papers, so that a part of the Examination remains in the dark, and candidates will not venture to disregard parts of their subjects because they do not find them introduced in the papers. If the tutor finds his pupils inclined to pass these matters by, he can urge that they may have to answer questions on them *viva voce*.

Moreover, a paper only shews the knowledge of the candidate, but not all his ignorance, except by implication. If a question raise points about which he is not clear, he passes on to something else, but in *viva voce* he has no escape; he must lay bare the state of his notions on the subjects on which he is questioned. If he shroud himself, as on paper he might do, under the words of a manual, the Examiner may ask him what they mean, or put some simple application which will test his grasp of the matter. The nerve, the presence of mind, and readiness of expression which are encouraged by a *viva voce* Examination, are also worth considering; they are mental habits, or the results of mental habits, and are evidences of character as well as valuable for themselves. They can only be formed from practice; and it is a good effect of this kind of Examination, that it will induce tutors to habituate pupils to oral questioning; to ensure this, however, it is necessary that the *viva voce* portion of the Examination should be made of considerable importance.

The University legislation of 1848 proceeded on the right track; it recognized in part the distinctive functions of Examinations, and provided separately for the discharge of each. Three days were allotted to the elementary subjects, which were to be treated without analysis, and every candidate had to obtain his degree by this Examination. This regulation was framed purely with a view to education. The distinctive conceptions belonging to the several physical subjects, which are of great educational value, are met with in the elementary parts of these subjects, and room was now given for forcing them on the attention of the student. Those who merely read mathematics to qualify themselves for the Classical Tripos found it advisable to confine themselves to the lower subjects, and in those they had an ample examination instead of a few scattered questions. After a short interval, the Examination was resumed, and questions in the higher subjects, treated of course by the analytical methods, were then set. This portion of the Examination was meant to answer the needs both of classification and also of scientific training. The places of candidates in the list depended on the combined result of the two Examinations.

Dr. Peacock and Dr. Whewell had also urged another point, viz. the limitation both of the range of subjects comprised in the Senate-House Examination, and also of the extent of each subject in itself. They prevailed so far, that a paper of directions to the Examiners was issued by the Board of Studies in 1850. The document is to be found in the report of the Cambridge Commission of 1852, in the evidence of the Rev. J. G. Mould, Fellow and Tutor of Corpus Christi College. It recommended the omission of investigations about which mathematicians are not agreed, and of those which lead to long analytical processes. Under the first head the mathematical theories of Heat, Electricity, and Magnetism, then somewhat imperfect, but on which a question or two had been asked occasionally, were excluded, and under the second the student was relieved of much dead weight. The result of these measures certainly was satisfactory in an educational point of view, and the Examinations retained their efficiency in determining the relative merits of candidates.

The Examination continued to be governed by this code of regulations for twenty years. The change that grew up in the meantime was in the direction of the extension of science.

The Universities have two aspects: they are seats of learning and they are places of education; they are regarded sometimes more especially in the one light, sometimes in the other. In former times the functions of the teacher and the *savant* could be perfectly well combined in an individual; science did not exact such exclusive devotion as she does now, and education did not involve the labor and anxiety of constantly preparing classes for Examination—the greater pressure of our time calls for a division of labor in this as in other things. The casts of mind required for a man of science and a teacher, though sometimes combined, are in one respect different. Sympathy with other minds is not essential for the former; with the latter it is all in all. The former must be devoted *avant tout* to the pursuit of truth in the abstract, the latter must look mainly to the improvement of his pupils. If he lights on a new problem or illustration, he takes an especial interest in it if it will serve to awaken clearer conceptions in some of his class; he is concerned in science chiefly as a vehicle of education; while his own special knowledge turns on the individual varieties of young minds and their laws of growth and action. To be a good schoolmaster, a man must first understand *boys*. The interest of the *savant*, on the other hand, is in science for her own sake — he counts himself rewarded if he can add something to the sum of human knowledge, as the other does if he have called out latent intelligence, and directed into a definite channel abilities which were running to waste.

Owing to this diversity, we mark in the history of the Tripos the action of an educational interest and a scientific interest—to use the terms rather in a colloquial sense. Those who looked mainly on the University as a place of learning were impatient of its being regarded as a mere school. They demanded that Cambridge teaching should embrace the sciences of Heat, Electricity, and Magnetism, which were becoming of immense importance and use, and were falling more and more under mathematical treatment; and their demand was most just. Scientific posts were being multiplied, men were wanted to fill them, a professional scientific education was required, and where, if not at Cambridge, it was asked, was this to be got? Cambridge, it was truly said, represented the mathematical learning of England, and it was derogatory to the country that the view of science she presented should be scanty or imperfect. This view was generally admitted, but it did not follow that these advanced subjects should be introduced into the Tripos Examination, which, as some maintained, represented only a *liberal* education in mathematics and not a *special* one. As, however, the main interest at Cambridge was fastened on the Tripos, there appeared to be no other way of drawing attention to those subjects than by admitting them into it. On the other hand, it was plain that the course would be so much extended by the admission of these new subjects, that no student could possibly master the whole in his three years and a quarter. After much discussion, a scheme was put forth including the above-named branches of study, increasing the length of the Examination and allotting certain proportions of credit to the different subjects. It was hoped that students would be induced to select a limited course for thorough study. Many persons of experience feared, with good grounds, that these hopes would prove vain, and that some students would do as they had done before, viz. attempt to learn scraps of the easier parts of nearly all the subjects. Much opposition was made to the Grace, but it was felt that if it were rejected the important subjects in question would for a long time be excluded from University teaching, and that the University might be thought indifferent to the growing needs of science; it was also suggested that if the evils anticipated came about, they would soon be practically felt, and therefore would soon call for a remedy.

This scheme came into operation in 1873, and has undergone no change up to the present time (1875). Prospects were held out that the Board of Mathematical Studies would issue a schedule curtailing some of the subjects, but this has not appeared. Such a schedule is urgently wanted; that which was put forward in 1850 has passed out of mind, and it would only apply to a part of the present course.

Our narrative of the History of the Tripos is now at an end. The principles which have come to light in the course of it may guide us in judging of the defects of the existing system, and of the direction in which we are to look for a remedy.

The Examination now seems to contemplate a liberal education mixed up with a technically scientific one. We ought to have distinct Examinations corresponding to each kind. Many of the more abstruse subjects, as learned by the great mass of students, convey few new conceptions, and merely load the memory. The value of these subjects lies in the application of them, and this application few students ever make. The course is now so long that the mind of a student who would carry the whole into one Examination is injuriously distracted, and his general education is, in a degree, sacrificed to the training him for the struggle. So long as the subjects comprised in the Tripos were not too extensive to be mastered during the student's course, there was no need for a boy at school to be pushed far forward in mathematics. The race was to be run at Cambridge, and formerly few arrived there bringing with them enough mathematical knowledge to be of importance compared with what might be attained at the University; but now, when no one can possibly master all the subjects in the allotted time, it adds greatly to the weight of metal a candidate can bring to bear in the final contest, for him to have read, before coming up, what would otherwise occupy his first two years. In consequence, we have in every year a dozen freshmen who might be high Senior Optimes at the end of their first Term, but who are sometimes defective in other departments of education. A provision, indeed, is made in the University for testing the possession of the elements of a general education. This is called the Previous Examination (Little-go), but as it does not bear on the great race in which the competitor is to win his prize, it is looked on as an interruption, which must be got over as soon as possible. If a boy at school shew mathematical talent, he is often withdrawn from part of his studies that he may be brought forward in that subject, by excelling in which he may gain glory for his school and advantages for himself in competitive Examinations. One side of his mind is thus early developed disproportionately to the rest, while some regions of it are left uncultivated and may become less apt to receive cultivation. Strong and genial natures will take care of themselves when they get to the University. They will have spare energy enough to create for themselves countervailing interests in literature and society, or, if their *physique* allow it, in outdoor sports; but with those of less general power and vivacity — especially if they are working with no love for their study, but are toiling prematurely as bread-winners by the sweating of their brains — the danger of unhealthy action of the nervous system from undue concentration is considerable, and such need to be watched over with intelligent care.

The great extent of our course not only harms some of the individuals who are training for it, but it will eventually thin our competitors, for it discourages all who are not already good mathematicians when they come to the University. It may be predicted that if the present state of things continues the Mathematical Tripos will decline in numbers. When a young man of ambition looks round him, on coming to the University, he will not choose a career in which he has no chance of high distinction; and if he sees no prospect of this in the Mathematical Tripos, on account of his having received a general education, and not a special mathematical one, he will take to one of the Triposes which deal with subjects like Law, or Moral Science, where he starts fair, and can cover the ground in the time allotted; or else he will put off his coming, and be so much the later in entering on the work of life.

The remedy must be sought, as I have said, in distributing the subjects into two Examinations. It had been hoped that each student would make a selection for himself: this, as was foreseen, he does not usually do, and it must be done for him.

Much advantage was found by dividing the Examination into parts to represent the Pass and Honor functions of the Examination. We must now make a further division, and this I think will be better done by dividing the subjects according to the purposes for which they are studied — whether for mental training or for scientific use — than according to the conceptions they involve. In place of the latter part of our present Tripos I would have two Examinations, one answering to our idea of a high liberal education in mathematics, and another framed to test the possession of advanced scientific knowledge, such as might be suited for persons whose intended course in life required them to be conversant with the higher branches of mathematical and physical science. The first list might be in order of merit as now, the second in classes with two brackets in each.

I think that a division of subjects, according to the end with a view to which they are studied, is the most convenient for our purpose, because the modes of reading and the appropriate kinds of Examination are different according as persons are studying for an Examination which is to test ability, or in order to get hold of the subject and to make use of it. It is one thing reading Law for Examination, another reading Law for Practice. So it is with Science. A student reading the higher Dynamics, for instance, for *Examination*, has not half done his work when he has mastered the theory and can make the plain applications of it he would want for any practical purpose. In the Polytechnic Schools abroad he stops at this point; if he would shew superior comprehension, he evinces this by drawing up essays or papers on particular points of the subject *at leisure*. He learns the subject because he wants to know it, but he does not require to have all the artifices which are effective for solving ingenious puzzles at his fingers' ends. The student who reads for a place in a class list has to learn, besides the subject itself, every possible application of it to problems, and must be familiar with those algebraical artifices which are essential for rapidly bringing out results : in fact Examiners regard the subject, in a degree, as affording an educational exercise, and furnishing a criterion to measure ingenuity by, while the *savant* regards it as a branch of science of which he wants to be master.

In the first of the two Examinations into which I propose to split that part of our present Examination which follows the "first three days" (for in that of the "first three days" I would make no serious alteration), the subjects would continue to be treated educationally, but with some view to discrimination— that is, much as they are at present. In the second of these Examinations, which would be the *third* of the whole system (if we call that of the "first three days" the first part), the highest subjects, with which alone it would deal, should be treated in a different spirit ; they should be regarded as instruments which the learner wants to be able to handle for scientific use and for the prosecution of research. He should have his eyes turned toward experimental investigation, and should be taught to estimate nicely the nature and value of the evidence thus obtained.

The Tripos system would then consist of three Examinations, the first and second of which would be combined as the two parts of our Examination now are, and the third, the higher scientific Examination, would stand to the rest something in the same relation which that for the Smith's Prize now holds. The Smith's Prizes* might be awarded by it, and the Professors might take part in it. I do not enter into the question of the *times* at which these Examinations should be held, because I am only

---

* These are two Prizes for proficiency in the higher Mathematics and Natural Philosophy. The Examination is conducted by the Professors of Mathematics, and is held soon after the publication of the Tripos list.

sketching an outline of a plan. The subjects of the second Examination should be chosen for their *educational* value, including, for instance, all those now placed in the first division and a few others. These might be mastered by able students in three years. The majority of candidates would not proceed to the further scientific Examination. The list in order of merit, drawn up from the combined result of the first and second Examinations, would furnish very nearly as good a criterion of *general* ability as the entire Examination now affords. Certain College rewards, not excessive in value, might be awarded for distinguished success in this portion of the Examination alone. Such success would indicate the possession of many of the qualities which go to make valuable men ; it would shew a trained memory, a strong head, much readiness of expression and fertility of resource, but it would not shew the same amount of positive scientific attainment as a high place in the Tripos now does.

The higher subjects, which would be dealt with in the third Examination, may possibly in time become so extensive as to require to be grouped in two divisions. The candidates for these would be manageable in point of number, and therefore a *viva voce* Examination would be practicable.* The subjects, also, would be better suited to it than the mathematics

---

* Some of the advantages of a *vivâ voce* Examination for the less advanced candidates might be obtained by *giving out, vivâ voce*, one by one, some plain questions on the principles of the elementary subjects and quite easy examples. These should not be published. The Examiners would not think it beneath them to give simple examples in this way, though they will not introduce into a paper that is to be published questions which do not shew neatness, and require ingenuity. In France, when an example is appended to a theorem, it is a simple application. The "riders," with us, have become problems, and many students therefore confine their attention to the questions from books. It would assimilate the action to that of *vivâ voce*, if negative marks could be given for errors in elementary principles, or for the declining to give an answer.

now commonly read.   The *principles* of these, which alone afford scope for *viva voce* questions, occupy but a small space of the whole.   In the higher subjects, however, the Examination might be to a certain degree practical, and this part of it should be held in a laboratory.   Candidates might then be called on to perform simple experiments, to point out the conditions required for accurate and trustworthy results, and to explain phenomena brought under their eyes.

The class-list, in this scientific Examination, would not, I think, require to be arranged in order of merit. There might be two or three classes, and two brackets in each class.   This would remove one of the objections to a *viva voce* Examination stated some pages back.   The candidates might take very different courses of reading, so that the Examination would be imperfectly homogeneous, and therefore attempts at closer classification might prove fallacious; while a place in the first class would be sufficient distinction to justify the colleges in awarding emoluments to those who obtained it, and would mark out those who shewed qualifications for the prosecution of scientific research or for high educational posts.

Having traced the growth of our Tripos system to its present condition, I have thought it worth while to point out the nature of the further changes which I would suggest for consideration.   They would present a development in accordance with the history. It would not suit my purpose or my limits, to enter into detailed proposals for a University measure.   Still less can I deal with the philosophical principles of mathematical education.   Should a treatise on this subject be required, a rich store of materials will be found in the Report of the French Commissioners to which I have referred, and also in the evidence on the Mathematical Tripos given in the Report of the Commissioners of 1852, much of which (that especially of Professor Stokes and Mr. Robert Leslie Ellis) is of the highest value, and contains material most deserving of being preserved in a more accessible form.

I have been struck, as I proceeded, with the amount of deep thought and practical sense which has been brought to bear on the framing of our Examination, and I cannot too highly estimate the advantages which our system has derived from its operation having been always under the eyes and under the control of an educational body, quick to observe the wants that made themselves felt, and thoroughly honest in endeavoring to remedy the evils that became sensible from time to time. I should be glad for our existing students to feel their obligations to those of whose foregone thought and care they are the inheritors.

I have had to speak of the evils arising from the too great extent of our subjects at the present time. These evils however it must be recollected, only affect a few students — perhaps a sixth part of the candidates for the Tripos. Those who have no hopes of the highest distinction are free from this undue strain, and they sometimes gain more in proportion to their powers from their University residence than those who have a prospect of much greater success.

My views of the action of the Examination on the whole are well expressed in a passage which I will quote from the evidence of Mr. William Hopkins, who, after making certain criticisms, concludes as follows : —

"Let me not be thought, in making these remarks, to undervalue the excellence of our present Examinations and the influence they exercise over our studies. The facility and accuracy with which our Students go through complicated processes of mathematical investigation, and the command they acquire over the ordinary artifices of analysis, are very remarkable, and very much facilitate their progress in any higher mathematical researches to which they may afterwards apply themselves. There is also another consequence of our mode of Examination, which, in considering our system of studies as one of mental discipline, can hardly be too highly appreciated. The necessity of giving brief and accurate answers to the questions proposed superinduces the necessity also of a distinct and logical arrangement of the successive steps of a demonstration and the habitual use of condensed and accurate language. The tendency to careless and illogical habits of thought, existing in most undisciplined minds, finds in this system as perfect a correction as the individual character of the Student will admit of. It has often been a matter of great interest with me to watch the gradual development of this exactness of thought and perspicuity of language. The young Student frequently commences his studies here with great defects in these respects; but where there has been sufficient intellectual power and activity, I have never failed to witness a rapid improvement, as the result of our system, from the moment he became sensible of his own deficiency, and (which is equally essential) that it could only be amended by his own persistent efforts, and not merely by the corrections which his Tutors might from time to time suggest to him. The perfect arrangement and style with which many of our higher Students answer the questions proposed to them constitutes one of the most striking results of our system. I could wish to see the same power called forth more effectively on a larger scale—in the exposition of the more general principles and results of mathematical science as well as in the development of its individual propositions." *

* " Report of Her Majesty's Commissioners, appointed to inquire into the state of the University of Cambridge, 1852," p. 243.—Evidence of W. Hopkins, Esq., M.A.

CHAPTER V.

THE FUNCTIONS OF EXAMINATIONS. SELECTION.

IT has been said that what is called scientific method consists in applying to abstruse matters the homely maxim of doing one thing or considering one train of circumstances at a time. This remark is illustrated by the foregoing sketch of the History of the Mathematical Tripos at Cambridge. By degrees it was understood that Examinations fulfilled many different purposes, each of which might be best effected by some particular mode of examining. We might not want a separate Examination for each purpose, but we ought to know how each purpose might be effected, and the relative importance we attach to it.

Clearly, then, the first thing to be settled about any Examination scheme was, What was intended to be done by it? The discussions that took place at Cambridge shew that the proposers of schemes were often by no means agreed on this primary point, and it was very much through these debates, and from people finding that they failed to understand one another because they were driving at different ends, that the complexity of the action of Examinations came to be perceived.

Having cleared their minds as to what they wanted, the next point to be considered was to what degree, if at all, Examinations could effect what was required. The practical acquaintance which most residents in the University had with Examinations shewed them that as means of selection these could only be relied upon to detect particular qualities, and that even for them it was very important to know under what circumstances the knowledge had been acquired. The efficacy of Examinations as a means of calling out the interest of a pupil and directing it into the desired channels was soon recognized by teachers. They were supposed to furnish a stimulus or motive power which could be applied to produce any required kind of mental cultivation : but as the Examination itself is not the motive to study, but only the mechanism whereby the efficient motive for learning — whatever it may be, the desire of gain, or distinction, or knowledge for its own sake—is embodied in a form in which it can be readily brought to bear on the pupil, this motive power is not got without something that is expended to obtain it. Some advantage must be in prospect. The Examination is the engine, not the fuel, and will only act as long as there are prizes or honors to be awarded. In the case, indeed, of one who can work for an Examination merely to satisfy himself that he is acqainted with a subject, the fuel, so to say, is self-supplied.

Finally came the question of what was the best way of using Examinations for the purpose we had in view. If we could answer this positively and fully we should see our way to that scientific system of Examinations which Dean Merivale, in his evidence given to the Cambridge Commission, pointed out as the most promising solution of certain difficulties that beset the higher education.

As yet, however, no step has been taken towards bringing the subject into that degree of order which it must attain before science can deal with it. In education, indeed, we may hope to see some scientific classification, of tendencies at any rate, though the deductions of theory will, owing to disturbing causes, often disagree with the facts. We may get some ideas of the most advantageous mode of using examinations for forming the mental habits, or testing the acquirements we want the pupil to possess ; but, as I said in the second Chapter, when we use Examination for *selection*, the matter becomes complicated by many social and political considerations over and above the difficulties naturally attaching to it.

No particular sort of Examination will produce one kind of effect or test one quality, and *that alone*, any more than any drug in the Materia Medica will produce one particular action on a particular organ, and no other whatever, on any part of the system. Hence we have "intermixture of effects," and we cannot sort our agents according to what we want them for, and label each of them, like cakes of watercolor in a box; all we can do, after settling what qualities we are looking for, is to find out by what signs we may judge of their presence, what kind of Examination will best bring them out, and then, what indirect effects this kind of Examination will have on education.

For though, to give some kind of order to our inquiry, I shall continue, as hitherto, to consider separately Examinations as employed to effect selection and to direct education, yet we must bear in mind that this distinction is only *actually* true when we regard the purpose in the minds of those who draw up the schemes, and that as soon as an Examination comes into operation, the two kinds of action must

necessarily take place together. There must be discrimination, or something equivalent, because the
candidates must aim at *success* in the Examination;
it has no effect if they do not, and by success they
mean either proving their superiority to others, or
getting a warrant of proficiency; and, on the other
hand, although the framers may have regarded the
Examination only as a sieve to sort out the article
they require, yet it must have an educational effect;
for the dimensions of the interstices will be accurately
measured by teachers and trainers, and an article will
be produced which, at the least cost of brains and
labor, will fulfil the conditions required.

The importance of this last consideration is seen
when we consider on what grounds the competitive
system is most fully justified. When applied to
Government appointments it may have some convenience as a mode of avoiding jobbery and solicitation;
but, as is said in the second Chapter, unless it can be
so carried out as to do more good than harm to education, we only get one kind of mischief instead of
another — and there is a large class of emoluments,
such as Fellowships at Colleges, and Scholarships
both at Colleges and Schools, whose *raison d'être* is,
in great part, to assist in promoting high cultivation.
We ought to find in such improvement a return for
the time, labor, and money, expended in competition.
I have shewn (page 49) that a high liberal education
will not generally be obtained by any but those who
have means and leisure as well as an appreciation of
learning, unless by means of endowments, as in
England, or by the enforcing of a thorough School and
University curriculum as a condition for entrance to
any liberal profession or for holding the higher Gov-

ernment posts, as is the case in Prussia. The latter course is out of the question in England; our ideas of the liberty of the subject would be outraged by the State taking possession of the boy, and denying to his parents their right of dealing with him in their own way. Hence, if we are to support a high general standard of liberal education, it must be done by making such education appear remunerative, and the cheapest way of doing this is to turn to account the hopefulness of young people and their parents by holding out rewards to competition; we hereby enlist on our side the spirit of contest of the younger people and the sanguine expectations which their elders entertain of them, and, as has been shewn, for one who gets a prize, forty may obtain a high education in aiming at it.

In this view, the effect on the learners is more important than the accuracy of selection. We have to do with the formation of the mental habits, and even the moral character of those who may be in positions of great importance, connected either with the Government or with the education of the country; and it is essential, not only that the knowledge should be genuine, but that it should be attained in a way which inculcates high views of the purposes of learning and a chivalrous feeling of honor. If we damage the general standard of truthfulness by leading young men to glory in having outwitted Examiners, and seemed to be what they are not, by the dexterous use of a scrap of information, then we lose far more morally than we gain in any other way.

When we set about selecting, by means of Examinations, the person who shall be most able or best educated, we at once become aware of how ill-defined our notions of ability and education are. A full analysis of these notions would fill a larger volume than I mean to write, and so I must limit myself to explaining what I mean by these terms, when it is necessary to do so, not with any pretence to philosophical precision or to completeness, but so as to establish an understanding with the reader.

We have then, now before us, the whole subject of Examinations, so far as their testing function is concerned. This gives us an unwieldly mass of matter to deal with, and we may be thankful for any mode of breaking it up into more manageable portions; we very soon come in sight of a distinction which will be of service to us in this respect. What Examinations elicit directly is always, either the knowledge of the candidate, as, for instance, an acquaintance with facts or the matter of certain books, or else it is the result of knowledge which has been assimilated, and out of which there springs a *faculty*, such as that of writing a foreign language, or of solving problems. But we may regard this knowledge in two very different ways,—we may want it for itself, or for what it tells us about the man. It has more or less intrinsic value, and at the same time it shews us something of the powers of the man who has acquired it.

We may go to an Exhibition, either to find a picture to our mind, or to pick out the artist who is most suited to execute some work for which we wish to give a commission. In these two cases we regard the pictures differently. In the first case the beauty of the subject of the picture will go far with us, in the second it is unimportant. We may perhaps get more insight into the artist's powers from a spirited sketch than from a highly-finished performance, and we shall especially pay attention to a picture eliciting the particular qualities wanted for the work we wish to get done.

Examinations may, in like manner, be used in two ways. They serve as the criterion of the possession of particular kinds of knowledge or skill for those who have to employ this special knowledge or skill for a particular purpose; but they may also be used to test ability of a more general kind. The capacity of the *man* may be shewn by the character of his work. One kind of work will test one quality, as taste or imagination; another, which involves patient labor, will shew industry and self-denial. Hence we should choose our testing processes differently, according as we are on the look out for attainments or for capacity, and scrutinize the results with a different eye, in the two cases.

But though we have here got a serviceable distinction, it does not go very far; after we have traced it a little way, the branches become intertwined and grow together. For knowledge helps to foster the development of matured ability. We may never mean to use the knowledge in displaying which the candidate has shewn the ability which recommends him to us, yet the possession of this may be a source of constant improvement to him. A man who has stored up a fund of knowledge has usually a greater copiousness of ideas — he has matter at hand from which to draw comparisons or illustrations — he has more sources of interest open to him, and therefore more of his faculties are kept bright from use. Hence, in framing an Examination to test ability, although we may in the first instance look to the qualities of the man, and direct our testing appliances to discover

this, still, if we look far forward, and wish to select
the man whose career is likely to be the most serviceable, we must have an eye to the knowledge with
which he has equipped himself before starting, not
for its practical use, but as an inner help to future
self-cultivation — this is more necessary the more
the nature of his future occupation will preclude general reading, when once he is engaged in his vocation
— and it will apply more particularly to those subjects
which necessitate some drudgery at the outset, or
which usually require a teacher, like languages or
mathematics. A man who wishes to acquaint himself with History, or English Literature, or even
Political Economy, has only to read the proper books ;
this he may do in spare intervals, but a busy man is
not likely to write exercises, or to familiarize himself
with mathematical processes. The two Examinations
for the Indian Civil Service afford good instances of
Examinations held with views of discriminating ability
and knowledge respectively.

The proposed object of the first Examination, by
which the candidates are selected, is to choose the
ablest young men out of a large body of candidates.
The way in which they acquit themselves in the different subjects which may possibly enter into a liberal
education, is taken as the criterion of ability. This
plan, under the conditions of the case, and as Examinations were then understood, seemed a good one.
The defects that I have mentioned have arisen from
the framers not foreseeing that an Examination backed
by large prizes would call forth a special sort of teaching ; perhaps, too, they overrated the sufficiency of a
single Examination, unaided by an acquaintance with
the way in which the candidates have been taught,
for testing the possession of the desired qualities.

They were quite right in having one Examination to test ability, and another to ensure the possession of the knowledge required for professional use. In the first Examination they regard the candidate's performances in Classics, Mathematics, English, and the rest of the subjects, with a view to judge of the man. He will probably rarely bring into actual use in his official life exactly what he has learned. He is not selected because the state wants to avail itself of these acquirements; they are only taken as the index of certain qualities shewn in the acquisition of them. Hence, in the examination for selection, it may matter much *how* the candidate's knowledge has been got. His German, for instance, may have been learnt analytically in England, much as a dead language is, and in this case, a good knowledge will betoken accuracy and the power of grasping the principles of grammar — or it may have been learnt as a child in Germany, in which case it tells nothing of the man's powers, and is only of service in estimating the *man*, from the effect which any real knowledge has in improving its possessor; one who can turn to a German book as readily as to an English one, has, no doubt, access to writers who are particularly valuable in keeping alive the process of self-culture. In the further Examination the case is quite different: a knowledge of Law and Indian languages is required for the daily needs of the man's prospective career, and all that the Examiner has to ascertain is that he has the knowledge that is wanted; this he esteems entirely for its intrinsic value. If the candidate knows Tamûl well, it does not matter how or where he got it. A language learnt analytically may, it is true, be more firmly held in the memory than one learned by ear — the more laborious method may perhaps leave a more permanent impression on the cerebrum — and this consideration would have to be taken into account, because the durability of knowledge is an element in its value; but in the case before us, that of a language which is to be constantly used, there is little fear of its being forgotten.

It is obvious that the results of an Examination can be more thoroughly relied upon to test the possession of knowledge, or of a faculty engendered by the assimilation of knowledge, than to determine the ability of the man. The business of the Examiner in the first case is much more simple. He wishes to see if a candidate possess some accomplishment, and calls on him to give a specimen of his powers. If he profess to know a foreign language, he may be asked to speak, to write, and to translate; if to know the principles of Law, he can be asked to state them and to apply them to some simple case; if he acquit himself with credit, then we may suppose that the bulk of his knowledge will answer to the sample, for the passages or cases put before him could not have been specially prepared. But in estimating a man's mental power from the knowledge he displays, we ought to know how long he has taken to acquire it, his age, and the advantages that he has had. No doubt, whatever be the subjects of Examination, unless the questions turn wholly on dry facts or mere terminology, the quality of a man's mind will be shewn by it in some degree; first-rate ability will contrive to peep out, and positive stupidity will stand self-convicted. But if the Examiner's object is only to ascertain what the candidate knows, and not what he is, he will not set questions in order to see the play of his mind, or consider his answers with this view; and an Examination so conducted cannot be trusted to indicate, with any nicety, different shades. of ability.

As I have said, in substance, before, the result that we get by passing the minds of candidates through the mill of Examinations, is a compound in which the elements of knowledge and ability will always be both present, but mixed in very varying proportions — frequently, too, they will be so intimately combined that it is no easy matter to disengage them. A man's knowledge is an element of his prospective ability, and his ability will appear in the character of his knowledge and his way of giving it out. But more delicate machinery and nicer handling may be wanted in order to obtain the greatest possible proportion of the more subtle of these two elements in the yield of our Examination-mill.

It will be convenient to deal first with the most difficult case, because in considering this we shall be led to a rough analysis of some of the qualities which characterize the kinds of ability which the framers of Examinations mostly have in view, and this analysis will enable us to see our way better in what follows. To consider, then, one point at a time, we will take a hypothetical case. Let us suppose that out of a body of candidates we want to select those who have the greatest intellectual capacity, those who, to use an old phrase, are "of the most superior parts."

Now we cannot lay bare the intellectual mechanism and judge of it by inspection, we can only infer the excellence of the internal apparatus and the perfection of its workmanship from the quality of the work turned out: this work, in the case of young people, is represented by the knowledge they have attained, and the powers they have acquired. We must form our estimate of the way in which it is probable that a young man will do the work of manhood by looking at the way in which he has already performed the proper work of youth. We should scrutinize, therefore, the character and amount of a young man's acquirements, in this case, in order to see what light they throw on his mental constitution and calibre.

The case is like judging of the works of a watch by its accuracy in keeping time, or of the machinery of a mill by the texture and smoothness of the cloth produced. We do not want, in this case, to set a value on the fabric itself. It depends very much on the quality of the cotton, and, besides, we are not thinking of buying the cloth, but the mill : so here, we are seeking not what the youth knows, but what he is. We are going to use him not as an expert, but as a man.

To carry on our metaphor a little further. The machinery of this mill will not go of itself. We must have steam-power or water-power at hand to drive it : this consideration affects the value. So in the case before us, we want to know, not only whether the intellectual apparatus is good, but what force there is to work it. In human beings this force is the will. We may find an admirable intellect, which either lapses into torpor, from the absence of moving power, or consumes itself to no purpose in ill-regulated or spasmodic action. Hence it is important for our object to find out all we can about the volition and energy of the minds that come under review. We can trace these qualilties in some small degree in combination with others, but the data furnished by

Examinations for judging about them are confessedly insufficient, and we can only give our conclusions as approximations. We may say that a man must have employed certain faculties with diligence and resolution for a certain time to learn what he has done, but we cannot say whether this industry came from his own strength of character, or whether it was due to the absence of temptation, the stimulus of an object eagerly coveted and a contest close at hand; or, what is possible, whether the apparatus in his case was really worked, not by his own energy and volition, but by those of his tutor transfused into him. In order to determine this, and therefore to augur confidently how he will turn out, we must know the circumstances of his education. In actual life private employers, or head-masters of schools, contrive to get good information on these points; but in our hypothetical case we are supposed to be investigating the question, "How far we may judge of ability by Examinations alone." I may say, however, in passing, that if papers containing well-drawn queries as to the energy of a pupil, his self-command, and his power of influencing others —all which qualities peep out at School and College— were sent to the tutors or masters of candidates, information would be obtained which would be worth having. Practical persons could soon tell to what answers they might attach credit.

Our hypothetical case may not answer exactly to anything we find in practice—the suppositions which we make to enable us to contemplate one kind of action by itself will, in most kinds of science, in Dynamics, for instance, or Political Economy, lead us away from the actual existing state of things — but we find many Examinations, in which the determination of the relative ability of the competitors apart from that of their knowledge, is distinctly contemplated. We hear it said of particular Examinations that they do or do not "bring out the cleverest man," and in certain Fellowship Examinations the avowed object is, not to reward proficiency, but to pick out the man who, from his mental calibre, is most likely to "do credit to the College" by making a figure in life.

And now we come to the question, "What do we mean by ability?" and here we seem to have opened up a wide question of mental science, but happily our range is limited by these two considerations : — first, we need only concern ourselves with those kinds of ability which the framers of Examinations have in view; and, secondly, we have only to consider the qualities which can be brought under review by an Examination.

The varities of human ability which Examinations are employed to discover and to measure gather into two groups ; of one group we may take the man of science, of the other the man of action, as the type. The strength of the one lies in dealing with general ideas or abstractions, while that of the other turns not only on his grasp of the principles he has to apply, but also on his comprehension of the nature of the persons on whom or with whom he has to act. We need not analyze all the qualities which go to make the ideal philosopher or statesman, though we must understand how our ignorance about the rest invalidates our results. We need only treat particularly now of those which an Examination can be made to disclose. Many qualities which go to constitute what is commonly called genius, act irregularly, and cannot be called into operation by the will when required, and so cannot be tested with certainty in an Examination. A man can no more display genius on demand than make a joke when told to do so. We could not call on persons to write poems in an Examination room : if we did, we should get a quantity of very fair verse, but the man who wrote the best would probably be as far as any one from all possibility of becoming a poet. Originality, and what is called brilliancy, will usually gleam out now and then, if the Examination be long enough, but if it consist only of a paper or two, it may happen that no sparkle shews itself, or, owing to some happy opportunity, we may meet with a brilliant display. Here, as in many other cases, we see the superior testing power of an Examination which extends over a considerable time.

Neither have we to look for an insight into human nature or for the wisdom of matured judgment, or the tolerant and appreciative spirit of the man who has gone thoughtfully through life, wishing to find "a soul of goodness in things evil." These are qualities which do not belong to the time of life of those who come under examination : and even if they did, I do not see how we could detect them by an Examination. The attempt to do so would cause them to be simulated, and would thereby perplex the Examiner, and do much mischief as regards education.

What I propose, then, to do is this :—I shall glance over those mental qualities which more or less come under our cognizance in Examinations, and which go to the making of some of those kinds of ability which Examinations are framed to detect. Then we must cast our eye over that large area which Examinations cannot explore, and we shall then be in a position to judge how far we may trust the verdict of an Examination. We shall find that both as to ability and knowledge, more particularly the latter, Examinations will furnish much information which cannot be got in any other way.

Further, the gauging of ability is a much more delicate matter than the weighing of knowledge, and it can only be entrusted to an Examiner of special skill. He must be able to recognize the qualities which are disclosed by the performances of a candidate, and he should follow the workings of his mind as if he were part of himself. Such Examiners cannot be readily found, though there are plenty who can judge of acquirements; this puts a practical difficulty in the way of the selection of persons, on a large scale, on the score of *ability*. It increases this difficulty if the public insist on having a list of numerical marks as a guarantee of fairness. There are some subjects in which, if a paper be marked question by question, the scores of the different candidates may ill represent their different powers; but such a plan gives a security that each answer has been carefully considered, and excludes the possibility of favor. Hence to deal with a number of candidates and to satisfy the public, a system like that of the Indian Civil Service Examination, which awards its distinctions by the aggregate of producible attainments, has great practical convenience. As a criterion of ability, this gives but a rough approximation; but then no very nice discrimination is required, because so many candidates are selected at once, that the action, as will be shewn hereafter, is not very different from that of a Pass Examination with a standard of about 1200 marks. Of the educational effects of this Examination I have said something, and shall have to say more.

The kinds of ability with which we are concerned are made up partly of natural gifts in the way of mental powers, and partly of habits of mind which have been formed, either by the strong will and self-watchfulness of the individual, or by the influences brought to bear on him in his youth. The general calibre of the mind will also be influenced by the mental diet and exercise, that is to say, by the supply of valuable matter to enrich the mind, and by inducements to exert it in a well-regulated manner.

The formation of mental habits, as has been said in a previous chapter, is more important than the imparting of knowledge, and in estimating ability, we must pay regard to these habits of mind, both for their intrinsic value, and because, since the individual must in a great degree, have formed them for himself, they speak well for his volitional power and his sound judgment in self-education.

This word volitional brings us to the consideration of two distinct modes of action of the mental powers, which are called by Dr. Carpenter, in his excellent work on Mental Physiology, volitional and automatic. For a full account of the nature of these modes of action, the reader is referred to the chapters on Attention, Memory, Will, and Imagination, in that work. The meaning of the words may be made sufficiently plain for the understanding of what follows by a simple illustration.

We will take the case of attention, which is explained to be a condition of *active* recipiency of the mind, as opposed to that of passive recipiency, in which it receives impressions without giving heed to them. A person walking through a street is sufficiently aware of the objects which come in his way, to prevent his running against them, but he may not pay any attention to them at all. If something in a shop-window strikes him, and he notes it as he passes, this is *automatic* action of the attention ; if the object recall circumstances connected with some past event, we have automatic action of the memory. What is thus remembered may lead to a further train of recollection. This action is still automatic. But if the person wish to call at a house with a certain number, his attention is volitionally directed to the numbers on the houses, and if he recall to mind the message that he meant to deliver, this is a volitional exercise of memory. So when a passage in a poem brings a vivid picture before the mind's eye, this action of imagination is automatic, but when, by dwelling on the part assigned to a character in a play of Shakespeare we try to form a conception of the sort of mind or person which Shakespeare had in view ; or when, from the traces on certain planes, we set ourselves to conceive the form of a geometrical surface in space, this is an exercise of volitional imagination.

The faculty which above all others claims our attention is Memory. All our knowledge, all that is got from books, and much that is learned from life, is trusted to her for safe-keeping. There is no Examination in which her fidelity is not tried, and there are many which try nothing else — except, of course, the power of expression. Memory, pure and simple, as philosophers tell us, is the reproduction of some past state of mind, and the recognition of the reproduced state as an old acquaintance; but we meet with it most often in combination with other qualities, and some combinations occur so commonly, and are so constant in their characteristics, that they may be treated of as being faculties of themselves. I shall mention some kinds with which we have to do: (1) what I will call the Portative Memory, which simply conveys matter, and whose only aim, like that of a carrier, is to deliver the parcel as it was received; (2) the Analytical Memory, which is exercised when the mind furnishes a view of its own, and thereby holds together a set of impressions selected out of a mass. Thus a barrister strings together the material facts of his case, and a lecturer those of his science, by regarding their bearing on what he wants to establish; (3) the Assimilative Memory, which absorbs the matter into the system, so that the knowledge assimilated becomes part of the person's own self, like that of his name, or of a familiar language. Further, I may name a variety less important as regards Examination—the Index Memory, that which does not recollect the matter itself, but only where to find it; an instance as seen in the lawyer, who does not pretend to carry the law on every point in his head, but who can readily refer to the case in which it is laid down.

Memory, in the words of Dr. Carpenter, "grows to" the circumstances in which she finds herself in a very remarkable way; this case of the lawyer is one illustration. People develop the kind of memory they want; the idle school-boy gets the power of learning a short lesson in a few minutes, which he forgets as soon as it is said; the *savant* readily acquires languages or sciences, but does not always recollect a commission in the matters of daily life; while a servant, who "has a head," but who cannot write down a memorandum, will recollect the directions given him on a number of points.

Memory may tell us of the existence of a power

beyond herself, for remembrance implies foregone attention, and if this attention have been volitionally exercised, as it is in application to study, memory is an evidence of the possession of some power of will. The power of attention is sometimes very defective, and the want of it is a presumptive sign of feeble intelligence or small brain power. It is this deficiency far more than idleness, or mere backwardness from want of teaching, that causes failures in pass Examinations. Most commonly the weakness is only a want of *volitional* attention; the power of attention exists, but acts automatically: it is drawn off by any incident or any suggested idea, and the individual has no power of applying his mind. He is, to use Dr. Carpenter's expression, "bird-witted."

In speaking of the different varieties of memory, it must be understood that I distinguish them according to the functions that we find performed, and that I am not dealing with the matter psychologically. These functions are displayed in Examinations, and are well marked and important.

The Portative Memory is shewn in the reproduction of what has been learnt, and from a display of it we see that the pupil has been able to set himself to work for a certain time with considerable activity. This shews some power of volitional attention, and in the Examinations of boys, and of young men who only aim at "qualifying," some regard must be paid to it, because it is nearly the only mental quality which we can look for. Subjects which turn on a reproduction of the contents of books, such as Literature and the outlines of History and Geography, as learned from Manuals, as well as the rudiments of Natural Science, which often consist very largely of nomenclature, are, nine parts out of ten, mere exercises of Portative Memory. If a youth be well taught, he may get, even from such rudiments, some general views which will remain by him; but there are in most "pass" papers enough questions, which only require this kind of memory, to enable a candidate to scrape through; and those who are not ambitious, being aware of this, will do nothing more than make sure of such questions. They will train their memory to carry a small amount of matter for the necessary time, whatever that may be. For instance, the translation of a Greek book must be held in the head for weeks and months, because only a little can be learned every day, while dates and facts and brief outlines are "got up" within the last twenty-four hours. Hence we may often flatter ourselves that we are examining students in all those branches of knowledge "without which no gentleman's education is complete," but what we really test is only this *carrying power* under various shapes: the matter that is carried soon disappears.

I am now concerned with the higher Examinations, and refer to the lower ones only as illustrations; we may often learn from them something that shews us clearly some general mode in which Examinations act. There are but a few subjects in which this Portative Memory does not come into play necessarily to a great extent, and very often to a greater degree than it is supposed to do or should do. The Examiner assigns no credit to it in Competitive Examinations, but, indirectly, it must bring its possessor an ample return. Its effect is at its minimum in those parts of Mathematics which consist largely of examples, in composition in foreign languages, and in translation where the books are not specified. Hence the value of these subjects to the Examiner; in them he sees exercised an acquired power as well as knowledge, and he need not be on the watch to detect what is merely remembered and not understood, as he is when concerned with the subjects which impart only information. A pupil may be made to learn facts, summaries, and general reflections, by the mere exercise of the Portative Memory. This is the faculty which renders what is called "cram" possible; indeed, the most intelligible meaning of this term is, that it is the process by which memory is made to simulate the fruit of other mental functions; the sound teacher tries to prevent the pupil from saving himself thinking by availing himself of his memory, and most tutors will rather teach a pupil than "cram" him; but when time is limited and success all-important, there is no resource but to trust to memory. Certain subjects and classes of questions throw students upon their memories, and drive tutors to provide formulated answers, more than others, and this should be carefully borne in mind in framing Examinations.

Mr. Todhunter* points out the mischief in this respect of demonstrations requiring proofs that are artificial, that is, which would not be suggested by the general views and methods belonging to the subject; and questions which call on very young men for the comparison of philosophical views, or for the judgment of ripe manhood—questions which belong rather to the Examiner's own time of life than that of the candidates—have this evil tendency. The Bishop of Salisbury remarks wisely, in his evidence to the Oxford commission, on the mischief which may arise from dealing with youth as if they had passed through

* *Conflict of Studies.* Macmillan & Co. 1873.

years of thought. One man in a hundred may be set thinking, the rest urge their tutors to give them *their* thoughts ready for production. This process is quite as injurious to the tutor himself as it is to the pupil, and the effect on the tutor should be at least equally considered. It is a sad thing to give able young teachers low views of learning; and one who has long done the work of "cramming" comes to have no more belief in the education got from books, especially with a view to Examinations, than the old statesman had in the truth of history.

Thus, in testing ability, an Examiner aims at reducing the effect of this kind of memory. In Mathematics, for instance, he would avoid asking for long burdensome demonstrations, and if for educational purposes he did ask them — and we shall see that there is an evil in omitting such altogether — he would attach little credit to them in selecting his candidates. This, it is true, can only be fairly done where the candidates have not been led to expect consideration for such answers.

But there is a deeper ground for mistrusting a glib memory than that it gives a facility in "cramming." An experienced Examiner can often detect "cram," and will not be far misled in discriminating between what is the pupil's own and what is his tutor's. "Cram" betrays itself in abrupt changes of style, and if several candidates have been prepared by one teacher, the Examiner may have his eyes opened by finding that the same striking phrase or illustration has apparently occurred to many candidates at the same moment. But the ready mechanical memory of a youth, besides enabling him to mislead unpractised Examiners, makes him deceive himself. Teachers find that a very ready memory is a bad educator; it stunts the growth of other mental powers by doing their work for them. A youth who can recollect without trouble, will, as it were, *mask* the difficulty in his classical author or his mathematics, by learning by rote what stands in his translation or text-book, and march forward without more ado.   Thus a quick memory involves a temptation which may enervate its possessor by suffering him to evade a difficulty instead of bracing himself to encounter it in front.

An Examiner may detect this superficial sharpness by various symptoms.   The man of mere memory keeps close to the words of his text-book, he shews what may be called the timidity of imperfect comprehension, like that theological candidate who dared not swerve a letter from the formularies of the Church, lest he should fall into a terrible heresy.   Occasionly, too, there will be a slip in some word which shews that the student has taken down notes orally and not understood them, or he translates from a reading not printed in the paper, and, generally, he confines himself to those questions which can be answered by memory, or he makes a comparatively poor show in the others if he ventures on them.

The Analytical Memory differs from that just spoken of in this respect; whereas the Portative Memory supplies the connection or succession of notions, by the help of a jingle of words on the ear, or by the position of paragraphs, or by some such aid which does not require any mental action, the Analytical Memory binds together the materials by weaving them into a structure, of which the mind has supplied the conception, or furnished some connecting view which holds together the matter like beads on a string.

For this there is need of imagination to conceive the view, and comparison to determine the relative importance of the items and subordinate some of them to others. In Examinations in "set subjects," this is one of the faculties which we want to see exercised. It is that by which a lawyer "gets up" his case, or a lecturer his dissertation ; he has supplied the view which enables him to comprehend the facts or the phenomena in one glance, and thus to print the impression on his mind. The memory in this case must be thoroughly under command, it obeys the slightest intimation of the will as to what it should record, and it is, in consequence, an indication of a disciplined and vigorous mind.

A schoolboy carries into an Examination the order of the kings of England, the dates of their accession, and the principal events of each reign, purely by help of the Portative Memory, as he would learn the parts of a Latin verb. When a student of History writes "a brief account of the foreign policy of England under Oliver Cromwell," he is exercising his Analytical Memory ; but when a portion of History has become *assimilated* in his mind, he can sit down and sketch an outline of it straight off, only requiring to refer to authorities for names, dates, and details, which, if his Index Memory be also cultivated, he can put his finger on in a moment. In the same way, a student who has thoroughly mastered Mechanics could write out a treatise on Elementary Dynamics without leaving his place in the Examination room. He would not have to "look over" this subject for Examination.

There are fatal objections to the introduction of "set subjects" into those competitive Examinations which are intended to give no advantage to particular places of teaching. It would interfere with school-work if particular subjects were prescribed. It is the great difficulty of the Indian Civil Service Examination, which is meant to afford quite an open field, that the English History and Literature, and the rudiments of certain sciences, act in the same way as set subjects; they represent acquaintance with manuals. The consequence is, that a particular kind of teaching *is* rendered advantageous; success depends much on the judicious selection of the subjects, and the teacher, rather than the pupil, is in fact the person under Examination.

In order to defeat "cramming," it has been proposed that all competitive Examinations should turn entirely on the exercise of powers arising from what has been stored by the Assimilative Memory; for instance, on the writing or translating of foreign languages, or on the application of those sciences which admit of the principles being applied to examples. But this would introduce an educational evil; a generation would arise destitute of common information; they would cultivate these powers and neglect everything else, so that they would have but a scanty store of mental food to nourish their minds in the busy time of life, when they cannot spare the time or energy for taking up a study. The best approximation to a solution of this dilemma will be found in making use of educational Examinations, not only those at the Universities, but also those carried on in the Schools and at various Local Centres and others that may be devised, as a means of making a first selection, to act in fact as *sifters*. In preparing for these, the student, being under authority, could be taught what was best for him. He might be examined in the information he had gained a little at a time through a long period — that so got lasts longest, and the capabilities he might be acquiring could be tested at the same time. Those who did well in these sifting Examinations, and those only, should be admitted to a further competitive Examination in a few of those subjects which endow the learner with a power of *doing* something, and are therefore suitable for our purpose.   I mention this briefly now, as being one reason for considering rather particularly how far an Examination comprising "set subjects" may give grounds for judging of the ability of candidates.   Such subjects must enter into School Examinations, and we want to find how far we may trust such Examinations for making a rough selection.   But apart from consideration of Government competitions, it is desirable to see how the introduction of specified books into an Examination affects its efficiency as a means of discovering the ablest men.

The case is best understood by taking an instance. Let us suppose that the Trilogy of Æschylus is the subject of study, and forms part of an Examination. This may be made the nucleus of a vast amount of illustrative matter.   It will bring under consideration the ethics and mythology of the time, the nature of dramatic poetry and its modern development, as well as much that is suggested by the form and matter of the plays themselves.   There is a vast amount of matter that may be made to illustrate the subject. A work like this, treated exhaustively, like the model book of Jacotot*, affords us a glimpse of what that writer was driving at when he said, "*Tout est dans*

---

* See *Essays on Educational Reformers*, by R. H. Quick.   Longmans Green & Co.   An excellent book.

tout." The man who is possessed by a great subject finds everywhere something that he can bring to bear on it. Illustrative matter clusters round the dominant idea like straws round a floating mass. Here we have volitional imagination warmed to catch impressions to which the duller mind is dead, and this faculty of seizing on and appropriating, in all that comes under view, those elements which may be made to bear on what we are about, is a marked concomitant of ability.

Some, no doubt, will speak of such a given book as a "cram" subject, by which they mean that he who does best in it, owes his success, not to assimilated knowledge of the language, but to a power "of getting up." Learners have a keen perception of the difference of these processes, and are apt to think that this "getting up" is a mere matter of time and toil. This is not so. The power of so mastering a mass of matter as to reproduce it with all its delicacy of detail shews a distinct quality of considerable value. The man who dashes off a spirited and fairly correct translation, and writes showy composition with much ease, may be utterly unable to deal with a quantity of matter in the thorough way that I have in view. One man has the power of grasping a subject in its entirety, he has a large mental field of view. The other sees but a bit at a time. Further, to attain high excellence in these set subjects a person must have the power of duly subordinating details so as to leave his main lines strongly marked, and a faculty of finding the idea which shall put form and order into the mass, as the statuary sees the figure in the marble block.

So far as the ideal pupil is concerned, there is here

no "cram" at all in a derogatory sense ; he may have to carry some dates and names and details into the Examination ; they are indeed retained by the Portative Memory for the time, and may therefore be called "cram," but these go for little in the value of his performance. These little matters have merely passed through his hands as it were, but a great deal of wisdom has been stored and accumulated, and forms part of his mental capital for evermore. What is valuable has been in fact assimilated. But the disparagement of such subjects is not hard to account for. Some of those who disparage them are quite right in feeling that if *they* got the subject up it would be "cram," and this leads us to mark the specific action of such a paper. Excellence shews much ability, mediocrity very little, while a display of mere scraps of information has no value for our purpose, and in selecting candidates on the ground of ability, it ought not to weigh against the display of any power. Upon passing in order down the list of those who might have attempted our supposed paper, a change would be found not only in the *degree*, but in the *kind* of merit. This is not sufficiently taken account of in any received system of marking ; some convenient formula is wanted for giving greater weight to excellence. It will roughly answer to give marks in the ordinary way and then *square* them*. If what is produced has not to be weighed against other kinds of knowledge, there is no need of numerical marking except as a record of impression, and the case is simplified. The question of different modes of mark-

---

* For instance, 20 marks might be given to a paper: then full marks would, after squaring, be set down as 400 and half marks only as 100. This would fairly represent the ratio of *ability*. If we want to reward *knowledge* and diligence the case is different. Fractional marks might be avoided by using one place of decimals.

ing will be treated of when we come to the mechanism of Examinations.

Given books may, then, be made effective for the purpose of discrimination, if we are content with selecting a few candidates out of many, and if, therefore, we need only take account of high excellence. If all the candidates have had the same sort of teaching within their reach, so that the difference between them is not likely to result from difference of opportunities, one source of complexity is removed. The number of such subjects in an Examination should be very limited, or the student will be distracted, which is injurious in an educational point of view, and the Examiner will survey his candidates when they have their minds burdened and jaded by a heavy load on their memory, whereas he wants to see them at their best and freshest. Students with all their possessions carried in their memories, shew the same uneasiness that a man does with great treasures about his person. They are in constant fear of letting something drop. Besides, if more than two or three given subjects be carried at the same time into an Examination, ability may be overlaid by a many-sided mediocrity, especially if the common way of taking an aggregate of marks be retained. But a small number of such subjects, not over-marked, will assist in bringing out a particular kind of ability. Thus a School Examination, into which set subjects must necessarily enter, may be made to give trustworthy results with regard to a few of the ablest boys so far as their *ability is actually effective at the time*. There will be many who do not ripen till they have left school, and these of course are passed over in any system of competition among youths. All such systems put a premium on *early produce,* of the effects of which I shall speak hereafter.

The kind of knowledge, however, which furnishes the proper field for competitive Examination is beyond doubt that which has been assimilated by a slow process, and becomes a permanent possession. This possession carries with it a skill or power which can be put in practice whenever it is called for. When a person is addressed in a foreign language with which he is acquainted, the words for reply come to him as easily as the proper motions do to a swimmer when he jumps into the water. But besides languages and science, the knowledge of facts may be assimilated, if it have been long enough present to the mind: the outlines of history, the general features of a map, and the fundamental facts and laws of a science often become so intimately associated with the man's nature, that he can hardly imagine that he can forget them; but it is not every one who has this power of assimilation in any considerable degree. It seems to be connected with a habit of unconsciously reviewing the stock of ideas, and is found mostly in persons of a certain degree of mental power and activity.

Many persons will forget in no very long time every word of a language which they have once spoken fluently, or of a matter with which they have been thoroughly conversant. Hence a good Assimilative Memory indicates vigor of brain, and also a power of steady application, for it does not yield its harvest in the way of a new practical capacity without long-continued culture. "Lightly come, lightly go," holds of learning as of other things, and what is rapidly learnt is rapidly lost, unless it be impressed on the mind in some unusually vivid way. A man cannot by working eight hours a day at Greek or Algebra get twice as much facility in dealing with them as if he worked four hours. Assimilation cannot be hurried; the mind will only absorb at a certain rate. The amount of a *book* which can be "got up" for production is much more nearly proportional to the time spent on it; but such knowledge soon passes away, because it is not taken into the system. Dr. Carpenter tells a story of an actor, who, having once had to learn a part in a hurry, forgot it altogether soon after he had played it, and had to learn it afresh, afterwards, whenever he had to act it, although the parts which he had studied at leisure remained always by him ready to be performed when wanted. These he had *assimilated*, the other he only *carried*. Dr. Carpenter explains the necessity of *time* for the forming of permanent impressions on the brain, a point which is also spoken of by Dr. Abercrombie* and Sir Henry Holland.†

I must here recur to the distinction I have so often dwelt upon, between the studies which yield an "Art," or capacity of applying knowledge, and those which terminate in the information acquired. I shall mention some of the advantages possessed by the former class of acquirements, considered as furnishing an arena for the exhibition of intellectual strength. One of these causes I have just mentioned; it is that a capacity cannot be suddenly increased for the occasion — in other words, cannot be "crammed" — and that knowledge can. A man's condition in respect of a capacity is more permanent than it is in respect of the knowledge of facts or of books, and the verdict of the Examiner, which is based on it,

* *On the Intellectual Powers.*
† Chapter on Mental Physiology.

will therefore hold good for some time: whereas a youth may succeed or fail in a competition, owing to the state of his knowledge of a manual of history, the contents of which he might acquire perfectly, or forget utterly in a fortnight.

Again, since it takes time and steady work to acquire an "Art," the possession of it is a proof of industry and perseverance. We conclude that the man can do good work, and, what is more, that he can go on working at the same thing, till he has thoroughly mastered it. This is important, for there are people whose minds have much activity, but little power, and these begin many things, but are stopped when the drudgery and difficulties appear. We get a glimpse here of moral strength, a quality of high value, and so hard to ascertain directly by examinations, that we must treasure up every hint they afford. A parent who intends his son for active life, sometimes values a University Honor more for the sustained energy and self-denial it takes to obtain it than for anything else.

Knowledge that is assimilated has also this advantage, that at the time of producing it the mind is not crushed by having to carry a load of matter, as in the case of the "got-up" subjects mentioned a few pages back: a man has his Latin and Greek, for instance, always by him; hence, when he sits down to an Examination in those languages, he has energy and vivacity to spare, and the Examiner sees him in his happiest condition, which it is his object always to do. Another valuable peculiarity for the Examiner of the class of subjects which result in a capacity is this— for most persons there is a *terminal excellence*, as regards this capacity, which is approached as a limit.

For each individual a certain *saturation point* may be marked in these studies, and by this we may fairly register certain kinds of ability. A school-boy who is learning Greek rises rapidly to a certain point, he then advances slowly, and at last stops. I was once told by a student who had been long occupied with classics, that latterly he had learned fresh words and books, but had not increased his hold of the language at all. In the same way, in sports, such as shooting, or playing cricket, there seems to be a limit of the skill which each individual can attain by practice. In Mathematics, also, the learner arrives at such a limit of skill in solving problems, or in performing analytical operations. But in Mathematics, as learnt for production in an Examination, there is also in most branches a certain amount of what is called "bookwork," and this is of the character of *knowledge;* it can therefore be extended in quantity by the outlay of more pains and time; but here also there will be a limit, for this "bookwork" must be understood in order to be recollected, and the student is often stopped short by finding that, as he advances, the subject involves conceptions, or requires a tension of mind to which his powers are not equal. It is an old remark at Cambridge, that if a man who has got to the length of his tether were to present himself year after year for the Mathematical Tripos, he might perhaps rise a place or two at first, but would soon become stationary, and then sink. This would not be so true in subjects depending on wide reading, like Law or History, or some kinds of Natural Science. If we were forced to judge of a man's general ability by some single proof which could be produced in Examination, the degree of his *Terminal Excellence*, in the

skilled work of the branch of Learning he might select, would be as trustworthy a criterion as we could
find. But the difficult point to ascertain is whether
the excellence *be* terminal or still progressive, and to
do this it will be necessary to know something of the
mental history of the candidates. Some indications
may indeed be drawn from the style of their work,
but conclusions obtained from such evidence cannot
be trusted implicitly.

By the excercise, then, of this Assimilative Memory, we obtain requirements which can be produced
in Examination when wanted, and which are not
mere temporary adjuncts, but part and parcel of the
man himself. Again, the more the candidate is
master of the art which results from his learning,
the less embarrassed is he by mechanical difficulties,
and the fuller play can he give to his taste, his
imagination, and his desire to express his conceptions
fully and accurately. The scholar who is not quite
master of the language he deals with, or the mathematician who is not quite at home in the use of his
analytical instruments, can no more fully bring out
upon paper all that he sees in his author, or all that
is in his mind, than the statuary who is imperfectly
skilled in using his chisel can give full effect to his
conceptions.

It is partly on this account, partly from the value
which attaches to all first-rate work — both from its
utility and the paucity of those who can do it — but
most of all from the fact that the power of advancing
to very high excellence shows various superior qualities of mind, that where it has been desired to select
the ablest men by Examination, more weight has
been given, as our experience has increased, to the

mastery of some acquirement admitting of application, and less to *passive* knowledge. It is then quite a canon of competitive examinations that the best criterion of mental power is to be able to *do* something — to perform some class of complex intellectual operations — with great perfection.

Every college tutor knows the type of man who might obtain a low place in the second class for several sorts of Honors, but who would never rise to a first-class degree in any one branch. Such a person may be very useful for many purposes, for teaching especially, but he will rarely prove to be a man of first-rate mental power. There is one sort of mind — that which is surcharged with native thoughts — which offers an exception to this remark. Moreover, the special excellence may be too dearly bought; a youth may be so narrowly trained in order to be rendered a remarkable performer in some one way, as to suffer in general capability, as well as in culture. This will be spoken of presently.

One very marked difference between minds of different orders is seen in the susceptibility, and the more delicate finish of the mental impressions of the superior sort. It is only fine intellects which are

"Wax to receive, and marble to retain."

The difference, I mean, will be best understood by an illustration. Suppose that we have a beautifully engraved intaglio gem of which we wish to get an impression; if we use coarse sealing-wax, and imperfectly melt it, the chief prominences and depressions will indeed appear on the seal, and the ordinary observer would say that the impression was quite sufficiently good; not so the connoisseur. He sees

that it has the form without the beauty and the life;
it is, compared to what it should be, what copies of a
Raphael painted to order are to the original, that is
to say, like it in everything but the charm. But let
us now take the finest wax specially prepared, and
have it thoroughly and uniformly liquefied, then apply
strong pressure, and the result is quite another thing.
The most delicate tracings, the perfect form of every
prominence and hollow, are now rendered with perfect
accuracy in hard and glossy wax.

This will help us to understand the difference in
the degrees in which the ordinary man, and one of
singularly fine perception, lay hold of the meaning
of a pregnant passage in a great author, or of a subtle
conception in science.

One man will see all the force that is conveyed in
an epithet, or in the emphatic position of a particular
word; he will catch the spirit of an author and the
genius of a language; he will not be satisfied until
he has got hold of the exact meaning of every technical and scientific term, and marked the reason for
every limitation in the enunciation of a theorem. At
every step of an analytical investigation he will
interpret the process, and follow the train of geometrical or physical conceptions to which the interpretation leads, while the man of more blunt perceptions
will be content with mastering the grammatical
meaning of his author, and with following the main
course of a mathematical investigation, or of a piece
of general reasoning. The images formed in his
mind's eye are like those seen in a telescope which
is not accurately brought to focus; and if the niceties
which he has missed be pointed out to him, he is apt
to think that his own notions were "near enough" to

correctness, and that the minuteness insisted on is over-refined.

This delicacy of perception is well brought out by the higher kinds of Examination at present in use. A candidate, in order to convey his conception, must be able to find language to express just what he wants to say; and thus we gauge his perceptive faculty in combination with the power of expression. This power generally accompanies vividness of conception, for when a bright and distinct image is formed on the mental retina, the right word will, with a little practice, follow the idea, if the mind be vigorous and fresh, just as the marksman's hand follows his eye.

We now come to a power which I have already spoken of in connection with the analytical memory, that of seizing on the main features of a subject, and comprising the whole compass of a matter in a single view. This faculty indicates mass and robustness of mind, while that last spoken of shows sensibility and fineness of texture. A strong mind, having made sure of one or two principles, will not take his eye off the beacon before him; the man who has great refinement and susceptibility, rather than power of mind, sometimes gets bewildered by the multitude of side-lights that claim his attention.

Connected with this power of intuitive analysis is a quality which comes much under the teacher's notice. I will call it range of mental field of view. There are minds which will master a small quantity of matter well enough, but which are utterly overpowered when they have to deal with a considerable bulk. If they be examined chapter by chapter — in Mechanics, we will suppose, or in Political Economy — they will answer intelligently, and even work out results in particular cases ; but as they pass on, one set of notion drives the other out ; a new slide has been put into the camera of their minds, and their view has "dissolved." When at the end of the course, they are examined in the whole subject, they produce much less than was expected from them. Such a failure (supposing the pupil to be diligent) is a sign that the mental range is small. The mind may be a very fair one as far as it goes, but it is on a small scale. There is no room in it for laying one conception beside another, and so forming a complete map of a province of knowledge. All such a man's acquirements will be fragmentary. On the other hand, a man of a large mental field of view is not overwhelmed though the extent of a subject be great, provided it be tolerably homogeneous (a great diversity of subjects I hold to be very injurious): with him it forms an organic whole, while with the others it is only a congeries of propositions. He sees the whole configuration of the subject, and its various parts are bound together in his mind by a general conception. Hence it is obvious that frequent Examinations, each covering a small portion only of ground, whatever their educational use may be, will fail to discriminate betweeen different degress of this sort of intellectual power ; for the extent of mental field of view cannot be tested in a small area.

It is well known that a very feeble person may pass an Examination in a considerable amount of matter, if he be allowed to take a very small quantity at a time. The case then comes almost to that of the "repetition" of a school-boy, who has trained his memory just to carry a week's work. The extent of this mental field of view varies very greatly in different persons, and from my experience, I consider its width of range to be a good approximate measure of general ability, while its dimensions may be pretty accurately taken by a well-conducted Examination.

Imagination has entered into many of the compound qualities which I have noticed. My business with them was not to analyze them, but to consider them as indications of ability cognizable by Examination. I must now make some remarks on Imagination as a distinct Faculty.

The term Imagination is variously defined by philosophical writers. I here employ it in its most comprehensive sense, so as to embrace both the series of operations whereby it forms or combines conceptions and also the power of readily evolving thoughts or expedients.

There is more variation in different minds in point of Imagination than in almost any other faculty. Persons deficient in it may be excellent men of business, or possess a great knowledge of facts and of books, but they can never attain the highest rank in any sciences (except those that are merely classificatory), or in any career which requires that they should understand the modes of thought of past generations, or influence those of the present one. This imaginative faculty usually acts independently of the will : it is called into play by a sight or a word, through association ; but in disciplined minds it is subjected to the will, and is set to do appointed tasks. In the first case we have the *automatic*, in the second the *volitional* action, spoken of in the earlier part of this chapter.

The volitional action of the Imagination is that

which comes most before us in Examinations. Indeed, we shall see as we proceed, that Examinations promote volitional action, and somewhat check spontaneity and profuseness of ideas.

The power of distinctly presenting to the mind some abstruse conception, like that of polarity or molecular action, is an exercise of imagination which is in a high degree volitional, and it is so in two ways. It is the result of a direct effort of the will on each occasion, and it could not be exercised unless the imagination had been habitually trained to severe exercise, and to obedience to its master. The power of concentration as well as imagination, is called out when the mind is directed to picture to itself conceptions like those just spoken of. This concentration is itself a very important faculty; indeed it was to his being able to withdraw his mind from distractions, and direct its whole energies to one point, that Sir Isaac Newton attributed his success as a discoverer.

The clearness and correctness of geometrical and physical conception can be accurately tested in Mathematics and Natural Philosopy. This is one of the peculiar facilities which, as was said in the last chapter, these sciences present to the Examiner. By scrutinizing the student's views on these branches, and making him apply his knowledge, we test, in addition to his knowledge, and power of carrying a train of reasoning, the degree in which he possesses a very valuable sort of imagination. It is by the want of the power of conception, rather than that of logical perception, that the mathematical student is most commonly checked in his advance. But besides being engaged in framing conceptions, imagination is required to seize on the relation of ideas in a way which cannot be better described than it is by the late Mr. Robert Leslie Ellis in the following striking passage :—

"Every one who has really studied mathematics must remember cases in which, after long and patient thought, the reason of a truth of a proposition, with the demonstration of which he may have been acquainted for years, has seemed to dawn on him; the proposition thenceforth becoming, as it were, a part of his own mind — a matter about which he is no more capable of doubting than about the primary conceptions of form and magnitude. The mind thus brought into nearer, if not immediate, contact with necessary truth is conscious of its own development; and herein, I believe, resides the special benefit to be derived from the study of mathematics, a benefit, that is, distinct from the exercise of patience and attention which it undoubtedly requires, but which is required also in other pursuits. The study of mathematics is especially valuable, not because it gives the student practice in ratiocination, but because it enlarges the sphere of his intuition, by giving him distinct and conscious possession of truths which lay hid in his conceptions of figure, number, and the like."

It might be supposed that Languages were more properly the domain of Imagination than Science; but Language, unless treated as a natural science, offers singularly little scope for the play of fancy. Grammar, as commonly taught, is in this respect the most arid of studies. As soon, however, as we come to Literature, the mind is brought into contact with the imaginative creations of great men, and in picturing them with nicety, as well as in grasping the full meaning which a few pregnant words were meant to convey to the author's readers, Imagination is brought into active operation. This exercise of it is strictly volitional; but the fancy is at the same time kindled into vigorous automatic action by contact with fine minds. The volitional play of imagination can be roughly tested, like that of the delicacy of perception of which it is a principal component, by translation on paper; but, as is the case in all attempts to test ability, it is only where the knowledge is very considerable that we can see in the student's exercise the free working of his mind. So long as he is struggling to recollect the meaning of words, or to apply rules of grammar, his imagination is dormant.

Dramatic power requires a powerful imagination and quick human sympathies; it is not confined to the writers of drama. We find it in the Prologue to the Canterbury Tales in greater perfection than in Beaumont and Fletcher. It resides in the power of transporting oneself into the character we conceive —of *becoming him*, as it were, in virtue of the cogency of our conception — of seeing matters from his point of view, and speaking from his lips. Marlowe and Byron place *themselves* in the positions of Faustus, of Edward the Second, of Sardanapalus, and Marino Falieri, and shew us what *they* would have said and done in the situation of their heroes: but Shakespeare puts actually new men and women before us, and we never think of the author at all. Many mimics will represent to the life what they have heard pass; but only one with some dramatic power will make his characters talk as we feel they would have done in a supposed case.

About this species of imagination, Examinations tell us little: it can only be tested directly by calling on the candidates to write a speech or a letter in the character of some personage whose life and writings they have studied; though traces of imagination of this kind will peep out in the course of a comprehensive Examination, in little traits and touches, either in translation or in answers to questions on dramatic literature. This kind of imagination is not required for literary men alone; no man will be quite successful in high offices of administration, such as the government of an Indian province, who has not sufficient tincture of it to give him the power of putting himself in the place of others, of seeing with their eyes, and feeling with their nerves. A Hindoo population will rather submit to be ill-used now and then by a tyrannical native prince, than to be steadily misunderstood by a benevolent Briton.

Hitherto we have regarded Imagination as being employed in forming the conceptions which are required in particular branches of study. This she does under the direction of the will. Examinations in these branches test the perfectness of these conceptions, and thereby the amount of the imaginative power, and the state of discipline into which it has been brought. But she performs also another function, which is better recognized as her duty. She perceives relations between ideas; and these perceptions which, bidden or unbidden, occur to her, are commonly spoken of as "thoughts." She may perform both of these functions, or she may perform one of them well and fail in the other.

A person may have a clear insight into the mode of action of forces in physics, or he may picture to himself the events of history, and yet his mind may yield nothing of itself. No apt illustrations will strike him; no happy expedients, no reflections, will occur to him. What he reads he will understand, and reproduce as he received it, but nothing more will come of it. Such a man may do good work in many ways; he may make a conscientious though hardly a suggestive teacher, and he may be an excellent man of business, and a useful subordinate as a civil servant.

On the other hand, there are men whose minds give off thoughts so freely as to hinder concentration of attention. They are impatient or incapable of steadying their mental gaze in one direction sufficiently long to form a well-defined and persistent image in the camera of their minds. Here we have automatic action of the imagination in excess of volitional power. Such persons may often hit on novel views, and may even urge them with plausible arguments and forcible illustrations. They may or may not have the power of will to marshal their ideas along the path in which they wish to proceed. A person may be rich in thoughts, and yet unable to carry on a long train of reasoning : he may start a notion, and hardly care to see whither it would conduct him. The capacity for making brilliant observations is most telling in conversation, for here a train of reasoning is out of place, and the play of the imagination should be automatic. In like manner the charm of certain essayists, Charles Lamb for instance, lies in the absence of set purpose, and in the exuberance of happy thought. We do not care whither we are going as we stroll along with him — our delight is to be in his company. To read the Essays of Elia is most recreative from this very absence of volition in them. The exertion of will involves effort, and even seeing it exerted prevents perfect rest by reason of sympathy.*

Examiners will always gladly note a copiousness of ideas. But if it be not controlled by will, if it end in brilliant talk, if imagination, instead of lighting its possessor along his road to a certain goal, leads him astray by its shifting gleams, then they discern a

* I have known a person suffering from the effects of over-work, quite distressed by the mere sight of laborers using violent exertion.

kind of person who is not what they are in search of. They do not want a great conversationalist or a brilliant essayist. The performances of such persons in life, they will observe, are usually small in comparison with their reputation among their friends, and they want to select persons, who, in some way or other, will do good work.

But though the value we attach to this automatic activity of imagination will vary with the purpose we have in view in making our selection, still we may want to know how far such automatic power exists, and therefore it is our business to consider how it may be made to shew itself in an Examination.

If Examiners wish to see free play of thought in the canditates, they must set questions which admit of being treated discursively; such, for instance, as turn on the grounds of scientific principles, or on the growth of certain influences in nations; the students being in either case supposed to have turned their attention to the matter. A man who has a fertile imagination can hardly avoid shewing it in his illustrations or remarks; sometimes he may be carried away by an idea, and the compactness of his answer may suffer thereby; but if the idea is a good one, the Examiner will give him credit for a creative mind, though he may wish to satisfy himself from other papers that the man has in general a good control over the course of his thoughts. In this way the quality of which we are in search is *undesignedly disclosed*—the candidate has not sat down with the intention of shewing his wisdom, or his thoughtfulness, or his smartness in criticism. He addresses himself to answer the question, and the ideas occur to him in so doing. If his thick-coming fancies injure the perspicuity of his answer, it is, as I have said, a defect which may be redeemed by other answers. If the illustration or paradox be evidently sought for, and put in, not to make his meaning clear, but to enrich his style — not to support the building, but to decorate it — then the Examiner will not augur favorably.

There are cases in which importance is attached to ascertaining the wealth of a young man's mind in point of ideas, and an English essay written under Examination is regarded as a mode by which "what there is in a man" may be brought to light, and pretty correctly measured. For my own part, I shrink from prying over-much into what is growing up in young men's minds, and I see little good in doing so. It is very hard to judge of the wine while it is working itself clear. Even if we thereby might improve our chance of securing in a Fellowship Examination the man most likely to "do credit to the College," I would rather, as a college tutor, forego my prospects of having something to boast of, than incur the danger of fostering unreality and intellectual coxcombry. Since, however, there are Examinations in which much stress is laid upon "fertility of thought," and in which Essays are used to discover it, I must consider the mode in which they operate.

The writing of essays shews two things; what a man has to say, and how he can say it. In reference to the latter, the essay is looked on as a mode of testing the power of composition. This it does in an Examination in the most simple and direct way. The student who professes to have acquired the art of writing English, is called on to give a specimen of his skill. Good sense, of course, may be expected in the remarks, and consistency of view, but originality is hardly looked for; the style is more thought of than the matter. Essays are regarded in this light in the Indian Civil Service Examination; the subjects there given are usually familiar ones, often calling chiefly for a power of description or narration.

But I am here concerned with essays used as a means of discovering the individual's store of wisdom, or his productiveness of mind. For this purpose, they are, as I have said, used in Fellowship Examinations; rarely indeed at Cambridge, but commonly at Oxford; the subjects are frequently such as lead to speculation or discussion, and are necessarily of a "general nature," that is to say, they may be treated of without precise knowledge of facts, or of scientific truths. If this were not so, the essay would be only a form of Examination in the subject to which the facts belong, and this subject may have been sufficiently represented in other ways. By setting an essay, we may, no doubt, often mark a particular kind of talent; we may bring out some clever men, though, if we give too great a share of consideration to the results of the essay paper, we may do injustice to many varieties of ability. There is, moreover, a danger of our being taken in by some plausible personage who has a knack of manipulating "masses of thought," taken out of his tutor's note-book, with such dexterity as to give the impression that he had gone through the process of thinking out these thoughts, that he is quite familiar with them, and tosses them to and fro with giant strength. We have heard of a mine in the far west, in which splendid diamonds were found by those who were sent to report on its value, but in which none have ever been found since; and I fear that some of these well-prepared essayists would prove as fallacious as the mine, if they were picked out on the score of the profound views that they appear able to evolve at will. It might be found that they, like it, had been " salted " for the occasion.

A man who has been thus provided with " views," and acute observations, which will " come in " under many heads, may have destroyed in himself the germs of that power which he simulates. He might have had a thought or two, now and then, if he had been left alone — but if he is made first to aim at a standard of thought above his years, and then finds that he can get the sort of thoughts he wants without thinking, he is in a fair way to be spoiled for a thinker. The higher and more speculative the nature of the subjects is, the more certainly will young men be driven to tutors in order that they may lay up a store of general reflections, or modes of dealing with such subjects, and, what is more important, the worse will be the effect on their own minds. I have heard of young men being allowed three hours, without notice of the subject, to deal with the following: "Trace the effects of Christianity in forwarding or retarding the progress of civilization." Here, it was said, we outflank the crammer, and must see the produce of the student's mind. Even, however, if such a mode of examining did baffle " cram," this would be a small matter compared with its educational effect. We may lose more even in our present point of view, that, namely, of selection, by deteriorating the whole body of candidates, than we gain by the increased chance any such means may afford of picking out the best.

If we lead a young graduate to think himself competent to dispatch in a forenoon a question on which a man's life-time might be spent, can we be surprised if he turn out a self-sufficient coxcomb? and can we wonder at his being incapable of reverence or conviction, when he has been led to look on Christianity, and progress, and civilization, as only a few of the counters with which students, and tutors, and Examiners, play the game of which a Studentship or a Fellowship is the prize?

I shall point out, hereafter, the way in which I think Essays should be employed so as to give us the most insight into the pupil's mind, without actually setting him down to shew how cleverly he can talk on any subject that is put before him. But I have now to consider the operation of the existing practice.

Whether we look chiefly to style and method, or to matter, we want to learn something of the pupil's habits of mind, and we want to see the mind working in its ordinary way. For us to do this, it is first of all necessary that the pupil should be at his ease with the Examiner — that is to say, he must banish the thought of the Examiner as much as possible from his mind. He must not be asking himself, "What will the Examiner think of this or that sentiment?" He must not "write up" to what the Examiner may be supposed to approve. We want him to be as unlike as possible to the author of the typical school theme, who is highly enamored of virtue and intolerant of vice. It is not always easy to persuade young people to appear without some conventional mask; their only stock of ideas and phraseology may belong either to the part of "propriety" or to that of "advanced thought," but sometimes they are natural enough. Young people are in more genial hands now than formerly, and a few words from an Examiner advising them to write just what they think, if only for the sake of the greater spirit they will throw into their style, will sometimes bring about a happy understanding, and induce them to open their hearts. But, supposing that our candidates are past this primary stage, there will still be, in some very important particulars, obstacles in the way of our forming a judgment by what we see.

I will specify two types of character which offer difficulty. There are some young men who are bad hands at making believe ; they can find nothing to say about a subject in which they have no interest ; they are too honest or too fastidious to put down the current commonplaces which they have never looked into — they cannot feign indignation or enthusiasm about " Capital Punishment," or " Female Suffrage." Sometimes unpracticed hands will declare that they can find nothing to say, and these are not the most unpromising. I have known an Examiner in such a case tell the candidate to explain on paper *how it was* that he had nothing to say, and in his doing this, some tokens of intelligence have appeared.

If we reject such candidates on account of their scanty performance in the way of an Essay, we may lose sight of persons who will turn out well ; the best course is, when we suspect that there are such candidates before us, to allow that, for them, this part of the Examination has been inoperative, and form our judgment on the rest of it, so far as we can do so without injustice to others.

There is a passage in Mr. Helps' *Friends in Council** which bears on this peculiarity of some young minds.

* *Friends in Council.* Second Series, p. 204. John W. Parker, and Son. 1859.

One of the personages of the dialogue says that a well-known man of letters told him that, as a boy, he was found to be " the stupidest little dog at original composition " in the whole school.   " I used," says he, "to take the heading of the theme back to my room, spend half an hour on looking at it, placing it in different lights — physically, not mentally — and, at the end, found out that I had nothing whatever to say about it."   This he explains to have come from a " deadly kind of sincerity — an almost stupid sincerity."   " I cannot," he adds, " talk from derived thoughts ; I must have seen or felt the things myself that I describe."   He continues, "The master read out, ' A great man is never greater than in adversity.' I took the heading down and stared at it hopelessly. I did not know what a great man is like, I did not know what adversity is, and, having a very sceptical nature, I should have doubted extremely whether the great man is greater in adversity."

If this " man of letters " had had the advantage of being prepared to compete for the Indian Civil Service, he would have learned that the doubt he speaks of was the very thing he wanted.   For one of the standard bits of advice is, or used to be, " When an aphorism is set, begin by contesting its truth ; there is much more room for talking, if you deny, than if you assent."   A form of opening much in vogue in such cases, I am told, is the following : " This is one of those apophthegms which are regarded as truisms, until, upon close investigation, they are found to be falsehoods ; " but pupils are cautioned against using the exact form of words, lest the similarity of their phraseology should strike the Examiner.

The other case in which the action of an Essay is

exceptional is that in which the activity of the brain, in originating thoughts, is abnormally great. I have already observed that persons of this character are frequently slower in attaining excellence in the "arts" resulting from certain studies than those whose calibre is smaller on the whole, but who are less diverted from what is before them by what is going on within. It might be thought that by setting such candidates to write an English Essay we were taking the best means of bringing out their peculiar powers. We find, however, that this is not always the case. If a subject takes hold of their fancy, they see so many ways of looking at it — so many arguments present themselves on different sides at the same time, that they cannot rapidly take a view clear and consistent enough to be put on paper. They may not necessarily be inferior to the rest in power of arrangement, but they are more embarrassed, because they have much more to arrange. Persons of this cast of mind suffer much from the limitation of time. Their mode of proceeding, if left to themselves, would be to begin by writing fully, putting down pretty freely the ideas that suggested themselves, then to review their composition, suppress much, and develop what was wanted to give coherence to the whole. This would not be a bad plan for them to follow; in time they would select what was apposite for their purpose as they went on. But such students are often overtaken by their Examination before they have reached this stage — for minds of original power do not always ripen early — and thus they are often bewildered by getting a view of the subject which cannot possibly be put on their limited canvas : they often begin with an introduction which occupies nearly all their time, and their conclusions have to be huddled in, leaving their best thoughts unsaid. Their work is like an architectural building which is all porch.

These cases exemplify the danger there is in using an essay as an absolute criterion. We must not always infer the absence of the powers wanted for good composition because they do not appear; and this mode of examining should only be used where great latitude can be left to the Examiners, where, in fact, the whole Examination is viewed simply as a means of arriving at an opinion on the merits of the candidates, and each Examiner is allowed to arrive at his conclusion by any means he thinks best. We can hardly give a definite number of "marks" to an English Essay.

The two cases I have just considered, would come before us if we took a body of candidates who were not expecting to be set to write an essay, and who had therefore never been "specially prepared." Another set of difficulties is introduced by such preparation; the Examiner has to separate what is due to the pupil from what is due to the tutor. We must not give way to the practice of branding as "cram" all that is received from instruction. For a tutor to give his pupils hints to work up into an essay is an excellent way of teaching; such hints may come into use in what is produced in Examination, and the Examiner may mistake them for the pupil's own ideas; but the fault is not that of the teacher. He must not refrain from doing the best for his pupil's mind because an Examiner may overrate his power, owing to his being well taught. The case is indeed different if the student is supplied, not with a few hints for an Essay, once a fortnight, which will furnish food for thought, but with particular ways of looking at or putting things, which are recommended to him for their likelihood to be of service in an Examination. If the pupil puts forward his tutor's views, with the hope of getting credit for them as coming " out of his own head," the morality of the proceeding is defective.

If we take the candidates who present themselves for any open Examination, we shall find that some few have been trained to write English well, a few more have had some assistance, while a large number have never been taught to express themselves at all. Those who have acquired a good English style, have an advantage which should quite rightly stand them in good stead. This is not a mere transitory possession, but one that permanently increases the efficiency of the man ; more than this, it is true that " Le style c'est l'homme," and if a person expresses himself with perspicuity and vigor, we may judge favorably of his general ability, and infer that he has some taste in English Literature. This taste will go far to induce him to carry on self-cultivation, and therefore, as I have before said, must be taken into account in selecting the candidates most likely to turn out able men.

But apart from the question of style, we find that out of a number of candidates about one in ten makes some striking remarks ; and sometimes such a candidate may not have attracted attention by his other performances. We may often feel confident, from the naturalness of the style, from the way in which the illustration seems to come readily to hand, and the genuine interest shewn in the point discussed, that the candidate is really saying what he thinks and feels, and not what has been put into his mouth. There are minds too elastic in substance to be moulded into set shape, and these will show freshness of thought in an English essay, and we may see from it, what we want, the real mind of the man. It is the success of the system in cases like these which has given it its repute.

Further, an essay acts effectively in what we may call a negative sense. It shews where the mind is arid, where there is *no* imagination or ideality. This is one of the indications on which experience shews that most dependence may be placed.

If a number of candidates for a scholarship be set down to write essays, there will be some — occasionally fair proficients in Classics, or Mathematics, or Natural Science — whose performances will shew that they have little or nothing in their minds. They do not belong to the exceptional classes spoken of just now, those who send up hardly anything, or else some disjointed matter. These youths write several pages each of grammatical English, without an idea, without a happy illustration, or a phrase which exactly hits the mark. It sometimes seems as if their special training for a definite object had repressed the romance of youth. Ask them to sketch their ideal of a career, and you may find it terminate in domestic comfort, or in earning money; for instance, in "a snug solicitor's business, in a country town, with an adjacent villa," or in a mastership in a school, with vacations spent with a few pupils in Wales, "whereby I might combine profit with pleasure." The English Essay does great service in laying bare minds of this description. The dull youth may have been studious, and his brain is the more receptive from the absence of any internal commotion, so that he may be brought up to the standard of what may be called the staple "trade article," which schoolmasters can dispose of at the Colleges which have small Open Scholarships. The thinness of the soil is often displayed by the English Essay, and frequently its prognostication proves correct.

Our inquiry then leads to the conclusion, that the English Essay serves the purpose of testing the fund of ideas in the minds of candidates well enough when the imaginative faculty is very strong, or very weak, but that in intermediate cases we cannot depend on it to detect shades of difference. Indeed, imagination is so various in form, as well as in degree, that we cannot expect to determine nicely grades of superiority in this respect; we should require, in this, as in so many other cases, to know how the candidates have been prepared.

For instance, a young man brought up in the society of grown people of cultivated intellect, imbibes, without any action of his own mind, the thoughts of those about him. He may have been accustomed to take part in the conversation that passes around him, and has thus possessed himself of a much greater range of observations on the subjects of the day, than falls to the lot of a school-boy, though possibly his mind has not worked so much; he has been imbibing without effort of his own. On the other hand, a lad restricted to the society of his coevals at school is often shut out from all intellectual suggestion, excepting through what is given him to learn; the conversation that passes between school-boys does not commonly tend to the development of ideas. Hence in an essay produced in a Scholarship Examination, or in that for the Indian Civil Service, a youth from a cultivated home may shew to advantage, but his greater supply of topics does not always represent superior power.

In these cases, I have been supposing that account is taken of the style and method, as well as of the matter of the essay. Style, besides being in itself valuable, tells us something of the man : when it flows easily, it shews that the mental apparatus works smoothly, and when it is vigorous and condensed, it shews energy and physical power of brain. Method implies a certain power of will ; in cases where the faculties act altogether automatically, there is usually an utter want of method. This quality is easy to observe, and it is of great value for practical life : its total absence would indicate a condition of mind incompatible with first-class ability of the sort wanted by the framers of Examinations.

It may be asked whether that variety of the imaginative faculty which is called out and tested in an essay, is wanted in a candidate for official employment, or only in one whose services we hope to retain for science or learning. I consider that, excepting in the case of a young writer of striking excellence, who might be worth securing for literature or science, the sort of ability thus discovered is most to be valued as an indication of capacity for administrative affairs.

What a good essay principally shews is a readiness in putting on paper, in a clear and orderly manner, a view that presents itself on applying the mind to a given subject. This is valuable for the drawing up of a despatch, a report, or a defence of a course of proceeding. A good essay will also shew some power of seizing on important points, and of putting things in new and striking lights. All these qualities are of great practical value in official life, but are not necessarily characteristic of an aptitude for original research. It may, however, be well to see that they are not wanting in a scientific man. We must not suppose that one who writes a fair essay with great ease will be able to write a book. The kind of qualities wanted in the two cases are very different. Hazlitt and Lamb wrote excellent essays, but never could write books which had a definite purpose. A man cannot lay down the scheme of a comprehensive work without much tension and concentration of mind, neither can he carry it to an end without steady power of will. Of none of these qualities does a short essay afford any sure indication.

Hitherto we have supposed the subjects proposed for essays to be of a general nature, and a very limited time to be allowed for their production, such being the usual conditions in ordinary practice. But these conditions are not essential; the subject of the dissertation required may be taken from the branch of study which the student has been pursuing, and ample time may be given. Changes such as these would furnish us with a different kind of test; one which would give us better means of judging of depth and solidity, but which would not discover readiness and versatility so well. To look forward to having to write an essay which shall embody some of the views which should form themselves in the course of reading, has a good educational effect, and as a means of selection, this mode of proceeding offers many advantages, and more especially this. It shews us what the candidate can do under the ordinary circumstances in which he would be called on to write, or at least under conditions less exceptional than those in which essays are usually written in Examinations.

If we set a number of young men down to write for three hours without their knowing, until they unfold the paper given them, whether they are to treat of "the Prince of Wales' visit to India," or "the influence of authority in matters of opinion," we are calling on them to perform a sort of *tour de force*, which is not a trustworthy specimen of their powers. The special circumstances under which they are placed, tell, as we have seen, to the advantage of some, as compared with others, in virtue of peculiarities of temperament which do not correspond to differences of intellectual capacity of the sort we want to estimate.

But when the subject proposed arises out of the branch of learning to which the student has addressed himself, we can mark the judgment shewn in selecting and storing up reflections as well as the comprehensiveness of his survey of the subject of study, and his power of writing with method and precision. These qualities are more to be depended on as evidence of the mental calibre of the man, than the readiness and productiveness of mind under pressure which may be displayed in an off-hand essay.

The complicated question of how much time should be allowed for answering a paper will meet us again, but thus much may be said on it here. A short allowance of time favors readiness, versatility of attention, and that kind of intuitive perception of the right things to say, or to do, on the moment, which Dr. Carpenter would class as "ideo-motor action." These are habits of mind of great practical utility, and likely to bring success in actual life; but while they are by no means inconsistent with the possession of the highest qualities, they do not indicate them of themselves. On the other hand, to be pressed for time paralyzes some who might shew power of thought. Hence, we have the common impression, which is, in the main, a correct one, that, in order to discover the men most likely to do well in active life, we should employ an Examination against time — the Cambridge Mathematical Tripos for instance — but to find the men most likely to serve science, we should adopt one in which abundance of time is allowed, like that for the Smith's prizes. Some minds are all the better for the stimulus of pressure, while others are driven by it into a fever.

I have already spoken of one or two cases in which a narrow limitation of the time allowed for an essay might give us a wrong result, but I would add one remark which applies to other kinds of Examinations as well. I have observed, as a constant symptom of young minds growing into fertility and power, that their best thoughts mostly come as after-thoughts. An idea occurs to them at first in a somewhat bare or imperfect form, and when they review their work, some valuable extension, or necessary qualification, or happy illustration, is suggested. We see the same thing in translation — the word that is interlined on revision, is often that which shews that the writer has caught the point — and, after solving a mathematical problem, some simpler process may strike the student when he reads over his performance. What the student has said or done in his first draft remains by him without his knowing it, while his attention passes on to other matter. "Unconscious cerebration" is taking place all the time, and when he recurs to what he has written, he finds that his ideas have grown, and his conceptions have become more exact. This perfecting power marks minds of a high order, and we should be careful to give an opportunity for its display ; whereas, if scanty time be allowed for revision, an advantage is given to men of quite a different type — men who never improve upon their first ideas — with whom the work " is done when it is done." The performances of such may often be better than the first draft of an abler man's writing, but inferior to the revised copy. Of course candidates should be given to understand how much more important quality is than quantity, or they may use the extra time in covering more paper.

But besides affording very ample time, I would also allow candidates, while writing their essay in the Examination Room, to have access to some standard authorities on their subject. What these should be would rest with the Examiners. This proposal needs some recommendation, because to many it will seem novel. It is a mode of carrying out the principle above stated, of making the candidate write in an Examination under circumstances as little exceptional as possible. What I mean will be most clearly understood from an example. Let us suppose that students have been engaged in studying the Language, Literature, and History of Greece. The Examination of such might comprise an essay paper, to which a whole day might be given. The subject might be : " The changes in the national character of the Athenians between the times of Pericles and Demosthenes." The candidates should then have access to the texts of the Greek Historians, Dramatists, and Orators, and also to works on Chronology and Antiquities. One effect of this plan would be to induce candidates to read their Greek authors in a less scholastic manner, and more in the way in which they would be read by a literary man engaged in Greek History. They would want to *know their way about* Thucydides and Demosthenes, but they would not be overburdened by having to recollect particulars. When they noted a valuable fact or observation, they would turn it over to their "Index Memories," and be able to lay their hands on the passage which contained it if they should want it. No man in writing a book would be justified in quoting from memory, however confident he may feel of remembering rightly. Authors no doubt did so in old times, when books were harder to come by, and vast trouble has been caused to their editors in consequence. There is now no object in forcing men to carry a number of details in their heads.

By this plan, moreover, the Examiner obtains a further advantage. The range of the subjects which can be given for essays is very much extended; for there are many points about which candidates could not write, without the help I propose to offer, even if the subjects were taken from their favorite branch of study, because so much would turn on questions of fact or on authority. It is one of the evils of the common system that, since facts cannot be made of great importance in an essay, those who look to the essay as their strong point, undervalue accuracy in point of facts, as compared with ingenuity of remark.

This method of proceeding is as applicable to some branches of science as it is to literature. The dissertations required in the Smith's Prize Examination at Cambridge, bear on subjects that have been studied, and ample time is allowed. Access to authorities is not permitted, and, from the nature of the subjects given, may not be very necessary, but the choice of subjects would be larger if certain books of reference, such especially as give information on the history of science, or on the magnitudes of the quantities that come under consideration, could be allowed.

It may be asked whether there is not more likelihood of the matter of an essay being drawn from the tutor, when the topic chosen is thus taken from a specified branch of study. I should answer that the Examiner has better means of judging of what is original in this case than in that of a "general" subject. He will have acquainted himself with the views of the principal writers on the point he selects, and he will expect to meet with these in the productions that come before him. He will give the candidates credit, nevertheless, if he finds that they have understood what they have read, and have selected the soundest views and weightiest considerations. He will not expect much originality, still less will he wish to force candidates to pretend to it. If he should meet with what strikes him as an original view, it will probably be really the candidate's own, for the tutor would not be likely to keep to himself any valuable views on History and Science, because these would gain him consideration by being made public, while smart sayings, or paradoxical views, which might be brought to bear on subjects of a "general" nature, would be of no great value for any other purpose.

Essays written altogether at leisure, such as those which are sent in to compete for University prizes, are also good tests of ability, but they hardly fall under the head of Examinations.

It may be said that practical inconvenience would be found in supplying access to books of reference, if the number of candidates were large; but I do not contemplate employing the method under review, except for distinguishing one or two out of a few candidates who have been already selected by some previous process. As far as my experience goes, the effect of an English essay in an Examination is this: A few, perhaps one-tenth of the candidates, write well; the essay brings their special qualities under notice, and gives valuable information about them; while the rest may be grouped as "fair," "indifferent," and "bad." In these groups, the evidence furnished by the essay usually agrees pretty well with what would be inferred from the rest of a General Examination, but among those who do poorly are found a few from whom (judging from their other work) we should expect something better, and here, the *negative effect* above spoken of is of practical value. Hence, for the purposes in view, their would be no need to admit any but candidates of superior attainments to compete by means of essays in the way proposed.

If I have dwelt at what may seem unnecessary length on the subject of the essay as a mode of Examination, it is because it may assist us in solving a considerable difficulty that will meet us when we have to deal with the question of Fellowships. It seems likely that two classes, at least, of such emoluments will be required: the one, as pure rewards for University success, involving no duties; the other, for those who shall be engaged in education, or who are likely to do good service in the way of research. There may be a difficulty in finding opportunities for some of the latter class to shew their qualifications, and if so, an essay written under the conditions I have just named, seems the least objectionable kind of Examination. I only state this now as an apology for having lingered so long upon the point; the consideration of the mode of selection which should be adopted for Fellowships and Scholarships will require a chapter to itself.

Connected with this power of engendering and expressing ideas which has occupied us so long, but different from it in very essential points, is that of reasoning. When we have considered this matter we shall have finished our rough survey of the chief intellectual qualities which can be revealed by Examinations. The reasoning power may be described generally as that capacity whereby the logical sequence of the steps in a train of argument is apprehended, and the investigation followed up to its conclusion. A thinker may hit on a valuable thought without being able to tell how he has arrived at it. He probably went through some unconscious process of mind, but the idea seemed to flash upon him all at once — just as the answer to an enigma comes on a sudden into the head.

Moreover, a man may have much fertility of idea, and may now and then light on a new truth, and yet be very averse to going through a process of proof to establish its certainty. He may be unequal to the sustained tension of mind required to do this; he may not have the patience and the knowledge of the laws of thought which are needed, or the habit of applying them. A speculative thinker is to a systematic reasoner what an exploring party, which makes a dash into a new tract of country, is to the regular force, which, acting perhaps on the news thus obtained, advances in regular form into the region, occupying station after station, and annexing the new domain. Those who are disinclined to put their own thoughts into logical order would be still more averse to going through the demonstration of a known theorem : they may have little perception of logical sequence, no pleasure in marking refined reasoning, or scrutinizing the validity of some novel mode of proof, and they are unwilling to encounter the mental fatigue attendant on this, to them, unattractive kind · of labor. On the other hand, those who find a pleasure in following out a demonstration, who comprehend thoroughly what is requisite to constitute proof, and what is the degree of certainty which can be attained in their subject, may have no invention, no happy anticipation of what they are coming to, and if they ever do reach anything new, they get at it by travelling along what the Germans call the carriage-road of thought.

By means of Examinations we may test this power of reasoning. Sometimes it is exerted by the candidate in the act of answering the questions put to him, sometimes it has been exerted previously, and is only recalled into partial operation in the Examination itself.

A person must, of course, proceed by steps of reasoning, in order to solve any problem in natural philosophy, but it is not in the process of reasoning that the difficulty lies. When the student has got hold of a right physical conception, and the right way to look at a case in order to bring it under some of his general theorems, then he proceeds to the proof by steps which are quite familiar to him. The student's ingenuity and resource are well tested by a problem paper, but to see his appreciation of reasoning, we must mark how he goes through the steps of a demonstration. Explanations of phenomena, and proofs of principles or of theorems (asked for in such a form as to preclude their being drawn straight from the book), are sometimes more effective than problems for trying the strength of the student's head. Indeed, it is beginning to be found that skill in solving problems is not an unfailing test of natural cleverness, or thorough comprehension of the science, but that it may come from a special knack acquired by long practice, and by confining the attention to subjects fertile in examples. In some sciences, Ethics, Law, and Political Economy, cases may be given for the application of principles ; these take the place of problems in Mathematics. The student, to reach his conclusion, must go through the process of reasoning in the Examination room, and thus such performances afford good means of judging of his logical power.

The reasoning produced in proof of some general proposition is rarely the fruit of the individual's own brain, but is valuable as the result of stored-up previous labor, which shews that he has, at some time before, exercised the qualities wanted for mastering a train of thought. He carries it in his mind in virtue of seeing the logical dependence of the links on each other, and memory, except in the case of a very artificial proof (and such artificial demonstrations are not well suited for Examinations), is only concerned in furnishing a recollection of the general course to be taken. The reasoning power must have been efficiently exerted when the theorem was learnt, and this past work forms a fund on which the student can draw for Examination purposes by merely refreshing his memory.

We see then, that the reproduction of a demonstration calls out a different faculty from that which is exercised in applying its results to examples. These two sorts of power supplement one another, and for an Examination to be complete, it should provide for eliciting both kinds. The "moral elements" involved differ in the two cases; in struggling with a problem or a puzzling question, the student is buoyed up with the hope of getting to the result, and of having a solution to shew; he is stimulated by the spirit of pursuit or of contest. But to work steadily through a given piece of hard reasoning, where every step has to be made good as he goes on, and which yields him no trophy of triumph, requires a greater fund of character and mental endurance — just as a harassing march is more trying to the moral stamina of troops than an assault.

No doubt a student, before producing the demonstration of a subject, will want to run his eye over it. However thoroughly the matter may have been assimilated, it can hardly be produced with the great rapidity now required in an Examination, unless it be fresh in the mind. Hence some who are always on the look-out for an occasion to cry "cram," will do so here. But the knowledge that can be rendered fit for production by a few hours of review is not "cram" — it must have been assimilated. The picture may have got dingy, but it only wants a coat of varnish to be as bright as ever. The knowledge may again lose its freshness, but the structure is permanent; the habits of mind, and ways of viewing things formed by the study are of lasting value. The barrister will need to turn to his text books, and the cases in point, before going into Court, but no one who is not a lawyer will be any the wiser for doing so.

We must, however, both in framing schemes of Examination, and in carrying them out, always recollect that attempts will be made to simulate the operations of the qualities which are supposed to be indicated by what is produced in Examination. It may be that the course of reasoning produced is a mere transfer to paper of what has been learnt from a book by rote, and that the logical processes involved have never been performed by the student's mind. This happens when the pupil learns propositions of Euclid by heart, and writes them out, as candidates will sometimes do in Pass Examinations. This practice is easily baffled by enunciating the theorem in a slightly different manner from that given in the text. With Pass Examinations I am not at present concerned; they will come before us hereafter. Something of the same kind is now and then attempted with isolated propositions in the higher Examinations, but the attempt very rarely succeeds, and if ever it does so, it is only in the case of those who are struggling to get through at the tail of an Honor list, that is to say, where the Examination, though competitive in form, is really a qualifying Examination only. In the hypothetical case we are dealing with, I suppose the object to be to discriminate between men of considerable ability, and such men would not engage in these practices. We may expect them to be above anything of the kind: besides, the inducement to learn what they did not understand would hardly exist with them, because they might always employ their time to more advantage in learning something additional which they could properly master. Students, no doubt, comprehend what they learn in different degrees — they may be more or less clear, both in their conceptions, and in perceiving the logical validity of the steps, and the necessity of the various qualifications which should accompany their statements. A haziness of view can usually be detected by an Examiner; very frequently it is shewn by the omission, or imperfect enunciation, of the above-named qualifications, and if, in putting the questions, a slight alteration be made from the suppositions under which the theorem is worked out in the book, this imperfection of knowledge will be brought to light. It is sometimes well to append a question or two on the nature of the proof, or on points which offer difficulty, and it may be advisable to have it stated that if such questions are not attempted, little or no credit will be given for reproducing the demonstration of the theorem.

What I have just said applies chiefly to an Examination in the exact sciences. In moral science and its kindred subjects, a far greater difficulty presents itself.

These subjects must, in great part, be dealt with historically. Where people are not pretty well agreed as to the fundamental propositions, or as to the conclusions reached in a branch of knowledge, the student will generally be called on to give the views of certain writers. A long list of books may be named, the student cannot obtain a precise knowledge of all, and he will look to his tutor to provide him with abstracts of the tenets of certain schools of philosophers, and an outline of the mode in which they arrived at their conclusions. Here the logical element is blended with an historical one, the phraseology and the ideas are usually less precise, and the sequence of the steps less immediate, than in the more exact sciences; there is also, frequently, a large proportion of definitive or formulated statement which may be committed to memory.

The subjects are usually so extensive that it is impossible to require the exact reproduction of the reasoning of the writer, in the close way in which a mathematical theorem is reproduced — and an abstract or outline of proof is all that can be expected. If the student drew this up for himself, and the teacher confined his assistance to giving a clear insight into the writer's meaning, all would be well; but unfortunately a strong temptation is held out to those who are preparing students for Examination to do this work of digesting for them; thus the pupil is furnished with the results of thought without thinking, which, as Mr. Mill observes, in the passage quoted early in this book, is a very enervating process, and the Examiner is at a loss to discover how far the pupil's answers represent a process of reasoning previously gone through by himself, and how far they are due only to his remembering what has been told him. Mr. Todhunter, in his "Conflict of Studies," observes that it would be convenient, sometimes, in Mathematics to ask for the outline of a proof only, but he remarks that if this practice became common, such outlines would be prepared by the tutors, and the students would not go through the processes which we want, and which we give them credit for having performed.

In mental science, there is little answering to the

separate detailed propositions of natural philosophy and much of which the pupil can only be asked to give a general account. Skilled Examiners can often distinguish tutorial manuscript from the student's own work, especially if they can employ *viva voce* Examination. But, though spurious knowledge may be detected now and then, still, if the profits be large, the manufacture of the counterfeit may be carried on to such an extent as to throw discredit on the results of an Examination, and I must therefore conclude that this subject, whatever be its educational or intrinsic value, is, like those which consist mainly of facts, ill-adapted to form the staple of a competitive Examination. We must reward proficiency in it, for the study of it will be given up if we do not; but we should not make it the wrestling ground for youthful wits in general, both for the reason above given, and because, though this science may be well suited for a few robust and peculiarly constituted intellects, yet mental physiologists seem pretty well agreed that for most young minds, introspection, or an attempt to view, as from without, the operation of their own brains, is positively dangerous. The few might shew their attainments by writing or by teaching well, or, if something of the nature of an Examination be wanted, by composing an essay under the conditions recommended above.

Further, the *style* in which demonstrations are reproduced, tells us something of the powers and habits of mind of the candidate. If he says all that is essential, and nothing that is not so — if he can put tersely what he enunciates, or what he concludes — if his mastery of expression is such that he can always find words to say exactly what he wishes — if he is never forced to suppress some qualification, or to append what is unnecessary by the exigencies of his sentence — then we may be sure that we have to do with a man of head, and with one whose ability is not confined to the special matter in view — that he is not merely a mathematician, for instance, or a moral philosopher — but a man who is able to think distinctly, and who is likely to speak plainly and act vigorously in any circumstances in which he may be placed. To bring out this capacity, it is essential that the candidate should not be over-hurried. "Mathematical style" is an expression constantly used in old writers about Examinations, but it is complained that in the papers sent up even by the best men now, excellence in this way is less conspicuous than it formerly was, and the Tripos at Cambridge has thereby lost a part of its efficiency for drawing out the sort of ability likely to make its mark in life. When rapidity is everything, the quality which a student values most is shortness. "My tutor," one will say to another, "has shewn me a way of proving that in half the time." Clearness and naturalness of procedure in a method of proof win it less favor with the student than brevity. He wants to write as little as possible consistently with getting full marks, and the qualifications needed to a statement are often hinted at in an epithet rather than expressed. Thus, there is a danger of our coming to a sort of telegraphic code, in our mode of answering, and even of this kind of conventional short-hand affecting the style of scientific literature.

If we want, then, to have the reasoning power of our candidates properly cultivated, and fully displayed in Examination, I must urge the importance of allowing the candidates ample time, and of leaving the Examiner at liberty to frame his view from all that comes before him. He may, of course, use marks for each question, as he likes, to aid his memory; but should not be bound by them, or feel in any way "under contract" with the student to give him credit for every scrap that is correct.*

We limited our enquiry, at starting, to those constituents of ability which the framers of Examinations have in view, and which Examinations test. This enquiry is now at an end — we find that we may expect to find power of attention, memory in various shapes, delicacy of perception, concentration, imagination and reasoning power, and that Examinations will help us to judge of how far these qualities exist. We see, moreover, that behind all these qualities lies something which a mental physiologist would call massiveness, or robustness of brain, and which we call energy of mind — of this, so far as it is brought out in dealing with books or ideas, we can judge fairly, we see that knowledge has been got, and know that brainwork must have been done to get it — and, in addition, we note indications of strength or feebleness of will: we can find out from a set of papers pretty well whether a man knows his own mind or not.

But, lest we should mistake the knowledge of a part for the whole, we must cast our eyes over the range of qualities which Examinations leave unexplored.

---

* When Examinations are used *scholastically*, that is, to see how students have learnt, we limit time in order to test readiness and thorough preparation. One who knows well what he has learnt ought to have an advantage over one who has to puzzle it out. It is also true that if Examiners are not bound to render marks, and have no personal interest in choosing the best men, they may be tempted to do their work less thoroughly than when their view of each question is recorded.

On so doing, we at once see another variety of that mental energy just spoken of, or rather another side of its sphere of work : we learn nothing of it when it is turned to dealing with *action*, or with *men*. Indeed, all qualities connected with action, and all that involve sympathy with human beings, or the power of influencing them, all that have to do with tact, address, and personal manner, lie outside the range of our testing apparatus. Most moral qualities do so also. We cannot even tell whether to refer an individual to one or the other of the two types, which are the foci round which a large portion of mankind is grouped. We cannot see whether he is likely, in any given position, to do as much, or as little, in the way of duty as he possibly can.

It is true that a student must have done work to get his learning together, but it may have been done under something approaching to compulsion, either that of masters, or of an overwhelming inducement. We can hardly guess at all, especially from a single Examination, whether the work has been done willingly and conscientiously, or by a person of good parts, but no intellectual tastes, who is looking forward to winning a prize, in order to indemnify himself for his drudgery by future advantages.

Mr. W. Hopkins once attracted much attention by his evidence as to the blameless lives led by those who, under his hands, had reached high University Honors; and there is no doubt but that to work freely for a reward three years distant, and that, too, where society, with all its solicitations and enjoyments, is close at hand, is in itself an evidence of moral steadfastness and self-command; but then, this guarantee comes not only from what is shewn in the Examination, but from the circumstances under which the knowledge has been acquired. It is indeed hardly likely that a person could master the great mass of matter required for the Mathematical Tripos, if he were liable to irregularity of conduct, but candidates for scholarships who have worked well under strict discipline at school sometimes prove unequal to being their own masters in the way wanted at college.

Competitive Examinations leave us most in the dark about those qualities which find their sphere in active life, but they also fail us in one important point, when we want to select men to fill posts intended for the "endowment of research." It is most important to know whether persons have a *taste* for their study, and about this, Examinations hardly tell us anything. We meet with cases of hard-headed men, who obtain high degrees in a course which they select as offering them the most favorable field, but who never care to open a book in their branch of study afterwards. Their object has been to win a place in the front, and they have done so, as one of the conditions for future getting on: the Examination was one of the hurdles in their race, and they cleared it, but they may care nothing whatever for classics, or mathematics, or whatever science they have taken up. Only, let me say, that as a man must go a little out of his way to acquire a proficiency in a branch of natural or experimental science, there is the greater probability that a proficient in these subjects will have a genuine taste for them. This silence of Examinations as to *tastes* prevents our placing reliance upon them as a means of selecting those who should be admitted to hold "endowments for research," although to have done well in educational Examinations must be regarded favorably as an evidence of general power.

It must be remarked that if we get wrong results by trusting to Examinations, it is usually because we use them to the exclusion of all other modes of judging — much as an invalid who pins his faith on a new nostrum, will sometimes give up taking ordinary precautions.   We have all the means of forming an opinion that we had before Examinations were introduced, and if these were used with care and method, we might get near the truth about some of the moral and personal qualities of candidates.   Insurance companies get information that they can trust as to the ways of living of applicants for policies, and some use might be made of testimony as to the way in which students have learned, and as to their behavior.   But the fact is that the public are afraid of the reintroduction of the patronage system, and would cling to Examinations "pure and simple," as a safeguard, even if they were less to be trusted than they are.   I need not consider further the qualities about which Examinations do not enable us to judge, but I must recur to one or two disturbing causes which sometimes interfere with their operation where they might be expected to be trustworthy.

I have said that in certain subjects, classics and mathematics especially, persons usually reach a kind of limit, not of knowledge exactly, but of power of using the knowledge — just as they reach a limit of skill in playing on a musical instrument — some are long in reaching this limit, and there may be some who go on improving all their lives ; but in general, one who after the usual course of study, is a second or third rate scholar, or mathematician, as shewn by Examination, would get but little more general grasp of his subject by further reading, although he may grow clearer as to some points, especially if he be engaged in teaching, and, of course, may become acquainted with fresh books on his subject. The limits so reached are important elements in judging of his ability, but the difficulty is to know whether a candidate, in an open Examination, has reached this limit or not. We do not know how long each candidate has been engaged in study, and some candidates may have been specially trained, so that the metal may have received all the working it will take, while others have had only a general education, and may improve much in their special line.

If we must needs decide by a single Examination, we can only make a guess about probable improvement, we learn nothing of the direction in which the student's mind is moving, and nothing of its rate of motion. We see it but at one point. If we can test the progress of students, as we do in a College course, year after year, we learn something of their mental changes ; some improve in grasp of a subject, and in general power throughout, while some remain stationary, and some decline. But an Examiner has seldom the opportunity of making more than one observation, and the testimony of teachers is inadmissible, or not to be got, and so it will be well to note one or two characteristics of the progressive and stationary conditions.

The following symptoms usually indicate a progressive condition of the student. We judge most favorably when he does steadily well in the earlier parts of his subject, and shews decided excellence now and then, and when, though he may be unequal in his performances, his errors do not come from unsoundness, or from inertness of mind, but from his having struck upon a wrong track, or from want of some piece of knowledge, or of trained skill in matters which, like composition in Classics, require long use. A practiced Examiner will also mark *vivacity* in the work as a good sign; a student who feels that he is making way, is full of hope and spirit, and he ventures with a happy audacity on what lies on the very edge of his range, or a little beyond. There is an air of good will, and of force to spare, in all he does.

The stationary or retrogressive condition has two varieties; the dull man may have reached his limit, or one who has been pushed on may have turned idle. The man who has a misgiving that he has got to the end of his tether, shews a chronic weariness of his work: he has gone over his books so frequently that he reproduces them mechanically, he is living on stored-up knowledge, and even his phraseology is found for him by his memory, he avoids fresh brain-work, he is quite contented with the conventional construings of common classical phrases, and the recognized methods of dealing with certain classes of problems. If, however, he be given questions of the sort he expects, he will make a good show, for he is rapid in "writing out" what he knows, and is provided with compendious forms: where long practice is of value, he shews himself expert, but he will not encounter what is new to him, and is more apt to outflank a difficulty than to face it.

The youth who has been pushed forward under a strict tutor, and who fails afterwards from weakness of will, or moral defects, is, like the advancing man, unequal in his performances, but in a very different way. His knowledge is disintegrating, and those portions last longest which he learnt, either when quite young, or most lately, or in which he has had long practice and some success. He may still produce a few good Latin verses, or hit on a neat solution of a problem, or talk plausibly on some open question in philosophy ; but all knowledge that requires *keeping up* is falling into decay, and he will attempt nothing that requires steady tension of mind; he roves daintily over the Examination paper, and will only touch what he has a mind for.

Another point is this. It is generally admitted that power is better shewn by first-rate excellence in one or two branches of study than by moderate proficiency in many, and those who have to dispose of places or emoluments, such as Fellowships, aim most often at securing power; hence they set much value on proficiency in one department. The evil of this is that as soon as a youth shews a turn for Classics, or Mathematics, or Natural Science, he is made to devote nearly his whole time to that study, with a view to gaining, first, some special Scholarship, and a Fellowship afterwards. General education, even at the Universities, is at present thrust, with some contumely, into a corner, and attention is concentrated on the production of Classical scholars, or mathematicians, or proficients in some Natural Science, or in some other special study. In fact, teaching is now too much directed to the training of prize-winners, instead of to the educating of men. This is done, not so much because people want *savants* for the sake of their knowledge, as because the attainment of special excellence is taken as a criterion of ability which promises distinction, or because a high class is "a credit to the College."

The educational effects of this state of things only concern us now so far as they render our criterion delusive. Special proficiency is only trustworthy as an evidence of strength when it has been healthily attained. Exclusive cultivation for several years of that branch of study for which a student has a particular aptitude is injurious to general power in several ways. We cannot keep a certain portion of the brain, or mind, in special activity, leaving the rest comparatively unexercised, and that from the age of sixteen to twenty-two, without causing a sort of hypertrophy of this part, and a starvation of the rest. The consequence will be that the student will lose the faculty of performing any mental operations other than those which occur in his particular study, and become a specialist, not only as to acquirement, but as to habits of mind; his thoughts will run in grooves, and the value of his judgment on matters of life be affected thereby. Moreover, if the student is led to believe that there is "no use" in his attending to any study but that which he has a fancy for — if he resent any attempt to make him give attention to any subject that lies out of the course in which he is to win his prize, and if, when forced to do so, he will commit to memory what he needs must learn, rather than call a new set of the mental muscles into play — then we are encouraging that habit of mind alluded to by Mr. Mill in the passage quoted already : we are rearing a race incapable of doing anything they do not like.

I now come to a matter which affords room for

debate. It being granted that excellence in particular subjects serves to show power, some subjects may show it better than others. We have then the questions, Which show it best, and why?

First of all, to recur to our old distinction. Those subjects are most valuable for our purpose which result in an "Art" or capacity. Next to these come those, the mastering of which calls into play the most important qualities or habits of mind, such as imagination, concentration, and reasoning power. Again, those subjects in which there is a gradation of difficulty, as we mount up step by step, are more effective than those which are spread, as it were, over a plain; for in these last we can only measure the *extent* of knowledge, and one student can travel twice as far as another, if only he have twice the time and sufficient memory, without possessing higher intellectual gifts. A student who knows French can learn Italian or Spanish, if he have the time, without needing any greater power than he has already shewn, and a student may learn the contents of half a dozen historical works without calling out other faculties than those wanted for mastering a single book. The extent of such acquirements tests only diligence and retentiveness.

Mathematics and Natural Philosophy have this particular advantage as testing subjects, that questions of any degree of difficulty can be given in them. In like manner, in Classics there are authors of different degrees of difficulty both in language and matter, and in the moral Sciences there are some portions which require more abstract conceptions and more reasoning power than others; but in History, and in some of the Natural and the Experimental Sciences, there is a large extent of matter presenting little variation in point of difficulty. If we take up Examination papers in a Natural Science, we often find that a large number of the questions turn on a knowledge of facts, or on the description of processes. A high place in an Examination may possibly be gained by answering numerous questions of this description, but all that it would shew would be a fitness for becoming a chemist or geologist ; it would not shew a capacity for attaining distinction in the pursuits of active life.

But there are other reasons why an academical Examination in Law, or History, or Moral or Natural Science, is less effective than one in Classics or Mathematics for selecting the persons of the greatest general power. The mass of educated men have acquired some proficiency in the latter studies, while, unless they have some special taste, or intend to follow a particular calling, they have little or none in the former, and consequently fewer well-qualified candidates present themselves for competition in them. Again, it has been shewn that to discriminate between degrees of ability we must examine the candidates in subjects which they have fully mastered. Now, what is learnt of Natural or Experimental Science in a University course bears a smaller ratio to the whole extent of that science than is the case with Classics or Mathematics; in these a young man leaves the University fitted to fulfil any functions for which a Classic or Mathematician is wanted, and in examining him we can look for close acquaintance with the higher parts of those kinds of learning ; but an under-graduate, who has learned chemistry, or geology, or botany, has done little more than develop an aptitude and lay a foundation for complete knowledge. To attain to this he must spend years in experiment, or in travel and observation. There are grand generalizations and profound researches lying in store for these sciences, and they afford scope for the most abstract conception and power of systematization ; but these problems lie at the extreme ends of the subjects, and cannot be dealt with (unless at second hand), except by those who have accumulated stores of facts by long-continued investigation. Hence, the part of these subjects which is best adapted to bring out *ability* is inaccessible to the ordinary University student, by reason of limited time and opportunities.* Nevertheless, students in these sciences may shew enough proficiency to deserve terminable studentships of moderate value. I would reserve all higher emoluments (supposing we conclude to award such to any not engaged in duties) for those who should have displayed qualifications in science of a nature not to be tested by Examination, or acquired in a merely academical course.

Further, in order that a subject may act effectively for the kind of discrimination we have in view, it should be one in which there is a positive right and wrong. When the matter is speculative, one school of opinions will pervail at one time and one at another. The Examiners will lean, or will be fancied

---

* Here we see how education may be hampered through rewards given by Examinations. The Colleges want men likely to make a figure in life, they therefore select them for proficiency in the subjects which afford the best test of their likelihood of doing so. These emoluments are the mainspring of the higher education, and all that does not lead to them is neglected. Thus, English Literature, which, though excellent for education, is unsuited for competitive examinations, is almost ousted; as were also, until lately, the Natural Sciences, but they have now attained full consideration; indeed, in the I. C. S. Examinations, a cursory knowledge of them, which is of little educational value, fetches more than it deserves.

by the students to lean, to one or the other,* and however impartial they may wish to be, this element of suspicion will exist. They have also to compare elements which are quite heterogeneous, such as the memory, which, rather than his clearsightedness, has led one man right, and the ingenuity, which furnishes another with excellent reasons for being wrong.

Speaking generally, we shall find that those studies are most fitted for use in discriminating ability which have the best disciplinal effect on the intellect and character, that is to say, those which call into play the greatest variety of important powers, and which tend to form the most valuable habits of mind.

The old studies, Classics blended with History and Philosophy, and Mathematics with its applications to Natural Philosophy, have proved their efficacy in this respect after long trial; the public learnt to attach a value to a first class at Oxford, or a high place among the Wranglers at Cambridge, not because they valued the Classics, or the Dialectics, or the Mathematics, or the Natural Philosophy — people had a very dim idea of the nature of the studies which led to these distinctions — but because they knew that they represented a liberal education as understood at Oxford and Cambridge, and that those who had won them often distinguished themselves in life.

The above studies, from having been long used as the instruments of education, have acquired a more

---

* Mr. Sayce remarks on this point as follows: — " Not very long ago the Oxford Class-list in the final Classical Examination was as much a monopoly as the appointments to the Indian Civil Service. It became an accepted axiom in the undergraduate world that none but the pupils of a certain well-known ' coach ' had much chance of getting a first; and when the Examiners tried to circumvent him by changing the character of the papers, they found themselves no match for the crammer, who had swung round from Mill to Herbert Spencer, and from Herbert Spencer to Hegel." — *Fortnightly Review*, June 1, 1875.

organized shape than others — teachers have learnt how to present them in the form most convenient for obliging the pupil to exercise his wits. They are well adapted for " setting lessons in " at schools, and are convenient subjects both for qualifying and competitive Examinations.

Some kinds of study, most valuable for mental improvement, as well as for the account to which the matter of them may be turned, are ill-suited for scholastic purposes at present, from defects of the form in which they are exhibited, and these are less adapted than others for testing ability in Examinations.

Fresh subjects may, from time to time, be put into a shape suitable for this purpose. Those subjects are most likely to be serviceable in this way, which, like Political Economy and Roman Law, are rigorously derived from a few principles, and which may be applied readily to a variety of special cases.

On the other hand, where the stock of principles is slender, and the mass of facts or opinions, large — particularly when the facts are disconnected, as they are in parts of English Law, in English Etymology, and in "Political Geography," as it is commonly treated,— the subject is less suited for use in mental training, and Examinations in it will try memory rather than strength of head.

The attainment, however, of distinction in a well-conducted Examination in any branch of systematic knowledge is a guarantee of the possession of a certain calibre of mind. It shews that a person is capable of gathering up his energies for a considerable effort, and he must, to do well, even in those subjects which are calculated to bring out information rather than intelligence, possess a good analytical memory, a clear head, a wide mental range of view, and a way of doing things thoroughly. Hence, he may be trusted to acquit himself well in any position in which he may be placed, more safely than a person who has a readiness in picking up what lies near the surface, but who has not shewn the power of attaining any special excellence. The deeper our Examination goes, the better it detects a " flimsy " mind.

It would appear then, that, supposing we look to proficiency in one branch of study as a criterion of general ability, we should rate the efficiency of this branch for our purpose by the importance of the faculties which it calls into play. But in order to settle what studies are most generous and catholic in their nature would require a laborous analysis of their action on the mind. For practical purposes we may get some help by considering them, in connection with the kind of *interests* which they awaken, or to which they correspond.

For a rough classification based on this distinction I would suggest the following : —

Interests of an intellectual nature are directed towards human beings, to other objects, and to abstractions. We meet with characters which serve as types of the men whose interest gravitates to one of these centres of attraction. We may find a person whose leading interest is in other men. Their doings, their feelings, their institutions, and their welfare, have a strong attraction for him, and he cares little for matters in which the human element does not appear. If one who is the type of this class be travelling abroad, he wants to see, not buildings, or works of arts, or natural objects, so much as the people themselves ; he longs to know something of their ways of living and thinking, he is full of human sympathy. He may be so wrapped up in his interest for *persons* as to be careless of external objects. He may have no observation for *things;* he may even be impatient if a companion stops to collect wild plants, or to examine antiquities.

The representative of those, whose interest is for external objects, may care less for history or poetry, or politics or sociology, than for what strikes his eye in the material world ; his turn will be for Natural Science, for Archæology, or Fine Art. Another will revel in contemplating abstractions, he will delight in mathematical, or metaphysical, or possibly poetical conceptions, and his main interest in what he sees, will be, not in the concrete objects themselves, but in some law or general view which they suggest or exemplify.

There are branches of learning which answer to these several types, some correspond to a single one almost exclusively — pure mathematics and metaphysics, for instance, to the last — while some represent a combination of two such interests, in nearly equal degrees. Natural Philosophy, for instance, combines the element of abstract conception with that of obervation. Political Economy, where it verges on Sociology, combines the abstract with the human element. Classical learning unites a sympathy with the thoughts and doings of great men of old with an appreciation of those laws of thought which underlie all human language. Some branches of learning embrace all the three elements, but in very varying proportions. There is, perhaps, hardly any one of them in which a person can excel who has no head at all for what is abstract, for we find this element in all that is intellectual; but a man may be wanting in sympathies with human beings, and be unobservant of the external world, and yet be a good linguist, or a great logician, or pure mathematician.

It would carry me beyond my limits to assign to every science its place as regards these elements. I can merely suggest this way of looking at the matter, and must leave it to the reader to make the application to particular cases. I only have to observe that a study which turns exclusively on a single interest is ill-suited to be the sole object of an Examination, which has for its object to enable us to select men suited for the work of life.

The natural philosopher may be too deficient in human sympathy ever to deal wisely with other men, and the same may be the case with the pure linguist — the man whose love is not for the literature, but for the vocables of a language, and who does not care to trace in it the mind or the history of the people who framed it.

Some sciences are spoken of as antagonistic. This antagonism is more easy to understand by considering the diversity of the *interests* on which they turn than by a more philosophical analysis. The sciences which deal with men, and those which deal with objects, are seldom equally attractive to the same minds. It is not precisely true that there is an opposition between Classics and Mathematics. A pure mathematician has usually some facility for languages, much more so than the physicist. The abstract element in Philology is often attractive to him, while a scholar of great mental power is seldom *incapable* of Mathematics, though his imagination may run more toward human beings, with their doings and affections, than toward figuring geometrical or physical relations in his mind's eye. A naturalist, however, or a man of a mechanical and constructive turn has often a positive distaste for languages, with little love for poetry or literature, and still less for ethical philosophy, while men of great literary talent have often been singularly inobservant, and incapable of doing anything *with their hands.* The classical scholar seldom takes a natural science for his hobby, while a mathematician often does so.

If then we wish to know that a man has been educated all round, and that he can think clearly on other subjects than his favorite one, we ought to ascertain that he has, at some time, attained a fair proficiency in some *supplementary* study.

The mathematician, for instance, and the student of Natural Science, in order to reach their full, free growth, should have gone through some literary training, and the Classical scholar should have been exercised in dealing with physical ideas, or with some science of observation, which may give him *eyes.* The actual knowledge thus acquired will no doubt soon slip away, but some conceptions may remain, and even if they do not, advantage must accrue from the more general development of the faculties, and even from the mere survey of a new department of learning. The men who indulge the most in contempt for all learning but their own, are either self-educated men, or those who have too narrowly followed their own bent with a view to the prizes now held out for special acquirements. Of course, a reasonable interval should elapse between heavy Examinations in different kinds of study.

I have before said that it is impossible to frame an Examination which shall place men in order of *ability*. We cannot judge with accuracy on this point, even between candidates who present themselves in the same branch of study. Knowledge, as well as ability, must be a factor of the result in any case, but in some subjects one factor, and in some the other, will be of the higher order. As we pass from place to place down a list drawn up in order of merit, we usually find well-marked differences both of ability and knowledge between those who occupy successive places near the top; as we go lower down, mere knowledge counts for more in comparison with ability, and, as the great mass of competitors have read pretty much the same books, the variations as we pass from place to place become smaller, till we arrive at what may be called the great plateau of mediocrity, where the slope is only just perceptible. When many candidates are selected out of a great body, as in the Examinations for the Indian Civil Service and the Army, we go down so far that this plateau is reached; and there is, in fact, no difference worth considering between the last ten who are accepted, and the first ten who are rejected.

To conclude this chapter we will glance over some of our results. We may rest satisfied that a man who gains well-marked success in *any* kind of Examination which deals with subjects of considerable difficulty or extent, must have a certain kind of power; he must know what *exactitude* means, he must have the faculty of applying his mind firmly to a matter, and taking off and retaining a perfect impression. If the Examination turns on the knowledge of books, as it must in parts of Law, History, and Literature, little else beyond the above power will be necessarily displayed, but when an acquired *faculty* is brought into play, as in Classics, Mathematics, and some other branches of study, we see the mind in more varied and complete activity, it is no longer mainly receptive, it not only gives house room to the material it brings together, but it works it up into some new product.

In many branches of learning two or three very different faculties are brought into play ; a Classical Examination, for instance, often brings out the strong contrast that exists between the two different types of the scholarly mind : we have the pure linguist, who has great imitative capacity, who writes Latin and Greek with something of the genuine ring, and who will by force of grammatical analysis unravel the sentences of a hard piece of reasoning from Aristotle or Plato, so as to send up a page of readable English translation without very precise notions of what it is about ; and we may have another who is weaker in dealing with *words*, who has less memory for them, and is less happy in hitting on the one he wants, but who is much stronger in perceiving the relation of *ideas*. He has enough knowledge of the language to make out the general meaning, and, by steady thought, one point after another will be cleared up, the sequences of the reasoning will be established, and the full meaning will reveal itself to him.

If we adopt the system of marks — and if we require to classify the candidates, we can hardly avoid using something of the kind — a high position may be due to great linguistic or great logical excellence, or to a moderate amount of both. Hence, if we wanted to discriminate nicely between two persons, or if we had to dispose of a post for which a person of one or the other type were required, it would be necessary to see how the marks were obtained. From the system of publishing all the marks, which is adopted in the case of the Examination for the Indian Civil Service, one who understands the relative value and action of the several subjects can arrive at a far better impression about the qualities of the candidates, by looking at the *items* which compose their respective aggregates, than by looking at the aggregates themselves. I shall discuss hereafter the relative advantages of lists arranged in order of merit, and alphabetically in small classes.

It may be well to remark that though we may fairly infer that a man who has done well in an Examination is likely to be an effective person, it is by no means safe to conclude that no one will turn out to be so who has *not* done well. It is safer to draw a *positive* than a *negative* augury. Some minds are not ripe till the time for examination has gone by, and some intellects of great thinking power are of this order. Moreover, a young man's work may, owing to disturbing causes, not shew all he can do, and when a person has to gain his bread by exertion, the stimulus sometimes calls up qualities which had been overlaid by youthful spirits or indulgent nurture. But it is by no means to be wished that our criterion should be infallible; it would be bad for clever young men to imagine that they had been discovered to have been born for success, or for the less gifted to believe that they had been pronounced dunces by an irreversible doom.

When we were considering what were the studies, success in which might be most safely adopted as an indication of the kinds of ability we were looking for, we found that we had to guess, as well as we could, from an *à priori* likelihood. But it would not be impossible, or even very difficult, to get something like statistical information on this subject. We may find out what the actual facts have been. No doubt we shall have to strip off some cases, as exceptional ones, and to apply corrections for disturbing causes in others, but a carefully drawn up table, putting early proficiency of particular kinds by the side of the doings of after life, might not only reveal something about the objects immediately before us in this chapter, but might throw light on the conditions most favorable to the preservation of mental health.

If we could see how those who in their youth were great classics, mathematicians, or mental philosophers, — so far as student greatness goes,— bore themselves in the work of their lives, we might find in what cases early promise was most frequently fulfilled, not only in the way of attaining advancement, for with this, fortune, family, and personal address have often much to do, but in winning, soon or late, recognition for commanding ability or good service done : some kinds of early distinction we might find were more frequently than others the forerunners of a career of usefulness. There are many cases in which men's lives are before the public eye, and in such a fuller analysis might be possible ; some minds would be found to grow, some to dwindle, some, ultimately, to ossify in a rigid form, some to take impression from every passing paradox, some to remain plastic and open to fresh ideas while retaining the mastery of their judgment to the last. By comparing such results with the nature of the early training, or early distinctions of the individual, we might perhaps learn that an original aptitude for certain kinds of study, and the mental exercise involved in such studies,— for the two elements would be combined, —were associated in different degrees with lasting activity and healthfulness of mind.

We have University records of academical performances for more than a hundred years, and if we were to tabulate a great number of cases of marked proficiency in different studies, and trace the careers of the persons, not neglecting the circumstances of their physical, and above all, their continuance in *mental* health, we might arrive at results which would be of value to mental physiologists. Differences of fortune and of opportunities would introduce formidable disturbing causes, but these would be partially eliminated if we got together a large number of cases. I believe that mental physiology will one day be recognized practically in education. The time may come when certain peculiarities of minds may be recognized as "indicating" or "counter-indicating," in medical phraseology, the use of certain kinds of mental exertion. A science of observation may be prescribed in one case, some study which enforces concentration of attention in another, while one which involves "introspection" may be strictly prohibited in a third. We may even have hereafter a medical branch of the educational profession, we may have persons who shall make it their business to understand mental constitutions, and to advise parents as to the course to be followed with youths of peculiar or slightly morbid turns of mind. I am aware that what I hint at would afford a tempting field for quackery, but, at the same time, I feel sure that immense good might be effected by a wise practitioner who should unite a sound knowledge of mental physiology with a practical acquaintance with the work of education.

CHAPTER VI.

EXAMINATIONS AS A TEST OF KNOWLEDGE.

IN this Chapter we have to consider a simpler question than that which occupied us in the last. Instead of scrutinizing what comes before us in an Examination to find out what we can of the qualities and general ability of those whose work is under review, we shall direct our attention to the knowledge displayed. We shall regard it as a possession valuable to the man himself, and also, in many cases, to others who want his services. In order to proceed more methodically, we have supposed first one purpose and then the other to be paramount, but we did not debar ourselves in the last Chapter from considering the value of learning as a constituent of ability: we regarded it as a store of mental food required as a provision for future mental growth. Neither can we in this Chapter consider knowledge apart from the intellectual qualities, the possession of which is implied in its attainment, or which are brought out in expressing it on paper, or in otherwise putting it forth. Knowledge only comes before an Examiner in very close combination with the power of producing it, and I shall in this Chapter consider this power as being bound up with, and forming part of, the attainment itself.

The case which in this Chapter I have to deal with is this ; — I suppose that we want to ascertain the degree of proficiency which those who present themselves have reached in particular branches of learning, and that we regard this knowledge, not as a test of diligence, or for its effects as a mental exercise, but as a good in itself, as an acquisition which will render service to the possessor, or enable him to render service to others. This function of Examinations was that for which they were first employed. As soon as people began to depend for help on the skill or advice of those who were supposed to possess certain "Arts," it became necessary to find out that these acquirements were genuine. Not only in what we call the learned professions, but in many other "crafts and mysteries" as well, we hear of provision for the appointment of "wise and discreet persons" who are to examine those who are at the end of their apprenticeships. No one could act as a pilot, for instance, till he had been pronounced qualified by a board of Examiners in a Court of Lode-manage. People would not trust their lives or valuable interests to persons for whose qualifications they had no security. Hence, qualifying Examinations grew up to meet a real need. In a short time prizes or distinctions were bestowed on those who acquitted themselves best, and the competitive element was thereby introduced. It may be observed that in all such actual instances the Examination was combined with some definite course of training, the candidate was never pronounced fit on the verdict of the Examination alone ; neither was this Examination open to all comers, howsoever and wheresoever taught. It formed the *finale* of a particular course of instruction, it strengthened the hands of the teacher or master by giving him something to hang *in terrorem* over the idle pupil or apprentice, and it served to detect decided ignorance or incapacity. There are many callings which turn so much on details that it would be impossible to ascertain by one or two Examinations that a person was fit for his vocation. There are others in which, if an Examination were the sole test employed, it would have to be inconveniently long, and the candidate should be required to answer nearly all the questions. Now we find by experience that a high standard in any sort of Examination can only be reached by persons who have more than the average calibre of mind. Dull students, however hard they may work, and however well acquainted they may be with their work *in their own way*, can never get beyond a certain point in Examinations, the talent for bringing out what they know, above spoken of, is wanting in them ; they are apt to misread or overlook questions, or to blunder about what they know perfectly well. Hence, if we fixed our Examination standard as high as would be necessary in order to ensure a satisfactory knowledge of a professional subject — and this standard would have to be higher if we had only one Examination than if we had two — we should soon find ourselves running short of Professional advisers.

Our forefathers thought they could secure knowledge by authoritative teaching as well as by Examination. They accepted the fact that a youth had had proper teaching for a proper time as a guarantee for his knowing what he wanted. This is not worth much by itself, but taken together with an Examination of moderate severity, it furnishes a test of some value which persons of moderate ability may satisfy — and by combining these two modes of proceeding our forefathers obtained as many persons as they wanted who were possessed of passable professional or technical skill.

I dwell upon this because it illustrates a point which bears on the conditions for the durability of knowledge. Durability, we find, depends in part on the length of time during which the matter to be acquired has been kept before the pupil's mind ; so that if one pupil has spent six months over his work, while another has been only six weeks at it, though the performances of the two in an Examination may be nearly on a par, the knowledge of the one who has been longest over his work will commonly be of greater intrinsic value than that of the other ; in fact, the latter should answer half as many questions again as the former to represent a knowledge of equal value. The practice common at many Universities of exacting attendance during a certain time at certain courses of lectures depends for justification on this principle. It is supposed that by such attendance the knowledge is taken in little by little, and that each portion will have had time to sink into the mind of the pupil. If these conditions are fulfilled they will, no doubt, be favorable to the durability of knowledge. That our forefathers should from practical needs have been led to adopt the course which our theory would suggest, is a testimony to its correctness. They combined an Examination of moderate difficulty with a disciplinal course of study of considerable length, and this we still find to be the most expedient course when we require a considerable body of fairly qualified practitioners for professional needs, or of persons fairly versed in any kind of learning.

The Examinations of old times, with the exception of certain inspections of schools, which do not concern us now, were all technical ones, using the term in the sense attached to it in the first Chapter. All that the Examiners cared for was to see that the person examined could do what he was going to be paid for ; they cared nothing for the cultivation of the person himself ; they certified, in fact, to the quality of particular kinds of skilled labor which were brought into the market. Many professional and other Examinations are still necessarily technical. These need not particularly occupy our attention here, not because they are less important than other Examinations, but because they have already been pretty well brought to compass the end they had in view. Professional Examiners know exactly the requirements of the profession ; they know exactly what the candidate will have to do with his knowledge when he has got it ; and they are not likely to be taken in by mere book knowledge got up for the purpose of an Examination alone. Moreover, the students they have to deal with, the better sort at least, look beyond the Examination, when that is over they will not have done with their knowledge, they have to win their bread by it, and though they may, and often do, look too narrowly to what will be of immediate use in practice, yet, on the whole, they are *willing* students. Another consideration relieves us from the great difficulty of all — the question of the durability of the knowledge. Professional students cannot forget any considerable proportion of what they have had to learn, because they have to use it every day of their lives. This observation, however, only applies to those portions of their Examinations which bear directly on practice. In most Professional Examinations, we find certain subjects included which are valuable because they force the student to take a broader view of the province of his labor than he could catch from the confined path which, at starting, he has commonly to follow, or because they equip him with the requisites for exploring new tracts, or for dealing with the philosophy of his subject. Such studies are Roman Law, Jurisprudence, and International Law, in the legal career; Botany, Mechanics, and some parts of Chemistry, in the medical profession. These studies are not kept bright by use in practice, and the student cannot see that they will help him on; they will not bring him briefs or patients, or enable him to do his routine work with more ease; and so it not unfrequently happens that he learns them with as much indifference, and forgets them with as much alacrity, as if he were a non-professional student who had to qualify himself in certain "liberal" studies for a pass Examination.

These parts then of the Professional Examinations belong to general education, and our remarks on the danger of artificial *Examination knowledge* taking the place of real knowledge, and of that which is flimsy and fading passing itself off as solid and indelible, will therefore apply to them.

In the Examinations employed in liberal education, three purposes are carried on simultaneously, we usually want to learn three things about the candidate, and the Examiner mentally, if not actually, assigns to him credit on each separate score; we want to guage his ability in the way spoken of in the last Chapter; we also want to see what he knows, and often we want to give a sanction to some course of teaching, and to ascertain that the student has gone through the processes of thought, which the educator intended him to perform.

We are only concerned here with the testing of knowledge, and with such knowledge as can be made useful to society, or which affords a sensible addition to a person's intellectual wealth.

This limitation must be borne in mind ; for a dull person may be learning all his youth long, and may get considerable good from the process, and yet may have nothing to shew — nothing that we can *measure* at the end of the time. What he does learn is how to get up on occasion what he wants, and to use such wits as he has to the best purpose. He may turn out useful for many positions, and yet he may possess nothing that can be called an *acquirement.* The brain gets indeed a little tinged with what runs through it ; most kinds of study, even with stupid pupils, leave traces which are of some good to the learner, but it is seldom that any one kind is sufficiently mastered to be made of use to other people, unless it is kept in exercise by coming into the business of life. As I said in speaking of the Mathematical Tripos, with the higher class of students the value of the knowledge itself is great, and often outweighs that of the training, while with the duller sort of students, nearly the whole good of education comes from its giving them the use of their brains. Some subjects leave much more behind them than others, but in general, unless the knowledge is kept up, it soon ceases to be available for actual use, and only serves for the general culture of its possessor.

The Examiner, in the matter now before us, will have three things to do.

(1) He must find out how much the candidate has learnt, how thoroughly he knows it, and how readily he can apply his knowledge.

(2) He must consider how far the sort of knowledge which he discovers is of the kind wanted for the purpose in view.

(3) He must judge of the durability of the acquirement — that is, how long the possessor is likely to retain it.

I shall consider each of these heads in order.

I. Attainments may be grouped in two classes, corresponding to the distinction we have so often drawn. One, comprising those subjects, the knowledge of which yields a practical faculty, and which for shortness we may call " Art subjects," and the other those from which no such accomplishment results. What is submitted to the Examiner by the student in the one case is a specimen of the skill acquired through a process of learning ; in the second he produces portions of information which he has derived from books, or teaching, and has put by in his head, arranged for use with more or less method.

It is much easier to ascertain what a person really knows in the case of an " Art subject," than in that of subjects of the other description. We can set the classical student to translate Greek or render English into Latin, just as we could give the musician a violin and call on him to play. There is no room here for " cramming," and we can judge of the order of his accomplishments *as a whole*, from a few specimens. But the knowledge which is of the character of *information* is different in this respect.

If we want to find out how far a person knows History or Geography, we can only judge by the answers he gives to questions on a few points ; hence we have to form our estimate of the value of the cargo by the quality of a few samples, the cargo not necessarily being equally good throughout, and these samples must therefore be selected — that is to say, the questions will have to be framed — with great care.

Returning to the first-named class of subjects, we find that we have comparatively little difficulty. Examinations properly conducted, whatever else they may be meant to effect, must shew in what degree the " Art " is possessed. If the workman displays the skill we want, we need not trouble ourselves how it was come by. If we want a good Greek Scholar to teach the language or to edit an author, we can ascertain by trial whether a candidate has the requisite knowledge ; it does not matter how this knowledge was got, it must be genuine, no " crammer " can " veneer " a person with the power of writing Greek Prose : if he can give it to him by a short way, so much the better. When we find the Greek good, we need look no further.

I assume that the Examination is extensive enough to test acquaintance with authors of different degrees of difficulty, and that it does not turn upon "set subjects ;" for these latter afford no criterion of knowledge of the language, although they may be of service in education, and a close acquaintance with a great work in its original language is an addition to a man's mental wealth. The branches of Mathematics which abound in *operations* are, so far, " Art subjects," and the above remarks apply also to them.

Whether the Examination be framed mainly for educational purposes, as in School or College Examinations, or with a view to pick out the person who gives the greatest promise of distinction, it will, if good of its kind, serve to test the range of the knowledge. It may go *beyond* what we want, but it will answer our end. We may make sure, for instance, that a mathematician is familiar with his subject without calling on him to solve hard problems in a very limited time, as we do when we want to test his power and ingenuity, or to produce long demonstrations, which, for educational reasons, we may want to know that he has mastered. But Examinations which involve these must bring out knowledge of mathematics, as well as ability and training. It may, however, obstruct the advance of the student to the more important parts of his science to be forced to prepare for a display of ingenuity, and so, if our view be solely to promote or to test *acquisition*, we should frame our Examination in a suitable way.

I now only give very general directions as to the best mode of effecting this, because when the object is clearly understood, Examiners soon find the way to attain it.

I have spoken in the fourth Chapter of an Examination which might be held in the highest branches of Mathematics in order to test advanced knowledge, such as would be required by persons intending to pursue mathematical science—these Examinations would be instances of the kind I am now contemplating. It would soon be found that the papers given in such Examinations assumed a style very different from that of those set in the ordinary Examinations which are directed to finding out the pupil's ability, and his adherence to the prescribed course of study, as well as his actual knowledge.

When we come to what I may call *information*

subjects, a point or two must be noticed. Every subject of Examination, of course, comprises positive information in some degree, so that the term "Art subjects" must be only understood to mean those in which a faculty of doing something results from the knowledge which is possessed. The classical scholar may not know the meaning of some word or idiom, and the want of this piece of information may prevent his translating the passage. This brings us to the first point that I have to consider, which is the relative importance of different kinds of information. Some are spread through the whole mass of a subject, others are isolated matters embedded in it. For instance, the scholar's ignorance of a very unusual word does not disclose to us ignorance of anything else; but if he mistake the meaning of a common idiom or of a legal term of frequent occurrence in Latin, he cannot have an intellegent acquaintance with Latin Literature or History.

Many subjects contain both principles and facts; the first take time to grasp, but when grasped, they constitute an abiding possession. Take Political Economy, for expample. It requires some thought to get clear conceptions about Capital, Cost of Labor, Rent, and the like; a person taking up the book casually, and beginning the chapters so headed, would not understand them. But some parts of the subject consist of *facts:* the history of the Bank of Amsterdam, for instance, or the account of the Metayer system — and these any educated person could comprehend on first reading them. The Examiner then must give far more importance to questions on principles than to those on facts, in order to estimate properly the cost and the utility of the knowledge.

In History, the *framework of events* answers in some degree to a principle. If this *structural* portion be unsound, the whole fabric will be in a tottering state, but there are certain parts which, if they should decay or be faulty, may be removed and replaced — like a decorative statue in a niche of a wall — without injury to the whole.

Thus questions on the concatenation of circumstances, or the spread of influences, or the general position of affairs at a certain time, should carry much more weight than those which could be answered in a few words by turning to a book of reference. Even in order to use such a book to good purpose, a person must have an idea of the skeleton of his subject, and this cannot be got in a moment; when he has obtained this, he can build up the body of his knowledge, if only he knows where to find the information he needs.

For instance, a person unacquainted with the History of France, hearing Cardinal Mazarin mentioned, turns to a biographical Dictionary, that he may learn "all about him;" but there he finds himself entangled with "the Pope," whose name is perhaps not given, with Anne of Austria, of whom he knows nothing, and with the wars of the Fronde, which he has never heard of, so that he is no wiser when he shuts the book than he was when he opened it. One who had got a *structural skeleton* of French History in his head would gather from the article just what he wanted.

Some parts of all knowledge must be built up by ourselves for ourselves, while there are others which, like articles of furniture, can be purchased and put in their proper places whenever we please. Questions on particulars of this sort should be sparingly set by the Examiner, both because they are of little service in helping him to assign its value to the student's knowledge, and also for a reason belonging to the next head — because they call into existence a special variety of knowledge adapted more for Examinations than for use.

As a practical rule, the Examiner is more likely to set suitable papers for the purpose we have now in view, when he sets them "*out of his head,*" than when he takes certain books and picks out questions from them. Besides, in order to set the paper from what he has in his head he *must* be full of his subject. This is a guarantee of his qualifications, and what has endured in his own mind is likely to belong to that more structural part of the fabric which I have spoken of.

But questions which can be answered in a word or two are easy to frame, and save trouble in the looking over, and such is now the pressure put upon Examiners, that they are forced to economize labor. They can hardly possess enough floating knowledge to furnish all the papers required, and they therefore take their questions sometimes out of books, selecting points which are perhaps isolated, and which belong to that part of knowledge which the student does *not* require to carry always about with him. Teachers begin to complain of the papers set in some educational Examinations as encouraging students to trust to the "Portative Memory," instead of assimilating knowledge. If Examiners were to draw the bulk of their questions from their own fund of knowledge without using books except for reference, the value of their Examinations, both as a test of attainment and as an educational appliance, would be greatly increased.

Answers that are erroneous throw much light on the state of a student's knowledge.

When a candidate's answer is wrong, he commonly receives no marks for that particular question, but the nature of the blunder may be such as to shew that his conceptions are wrong altogether, or that he cannot be said to have any conceptions at all, right or wrong, upon the matter; in this case, those of his answers in this subject that happen to be correct will not indicate knowledge of any value, but only the recollection of the words of some manual, and no credit should be given for them.

Again, various sciences of experiment and observation are now made the subjects of *paper* Examinations. Such Examinations are never quite satisfactory, but if the student answer nearly all the questions rightly, this will shew a valuable knowledge of his science. When, however, a student gets only a small proportion of the marks — one hundred and fifty marks, for instance, out of five hundred in Geology — this does not indicate knowledge of *any* practical value at all. If we were to shew such a student a piece of domite, he would probably call it chalk; he has never made out how the strata lie in a district, and does not know how to set about it; what he *has* learnt is the nomenclature of the science out of a manual. The geological student should know this nomenclature, but its value lies in its being applied further on; and if the student do not go far enough to use it, he might as well have learnt a page or two out of Johnson's Dictionary. Hence *no credit whatever* should be allowed on the score of acquirement for scanty knowledge of a subject of this nature displayed on paper. If a candidate can perform even a few practical processes, or identify specimens in branches of Natural History, he may claim some credit. An aggregate made up by a few marks in several subjects shews no knowledge, but rather dissipation of mind.

When it is *not* the purpose of the Examination to test acquirement, the case is different. For instance, in examining with an educational view, we must recollect that with beginners, knowledge comes, not steadily, not advancing as it were *in line*, but by patches — a bit here and there becomes bright, and the brightness may spread over the whole field of view. Hence, in such cases, the Examiner will be less ready to pronounce that all is dark because he comes on a very bad blunder. But in an Examination which is regarded as final, and to show that a candidate possesses acquirements of service to himself or to others, knowledge which stops short of the fruit-bearing stage should not be allowed to count for anything at all. When we regard the possessor of knowledge as a skilled laborer we require a certain completeness of skill. Knowledge, in order to have any exchangeable value, must be tolerably perfect in its own department : the *foundations* of edifices are not marketable at all.

But in education the case is different ; we give credit, then, for mental training. The plan of allowing marks in proportion to knowledge is quite justifiable on *educational* grounds, because a pupil must have used his wits a little to have learnt a single book of Euclid : and even the elements of Latin or French grammar are worth something as scaffolding, supposing that the owner is going on to build. Even if the learner at the end *know* but little, he may not have lost his pains — he may have got clearer conceptions and more of them, as well as a better use of his faculties, from the discipline he has gone through.

II.   I now come to the second of the purposes which the Examiner has in view, that of ascertaining that the knowledge which has been acquired is of the sort which will be wanted in the position the candidates hold, or be valuable to them as a personal possession.

When Examiners have to test the qualification of candidates for admission to the Professions or to appointments — as in the case of the Further Examination for the Indian Civil Service — they understand exactly the duties which will have to be performed, and have only to adhere to a general rule, which may be stated as follows :

Examinations employed to test the value of acquirements should turn on the exercise of these acquirements as much as possible in the way in which they are employed in actual practice.

Of late it has become necessary to examine in some subjects of a practical kind, which it is difficult to treat in the way indicated by our rule.   Examinations framed like those employed in education have been introduced.   We are in consequence driven to examine on *paper* in subjects which, in a great degree, turn on acquaintance with objects or experiments.   Instead of performing an experiment *himself* before the Examiners, the pupil describes on paper the way to do it, and this description comes out of a book.   The consequence is that the "bookwork" element in many subjects has been made unduly prominent. Thus students reading for an Examination may get one aspect of some studies, and those who pursue the studies for use in the business of life may get altogether another. Indeed, it is possible that the student who has passed his Examination may have to begin again, and learn his subject in a different way when he wants to make use of it.

An instance of this occurred when Civil Engineers for the Indian Service were selected by competitive Examination. Those came to the front who were "well up" in the text-books, and had a facility in solving a certain kind of Mathematical problems. The Engineer, in the course of a series of great works of construction, might have to address himself to half a dozen of such problems, but in the Examination, success turned mainly on a facility in solving them, and on the power of reproducing text-books. In actual service, the Engineer would take these text-books with them, and all he would want would be to recollect where to turn for what he needed; hence what was wanted for Examination differed from what was wanted in practice. Moreover, in the course of an Examination of a few days, it was impossible to see with what handiness each candidate could use a theodolite, or how he could lay down a map; much less was it possible to ascertain whether he knew good materials from bad ones, or had an eye for the capabilities or difficulties offered by a line of country, or the power of estimating the amount of work in an undertaking. In consequence, the men sent out, selected by competition, were often found to be useless, and the evil was remedied by recurring to the sound practice of providing a special course of instruction, and using Examinations along with it as a sanction for the teaching. The establishment of the very successful College at Cooper's Hill has met this difficulty.

In Germany, as I am told, the Examination employed falls in with the rule I have laid down. The students have not only studied at a Polytechnic school, but they are called on afterwards to do exactly what they will have to do in their profession — they are directed to prepare plans and specifications for a line of railway, or a canal, or for drainage works in the neighborhood of their place of study, and are allowed three months to do it in ; they are examined in the text-books and scientific parts of the subject during their course of instruction from time to time.

But it is not only in technical subjects that the Examiner has to distinguish knowledge available for use, from *educational*, and from *artificial* knowledge. Many subjects comprised in a liberal education may be studied in a different way for an Examination from that in which they would be learned if only wanted for the student's own use ; but the knowledge is not the worse on that account, if the Examination be framed on sound educational principles. A person who learns what he wants simply for his private use, may look too narrowly to his immediate purpose. Gibbon tells us that he originally picked up Greek only to enable him to get at the contents of Greek books, and he found that his knowledge of the language was, in consequence, very inaccurate; and persons who only learn a modicum of mathematics for purely practical purposes, for navigation, for instance, are thrown out by any case that deviates from the normal type, and work with an uneasy sense of the insecurity of their footing. Thus study may be cramped by too exclusive a regard to practical use, just as it is by looking to Examinations.

By *educational* or *student* knowledge, I mean such as may not be in itself effective, but which will serve as a basis for real knowledge : by *artificial* knowledge I mean that which is only frabricated for Examination purposes.   There is less chance of meeting with this in some subjects than in others, least of all in the case of languages.   For every one who learns a language wants to be able to read it, write it, and speak it, the very acts he is called on to perform in Examinations ; and though if it is thought necessary, in University phrase, "to separate the men," *crabbed* passages may be picked out, and an artificial kind of reading thereby encouraged, still enough that is wholesome must be learnt to make the student's knowledge profitable for use.

With some mathematical subjects the case is rather different ; for the object of them may be to enable the student to work out practical problems, or to proceed to higher investigations, and if he cannot make these practical applications of theorems, and does not go on to higher investigations, then we have an article produced for Examinations only.   Some educational advantage may have accrued from the study, but the knowledge, looked at with a view to usefulness, is not what we want.   A student, for instance, may "write out" Trigonometrical theorems, and yet be far from at home in using logarithmic tables, or in applying what he has read, to the problems that would actually arise in surveying. He may have got up his "De Moivre's Theorem" without any idea of what it helps people to do ; or he may have learned his Lunar Theory, and have no notion of how it is to be applied to form Lunar tables, or of how the "coefficients" in his expressions are deduced from observations. Hence, if an Examiner would satisfy himself that a candidate's knowledge is of value for scientific purposes, he must make sure that he knows on what experiments or observations his science rests, how they are performed, and, above all, that he can make use of his knowledge when he has got it. To effect this he must introduce some questions of a different character from those usually set in competitive Examinations, and it may be necessary to allow students under Examination to have access to Mathematical Tables, or other books of reference, with the use of which they ought to be familiar.

Rapidity of production is not wanted in the case of knowledge that is acquired for use and not for display ; hence, the student should not be set to write against time, nor should problems be proposed to him which do not aim at bringing out correctness of apprehension, or the power of applying knowledge. Ingenious puzzles may be of service in detecting cleverness, but they do not test what I am now supposing the Examiner to be concerned to discover.

The most difficult subjects to deal with in Examinations are the literary ones ; of these the good comes less from what we recollect of the matter, than from the images formed, and the trains of thought set going and carried out in our own minds. History, and the Literature of our own and of foreign countries, are in this condition, and will serve for instances of the class of subjects I am speaking of.

The main use of such subjects is for the pupil himself; but some of them have also a practical side. For instance, we may want to find a person to edit old authors or historical papers, or to write articles for an Encyclopædia, and then an Examination might be employed to tell us where to look for people provided with the apparatus of learning required. The sort of knowledge wanted for this purpose is just what an Examination can easily be made to test. We do not need comprehensive views, or the wisdom which should result from study, we only want to see that a person knows *his way about* the old authorities, that he can read the language in which they are written, and knows what credit to assign to their statements. We want, in fact, a man whose mind is an index-map of the subject, and who is also an adept in Palexography.

We are here dealing with the technical side of the study; we do not consider whether the individual is benefited by knowing the Latin of the tenth century, or the dialects of the earliest forms of other European languages, or by being able to read the handwriting of the middle ages. We regard these kinds of knowledge as tools, and we are looking out for one who can use them.

But to leave this special sort of Historical knowledge, and to turn to what is generally understood by the name, we have to consider whether a student reading with a desire for his own improvement would study in the same way as if he were reading for Examination. We shall find some differences in the mode of proceeding. A person reading for Examination will have to note details and to acquaint himself with the terms of statutes, Proclamations, and Constitutions, where the ordinary reader would be content with their general purport, and he must be familiar with dates and genealogies.   So far the *student* knowledge required for Examination only differs from that which would be acquired by a person reading for his own improvement, in being fuller and more minute; but the main difference between the two cases is one of spirit.   A student who is "getting up" an historical book keeps his thoughts to his task, he will not follow suggestions which lead him off it.   If of a discursive tendency, he is the better for being thus tied down, but the knowledge he gets savors of the "lesson."   He is always asking himself whether he remembers what he has read, and perhaps he frames questions for himself as he goes on.   The matured reader notes his facts for future reference, keeps his brains free for thinking, and gladly treasures up the thoughts which come into his head as he reads.

Examinations belong naturally to education, and they fling an educational hue on all that comes under their influence.   To prepare for an Examination in History the student must go over his work, pen in hand, with maps and tables of chronology.   This is admirable discipline, but it belongs to *educational* study; it makes the well-informed youth, rather than the wise man; nothing but self-culture can give an eye for grouping events in due subordination, or a mind peopled with historical characters.   Students, however, would do well to get this *educational* knowledge, even if Examinations did not exist, for its intrinsic value as well as for discipline.   It is not *artificial,* it is genuine, as far as it goes; it is that part of knowledge which can be communicated by a teacher, as distinguished from that which grows up slowly, and is fed by observing, reading, and thinking. In many other cases we shall come to this same conclusion, viz., that our ordinary Examinations test *student knowledge* well enough, but tell us little about that of the *savant.* Happily the latter is not in danger of being long overlooked ; first-rate excellence in any department of learning is sure enough to find a field for display in time.

There is, however, a sort of knowledge of history which is got up to be "written out ;" which does not come from reading authors — for a good author can never be read without profit — but from compendia and tutorial help ; and this is *artificial,* in our sense of the word — it is acquired for use in Examinations only. The essence of history lies in its being a *chain* of events ; but the examinee sometimes resembles one who is in possession of a handful of the *links* of the chain, only they are all loose in his pocket. This may properly be called "cram." These *links* are scraps of information sometimes given by tutors, or taken down in Lectures, or "got up" from a note-book borrowed from a friend, or looked out in a manual the day before. They consist of "short accounts" of "leading events," and of "brief notices" of "eminent personages."

An Examiner can hardly set a paper so as to give no opening for such scraps of information. But when a candidate picks out a date from one question, and a name or leading event from another, but treats no matter as a whole, and there is no appearance of there being any framework of knowledge in his head — anything to fit his isolated facts into — then whatever be his aggregate of marks, the value of his knowledge is nothing.

There is another kind of spurious knowledge of a more ambitious description. It consists of what may be called ready-made "views." The student is always ready with an opinion on the leading questions of history, but he has never formed an opinion in his life. "The tendencies of events," and the "influences of principles" are described in tutorial manuscripts and given to pupils. An Examiner will be on his guard when he meets with stupendous wisdom, or patches of reflection, in a different style from the rest of the pupil's work.

I would recommend as part of an Examination for testing the possession of historical knowledge, as I did for the testing of ability, that dissertations should be composed on given subjects, and that the student should have access, while writing, to the necessary books of reference and to original authorities. By so doing, we should conform to our rule. We should see how the student can use his knowledge for the purposes for which it is properly intended, and should free him from artificial conditions.

English Literature is, above all, the subject in which Examinations have called a particular kind of study into existence. A person who has read much, and enjoyed his reading, would often be puzzled if he were asked what he had to show for his knowledge — many happy hours, and a mind rendered alive to many interests, he would indeed be conscious of — but this good is not of a kind to be tested in any Examination. Yet a well-read man carries a certain superiority about him, and when we are weighing the advantages of competitors, we must give its proper weight to this superiority ; hence, we may be obliged to examine in Literature, if we want to give credit for all intellectual acquirements, and we are also forced to examine in it on educational grounds, because a subject which is not represented in Examinations gets squeezed out of sight.

I believe it to be impossible to frame a competitive Examination in the *entire range* of English Literature, which shall not favor the growth of artificial knowledge, and for this reason, that a person may be a well-read man, and have derived great advantages from his reading, and yet not be able to produce any particular knowledge; and, on the other hand, a man may learn many things *about* books, and may commit many scraps to memory, and get marks in Examinations, and yet obtain no good from this knowledge worth mention.

When a paper of questions has to be framed on English Literature, the Examiner is driven to the History of Literature. He can ask for an account of authors and their works, and the variations of different editions, as also for information about the hard passages, for the context of familiar quotations, and for the names of the plays of Shakespeare in which certain characters occur. But these quotations, etc., are matters which might be the *accompaniments* of the knowledge of a well-read person, but they would not constitute the gist of his knowledge itself; they would in no way represent the good he had got by his reading. If he wanted such information he would know where to look for it, and this would serve his turn.

But when Examinations were applied to this subject, these shreds and patches of knowledge were found to have great exchangeable value; they afforded the simplest and readiest questions. Whether a student entered into the spirit of a play of Shakespeare we could not find out. But we could set questions about the explanation of allusions and grammatical peculiarities, or on the sources from which the plays were taken, and the changes made in subsequent versions. When this subject was first introduced, such knowledge could only be obtained by something approaching to research, or from a lecturer who had got together all there was to say on the subject. A student could then hardly know these little niceties except by being a literary person: they served as *symptoms* of something better. Now, however, all for which lecturers formerly used to refer pupils to authorities is found in the school-books; and what is meant by "English Literature," as far as competitions go, consists mostly of the reproduction of footnotes and manuals.

If people must be examined for such competitions in English Literature, an Essay to be written with access to authorities is the best course that I can suggest. Educational Examinations on specified books, or on epochs of Literature, may be most serviceable, but then such Examinations must be connected with some particular course of instruction. Educational Examinations are meant to show that the student has made his own what he has been told in Lectures or has been directed to read, while the *Open Examination* is a mart for knowledge brought from any quarter, and in this case no particular kind of teaching can be presupposed.

III. I now come to the important point of the permanency of knowledge. Examinations shew us the state of the pupil's acquirements at a certain time. The question then arises — what judgment can we form as to how long this state will last? Our conclusion must be uncertain if it be based on Examination only, but least so in the case of what I have called " Art Subjects." For the knowledge to have borne as its result a power of doing something, it must have been assimilated, and as assimilation requires time, it must have been present to the pupil's mind for a long time: thus one condition required for permanence is secured (see page 244).

About "Art Subjects," then, I need only make two remarks. (1) The durability increases with the thoroughness of the knowledge, and in a higher ratio ; that is to say, if A knows twice as much as B, A's knowledge will last, not only twice, but three or four times as long as B's. Here our judgment turns on what the Examination can shew, viz., the perfectness of the knowledge. (2) The more labor the mind has undergone in connection with the subject, the deeper the impression will generally be engraved on it.

Knowledge which is imbibed unconsciously, such as the French or German picked up from conversation, soon disappears ; it depends on ear, and when the ear ceases to supply the phrase required, the learner is unable to put one together. To arrive at a probable estimate, therefore, of the durability of knowledge, even in the case of these "Art Subjects," it is necessary to take into account the mode in which the knowledge has been obtained.

With regard to subjects learned for the information they furnish, the case is more complicated.

Few people are aware how completely a small quantity of such knowledge disappears, especially if, when after being poured out in an Examination, it is thought to be "done with." When men of learning frame schemes for general Examinations, such as those in the University of London, each *savant* is likely to urge the introduction of his own science. For the University to ignore, as it is called, a branch of knowledge, that is to say, to omit it from the Examinations, is to give an opening for attack to its adversaries. No educated man, it will be said, should be ignorant of this or that science; this may be so, but an Examination does not ensure such knowledge; where bits of eight or nine subjects are taken in at once to an Examination, the traces of them left in the pupil's mind at the end of a month will be hardly worth considering. All that the Examination tells us for certain is, that those who have passed have been able to carry in their heads for a short time a certain quantity of matter out of a book. We may extract answers in English History, Physical Geography, and Moral Philosophy, and may boast of the broad character of our system, but to suppose that the successful candidate necessarily knows something about these subjects is a delusion; all that we have found out is, that he has been able to "get up" so many subjects for Examination, and that he could therefore probably "get up" these same again, or different ones, if he should require to do so.

I shall now note some of the circumstances which are favorable for the retaining of what is learnt.

1. The first requisite for remembering a matter is that it shall have made strong impression, and that this impression shall have had time to fix itself.

We recollect that best which it took pains and time to learn. What we get by being simply *told* is soon forgotten — the student who finds all his work done in a translation, and uses it, not to see whether he has made the passage out correctly, but to avoid having to make it out at all, learns nothing. What we puzzle out for ourselves remains by us longest; that which is explained by a tutor before we feel the difficulty soon goes. Hence it is that the reading of solutions of problems is of so little value compared with the working of them for ourselves. In fact, in this case, as in most others, no possession of value is to be got without corresponding effort, and to get what is of lasting good we require sustained exertion.

2. The frequent recovery of an idea is what seems to grave it most deeply in the mind; the process of recalling it seems to clear out the tracings on the cerebrum which might be filling up, and our memory gets a fresh date to start from. Hence a system of Examinations which obliges a student often to review his old stock of knowledge helps much to confirm him in the possession of it.

3. As long as we think that we are likely to want a certain kind of knowledge, we keep it, often without being aware of it, stored in our mind, and it ripens by "unconscious cerebration." In the intervals between visiting a foreign country we may almost drop the language, but if our knowledge of it have taken root, we may find on our return that after a while we speak it better than before. Mathematical and other scientific conceptions also work themselves clearer in this way, even without conscious study, provided the conditions required for this unconscious ripening are observed. The first of these is that we should not feel that we have done with the subject for ever. When we experience this sensation — like a boy who escapes into a modern department, and burns his classical books — all the creases in our brain, so to

speak, caused by this study, seem to be smoothed out, and the mind, on this subject, becomes a blank.

Secondly, for this ripening to go on, the mind must not be distracted or disturbed by a rapid succession of different sorts of action. I once heard of pupils preparing for a very heterogeneous Examination, whose morning course was this. "A master in French comes for an hour, then we go to a lecture in chemistry for an hour : this is followed by an hour of English Literature, then an hour of Greek, and then one of Mathematics." Here there would be no possibility of the ripening process going on, for no knowledge could strike root. A certain amount may, in such cases, be kept suspended in the mind till it has to be discharged, but this is all. Just as one faculty has got into action it is stopped, and another part of the machinery is set in motion, this must jar the whole fabric, and there is an excitement in this constant change which after a while becomes necessary to the pupils. When pupils have been trained under such a system, it is difficult to bring them to apply their minds under a less stimulating one. The evil of this is more apparent with young men than with boys.

4. Again, for us to carry a subject in our minds, it must form a whole — fragments are troublesome to carry and are soon dropped — I do not mean that a science must be mastered in its full extent, but the portion of it learned must be so complete in itself that it shall be possible to regard it in one view, and to use it for the purpose proper to the subject. If we have been learning a language and stop at the grammar, it disappears in a moment ; but if we can speak, write, and read it, then the language has given us a new nationality, and it abides by us.

So, if we learn any science, we must get beyond the *information stage* for it to rest in our minds. By the *information* stage I mean that in which we get the results of science *told* us, as useful information, without arriving at them by investigation. Such is the sort of knowledge commonly furnished by a popular lecture ; we may go away pleased to have become acquainted with certain facts, but if we have no grasp of any principles which hold them together, and no general conceptions which we can apply to what we see about us, then our knowledge will have no principle of vitality, it cannot renew itself.

5. The nature of the knowledge has much to do with its permanency.

The kinds of learning which result in an " Art," as I have already said, are the most permanent of all. In the case of these the foregoing conditions are all fulfilled. But of the other kinds of learning some are more abiding than others. The more compactly a body of matter is held together by a system, the more easily it is carried in the mind.

The kinds of learning which are made up of ramifications from a moderate number of fundamental truths, or laws, or principles, are much more lasting mental possessions than those which are made up of detached facts. For instance, French Etymology, in which certain laws of derivation from vernacular Latin are of general application, is more easily remembered than English Etymology, which has few laws.

Again, many physical sciences are wrapped up in a few elementary principles which can easily be carried, more especially as they may be recalled by what may be seen every day by one whose eyes have been

opened to the ways of Nature. The brightness of a
crack in the window-pane, for instance, the height of
the December full moon in the heavens, the unequal
lengthening of forenoons and afternoons, and a hundred things of the same sort, serve to exercise
pleasantly the student's recollections of Optics and
Astronomy.

To know the why and the wherefore even of such
simple facts is real knowledge, as far as it goes:
to have trained his eye to mark natural laws in operation makes a man happier and fuller of resource.
If we want a pupil's knowledge of Physics to last for
life, we should try to bind it up with what he may
see day by day; and it will help to give him the
habit of being observant, if in the Examination
papers which guide his reading he sees that the
explanations of familiar phenomena are asked for as
illustrations of principles.

The above remarks apply with still greater force to
Chemistry and its kindred sciences, which require
work in a laboratory or workshop. The examiner
should ascertain whether such work has been duly
performed; when it has been so the residuum of
knowledge that will be permanent will be considerable. Any manual facility that has been acquired
remains by its possessor; and this facility, in the
case of Chemistry, &c., is connected with knowledge, and will keep it alive. In all Experimental
Physics the student should, if possible, have instruments given into *his own hands*, and be made to
use them for himself; for instance, he might be
set to find the specific gravities of substances. For
the teacher to perform the process while the student
looks on, is a very different thing, especially if the

latter does not expect to be called on to perform the experiment for himself.

In answer, then, to the question proposed, " How far can 'we judge by Examination of the length of time that a student's knowledge is likely to last? " we reply that by far the most important requisite is, as seems natural, that the knowledge must be thorough enough to be readily used. A man who can read French as easily as he can English, is sure to take up a French book now and then ; but one who has to turn to a dictionary will not do so unless he designedly sits down to study. So, also, in subjects which turn on information. Very exact and complete information fulfils most of the above conditions. Moreover, a person is better inclined to keep up a study from having attained excellence or distinction in it ; for it will then be stored away on the sunny side of his memory, to which he most readily turns.

If, then, we want knowledge that should be permanent and useful, we should be satisfied with nothing less than very thorough knowledge ; but if we are forced, from professional or other needs, to put up with partial knowledge, we should ascertain that this knowledge has been slowly taken in, and not run hastily up in a few weeks in order to be poured out in an Examination, and then done with for ever.

Again, we should have more hope that the knowledge of a subject would last if it were taken in to an Examination by itself than if it were one out of many branches of knowledge taken at once ; and we should prefer a system in which the subjects are carried on from Examination to Examination, a part at one time and a part at another, to one in which each is cleared off in a single Examination.

There are some subjects which are bundles of detatched facts, like English Etymology, and some parts of English Law, in which it may be necessary to examine for educational or other purposes, but for the retention of which we can never make sure unless they are constantly in use. A person may pass a creditable Examination on a given day on such points, and be unable to answer a single question on that day month. This same person could, however, recover his knowledge in a short time. These are subjects which ought to be entrusted to the "Index memory" above spoken of. The student only wants to know that such knowledge is to be had, and where to find it. Even if a lawyer did recollect the substance of a case in point, he would not be justified in citing it without having previously turned to it. It would have saved editors a vast deal of trouble if some writers of great erudition had taken this proper precaution with regard to their quotations and statements.

We have now considered the three points that came before us, viz., the extent, the suitableness, and the durability of a student's knowledge. In all cases we have found that the subjects which yield a faculty, which we can see in action, are the more easy to deal with. They have this additional advantage, that they in general require little special preparation to be fit for production in an Examination. A person has his Latin and Greek and French, so far as the *mere languages* go, always about him. But the knowledge of a true classical scholar involves something of a higher kind, and this difference causes difficulties in the relative adjustment of "marks" in Competitive Examinations.

A modern language affords the best instance of a subject learned solely for its value as an acquisition. That a man can speak and write French tells us nothing for certain about his ability, or his powers of application. He may have picked it up abroad as his mother tongue, and, whether this has been the case or not, the more nearly, in learning it, he follows the process by which a child learns to speak, the sooner he will acquire it, but it will not serve as a mode of educating his faculties so well as if learned by grammatical analysis. He goes through few conscious mental processes, and, therefore, he gets little training from the study; but he does not want to get education, but to know French. And thus the French master very properly aims at producing a system which will enable people to learn French with the least possible call on their brains, whereas an educator looks *first* to the kinds and amount of brain action that he can call into play in his pupil through his teaching.

This difference between modern languages and the more educational subjects causes a difficulty when such a language is made in an Examination to rank against subjects of the other description. This difficulty is the greater because French or German *may* be, and at English schools often *are*, taught just as if they were dead languages. Less is thereby learnt of them, but more general good is got from the process. Hence, to judge fairly of ability or application in such cases, we ought to know by what method the pupil has been taught, though if we only want the accomplishment itself this does not matter.

On this account Modern Languages are not well suited for an arena for a contest of wits. They cause uncertainty in the Indian Civil Service Examinations; and where it has been attempted to award Prizes or Scholarships to them at the great Schools or the Universities, it has been found that this amounted to giving a man a prize for being of foreign extraction, or having had a Swiss nurse, or having been brought up abroad. Those who did not possess some such advantage would not venture to compete, and the prize failed to encourage the study. Yet if no advantages are attached to a knowledge of Modern Languages, all attention is turned to more remunerative subjects; and, as we confessedly want young men to know Modern Languages, we are in a dilemma.

One solution that has been attempted is to introduce into the Examination what I may call *literary* knowledge of the language as contrasted with *working* knowledge, for example, " Historical Grammar," Philology, and the History of the Literature of the country. This, no doubt, would tell against those who had *only* the knowledge of an uncultivated native; but still a great advantage would remain with a cultivated native.

By this mode of treatment, however, we give a new character to the study, and its claims to consideration are no longer the same as before. Modern Languages rest their claims greatly on their usefulness; but an acquaintance with obsolete forms and dialects, though interesting, is not useful knowledge. German philology involves an acquaintance with Mœso-Gothic, which is as much a dead language as Greek. An acquaintance with the Lay of the

Nibelungen is a possession of the same kind as a knowledge of the Iliad. One takes as much time as the other to acquire; and they are of about the same service in the business of life. The History of a Foreign Literature as a subject of Examination is open to the objection which is made to Examinations in that of English Literature, but the reasons for introducing it as an optional subject may in particular cases outweigh the objections. It should be kept distinct from the Examination in the Language.

I would resolve the dilemma in a more trenchant way, and, except in case of marked excellence, remove Modern Languages from the Competitions, but exact a serviceable acquaintance with them, as being desirable, and often necessary accomplishments, by means of a qualifying Examination.

They are quickest and best learned in early youth, say from twelve to fifteen, and in the countries in which they are spoken: they require but little head; they may be picked up by ear at a time when a boy usually learns little, and though, if dropped, they will be quickly forgotten, they may be kept up by the three hours a week spared for them at English schools. A boy might translate his Latin, on paper, into French, and read his Physical Science in French books.

In this way Modern Languages, considered *linguistically*, would not be brought *into the same account* with more strictly educational studies, with which it is difficult to compare them, though high excellence in translation, or in the rendering of a version, might carry credit for the competition, because excellence of any kind shews a mental power. In Examinations on leaving school or entering the

University, Modern Languages would find their proper place : a knowledge of one, at least, might be expected.

We come then to this. Where a subject is wanted purely for utility, and is of a different nature from educational studies, it should be made the subject of a preliminary Examination, which might give a certificate of mere qualification, and also one of merit. The certificate of merit would be rated at varying values for the competition according to the intelligence, accuracy, and power of expression displayed. Supposing that it is desirable that all Indian officials and all officers in the army should know French, I would exact a serviceable knowledge of that language in a preliminary Examination.

There are few subjects in which knowledge is so purely regarded as a useful acquisition as it is in the case of languages. The direct *usefulness* of knowledge for practical purposes, excepting strictly professional knowledge, is so small as to be discouraging to the teacher. People boast in the presence of the young that they have got on very well without knowing anything, and there are indeed few occasions in actual life in which a person suffers seriously from his ignorance. Even in the case of professional knowledge, science and practice are less closely united in England than they are abroad. Three out of four successful English barristers owe their advancement more to their insight into human nature, and their practical sense, than to a philosophical knowledge of Law. In England a "leading lawyer" means a leading advocate ; but in Germany, where there is more of scientific system in legal procedure, promotion comes more from the State than from the public, and the lawyer's claims often rest on his learned treatises, or his repute as a jurisconsult. Scientific Law comes so little into common practice in England that we have to enforce a knowledge of it by Examinations backed by Prizes.

We must come to the same conclusion as to competitions in the display of knowledge that we did when speaking of ability; we cannot nicely discriminate between degrees of knowledge, for we can only explore certain provinces of learning, and even in them we may pass over some regions in which the particular strength of one candidate may lie; but we can make sure that a person who does well possesses high attainments, and that one who makes blunders of certain kinds is altogether unsound. We cannot say that a person about whom we form a judgment may not possess more knowledge than we see displayed, or that he might not extend some descriptions of it considerably in a short time: in other cases we might see that he had reached his limit, as was explained in the last chapter (177).

What we can gauge most closely is the degree in which students have drawn advantage from a prescribed course of study. This leads us to conclude that we should not attempt to make nice distinctions, except where the Examinations are connected with some such course. All Examinations, as I have said, imply *pupillage;* the older a student is, the less is the discipline they afford needed for his case, and therefore ,the less he should be shackled by the trammels of close competition. Examinations used for testing knowledge should be like those which the student would frame for himself in order to direct his work, and to shew him whether he had really learned what he wanted to know.

I now come to a practical point. In some Examinations — that for the Indian Civil Service, for instance — various kinds of knowledge are comprised, and marks are to be assigned to each. Can we find any principles to guide us in fixing the proportions in which we are to allot the marks? We may object to the system, but that will not justify us in evading the question.

Not to embarrass ourselves with two considerations at once, we will for the present suppose that all the branches of knowledge comprised in the Examination are of equal utility, and the proportion of marks due to each will then depend on certain elements which enter into the cost of production.

(1) There are some kinds of knowledge to which only a few choice intellects can attain. High mathematics, first-rate classical scholarship, and parts of mental philosophy, are of this order. A high value must be assigned in a competition to studies requiring these peculiar faculties, or those who possess them will seek, and in the present state of things will probably find, some other sphere where their peculiar powers are better appreciated. If any desired product could only be raised on an exceptionally rich soil, it would on this account be more costly: this answers to the case before us.

(2) Other kinds of knowledge stand near the top, as it were, of a long ladder, which the learner must have climbed rung by rung to reach them. A person cannot take up a book on the Polarization of Light, or on Greek Philology, and begin on it without being versed in preparatory studies; but if he want to instruct himself in History, or Political Philosophy, or Physical Geography, he requires no such special

apparatus, but only what a fair education would have provided him with. The time and labor required for providing this special apparatus are elements in the value of the knowledge, and must be considered. A question which arises in elementary Examinations may be noted in illustration. A knowledge of the sixth book of Euclid involves that of the previous ones. Are we, in marking a proposition in the sixth book, to take account of the labour required to arrive at it, or only of its intrinsic difficulty and value? My answer would be, that if, in a miscellaneous paper, we set a single question in Euclid, and that one taken from the sixth book, we should attach to this the value which we assign to a knowledge of Euclid as an entire subject; but if we set a paper with propositions from each book of Euclid, the candidate, in doing the paper, obtains credit for his knowledge of each book, and therefore the proposition in the sixth book must only be valued for its intrinsic difficulty. For educational purposes a little extra credit may be given to the latter part of a subject, because pupils get weary; and it may be necessary specially to reward those who "keep on to the end."

(3) We have also to consider the length of time it takes to learn a subject in the case of a pupil of fair intelligence who is properly taught. The old question then arises, as to how we are to suppose the subject to have been acquired. This especially affects Modern Languages. My suggestion (p. 277) would remove the difficulty, but I must deal with things as they are.

To learn German passably in England, by grammar and dictionary, will take two-thirds of the time required to learn as much Greek. But a valuable knowledge of it can be obtained in Germany much more quickly. How are we to rate these languages? I think it safest to suppose all goods to be purchased in the cheapest market, supposing always that no educational evil results from so doing. I should, then, so far as the consideration of time goes, rate German on the supposition that it is learned in Germany, because an English boy may very well go to a German gymnasium.

There may be cases in which a vicious system of cram would offer the shortest road to some kinds of learning; but, in that case, the Examination should be recast as regards those subjects. At any rate, it would be essential not to over-mark a subject which offered such a temptation.

Another point is this. Those subjects which require a master, and especially those which must be taught for a long period in youth, should carry more weight in examinations of young men, than those which a person can learn for himself whenever he has a mind. These studies will otherwise be superseded by others which can be got directly they are wanted, and this may do harm. For if a student do not learn the former as a pupil, he will never learn them at all, and will thereby be shut out from those fields of knowledge to which these studies give access. For instance, a person who has never learned geometry at school is not likely to begin it in after life, and is thereby precluded from knowing anything properly of any physical science. Hence, the kinds of learning which require that a youth should have had schooling, and which must have been taught him at school, should in an Examination of young men be more highly considered than subjects which can be acquired later in life.

But instead of fixing what I may call the market values of different kinds of knowledge, by the relative cost of production, we may in some cases be guided by their relative utility. When we know exactly what kinds of knowledge the successful candidates will require, in what degree each is essential, and what difficulties or facilities they will have in perfecting a kind of knowledge after they are started on their duties, we have all the data wanted for properly apportioning the credit to be given to the various subjects. In this case, even if the subjects be fitted for a liberal education, they are regarded in a technical spirit; the candidates will be reading with a particular prospect in view, and will only aim at reaching a certain standard in each subject required. If it is desired that particular attention should be paid to a particular study, all that will be necessary will be to mark it highly and to set a high standard for qualification. When we want, then, to test specific qualifications the case is comparatively simple.

The Further Examination for the Indian Civil Service affords an instance. Its object is to ascertain that candidates are fitted to exercise certain duties, and it is, therefore, a qualifying Examination, with enough advantage, in the way of prizes and seniority in the Service, attached to doing well, to give a student the requisite interest.

This Examination comprises Law, Indian Languages, the History of India, and rudiments of Political Economy. The highest marks are allotted to Law, because this knowledge is essential for the

Indian official, and can rarely be attained in India; the languages are less highly marked, because a civilian can hardly help perfecting himself in these afterwards; and the other subjects carry comparatively little weight, because they are not essential, and can be studied without help from teachers whenever a knowledge of them is required.

If, in allotting the marks to our subjects in a Competitive Examination, we have to take the so-called cost of production, and also the utility of different kinds of knowledge into consideration at the same time, we shall be involved in difficulties similar to those which met us in the case of Modern Languages. We shall then be considering knowledge partly as the criterion of ability, and of the mental training got from a liberal education, and partly as a qualification for particular duties. If a person cannot set about his duties without a certain knowledge, the value of this knowledge to him, mathematically speaking, is infinite — it must be made a *sine qua non :* but if a kind of knowledge is not likely to come into practical use till the student is high in his profession — as is the case with Jurisprudence in the Law, or Political Philosophy in the Civil Service — the value of this lies in its furnishing a proof that the student knows how to set about applying to such studies, and can take clear views of their principles. What he has actually learned for Examination will have been forgotten long before occasion comes for its use, and possibly will have become antiquated before that time. When utility, then, has to be taken into account, we must understand whether a kind of knowledge is wanted for *immediate* use or not. If it be, a sufficient amount must be rigorously exacted, and if in the display of this the candidate shews that he can seize on the gist of a matter, grasp it firmly, and put it forcibly, this should carry marks in the competition, as indicating the kind of ability we want. But the subjects on which the competition is to turn should be marked on the principles above laid down. To overmark an easy subject because it is, or may be, useful, is to leave a weak point which will certainly be taken advantage of. By restricting the subjects of competition to those which are useful for the object in view, we force candidates to adopt a special kind of preparation, and thereby we limit the area from which we draw our candidates, as will appear below.

In the Examination for the Selection of candidates for the Indian Service, which precedes that just spoken of, the object is to obtain, not young men with special attainments, but those who are likely to make efficient public servants. It was therefore wisely determined that the Examination should turn, not on what was likely to be of service in the position contemplated, but on the ordinary subjects of a liberal education. Had it been otherwise the competition would have been confined to those who were disposed to risk their whole education on the chance of success, for the special knowledge wanted for the Indian Service would not have fitted them for English professional life. The aim of the Examination was to secure ability, but it was necessary to admit *knowledge* as evidence of this ability ; and it is on this ground that I consider this Examination in this chapter instead of in the last. Knowledge, as we have seen, is only an indirect measure of ability: some kinds of knowledge, that of " art subjects," for instance, represent it better than others, and excellence in a few points shews infinitely more of it than mediocrity in many. But an Examination directed solely to picking out the clever men would have had a much worse educational effect than that which is in use — it would have generated a straining after point and effect, and an affectation of premature wisdom. The difficulty of framing an Examination to effect what is wanted, without doing educational mischief, is caused in a great degree by the variety and irregularity of secondary education in England. In Germany such difficulties do not exist. If the Government there wanted to select candidates for appointments they would know that they would all have been educated at Gymnasia much in the same way. But in England the Examination must be fair for persons educated in different ways : this involves the offering of a very wide option of subjects. The framers of the scheme might estimate the subjects according as they brought out ability or valuable habits of mind : but in marking them one against the other, the chief point to be considered would be the cost of production, because if a subject were over-marked — as was once the case with Italian in the I. C. S. Examination — it would be largely taken in, to the exclusion possibly of more desirable knowledge; and if undermarked — as was once the case with mathematics — it would soon be taken in only by a few.

If ever such an inequality exist in the relative marking of subjects, indications of it will appear after a few trials. When the weaker men are found to take in very generally a subject that would not usually come into a regular educational course, it may be suspected that this offers them some undue advantage ; probably some way has been discovered of communicating enough of it to bring in a good share of marks, in a shorter time than the Examiners reckoned upon : it may have been, for instance, reduced to a matter of mere memory, or put into such a shape that the tutor can do for the pupil what it was supposed he would have to do for himself. Again, if a number of students, who have failed in one trial, select a particular subject as an additional one to increase their weight of metal in a subsequent conflict, it may be suspected that this subject is over-marked in relation to the time it takes to learn.

The ablest men, indeed, will not care thus to pry into the system in search of a weak point — they know that they can carry the position by a front attack — but when fifty candidates have to be chosen, the last twenty taken and the first twenty rejected do not differ much in calibre, and a sufficient difference in the marks to decide success may be due to a nice perception of an advantage offered by one subject or another.

The relative productiveness of subjects depends of course on the relative difficulty of the papers set in them, and on the proportion of questions that can be done in the time allowed. One Examiner may have a higher standard of excellence than another, and one subject may yield marks more freely than another. For instance, a much larger proportion of candidates can, in general, get three fourths of the marks in a translation paper than can do so in a mathematical paper. This must be allowed for. Tutors arrive at a marvellous intuition as to the subjects which each candidate had best select, and can predict his " score " with great accuracy — indeed, a talent of this sort is a main requisite for one who makes preparation for these Examinations his special work.

As I have said, it does not matter much, as regards the actual convenience of the service, even if a few of those selected do owe their position to skillful tactics, because so many are accepted that the list extends down to the "great plateau of mediocrity," and with the candidates in that region the intellectual differences vanish as compared with moral ones, such as the differences in volition and energy, about which Examinations can tell us nothing. But all that encourages tactics, all that leads a man to trust to cunning, and to glory in outwitting the Examiner, has a deteriorating effect; when a student reads in a narrow spirit, every sentence is considered as to its probability of being set, and when the Examination is past, all reading seems to him intolerably flat from the want of being seasoned with this gambling element to which he has been accustomed. This evil in some degree attends all Examinations, though it does not become serious unless they are too often repeated; but it is increased by its being supposed that there is room for adroit management, and for this there is more scope when the subjects are numerous, and some more productive of marks than others. This idea leads to the study of Examination papers, and to the looking too narrowly to an *immediate return.* By avoiding inequalities, then, we reduce the educational mischief, and this is worth our consideration, even as regards selection only, because, by the prolonged operation of a bad influence, the mass of candidates may so deteriorate, that we may hereby lose more than we gain by the increase of the probability of getting the best among them for the Public Service.

This chapter would be imcomplete without some notice of what I have called Pass or Qualifying Examinations — such Examinations should indeed be framed chiefly according to the educational needs they are to answer; but still we may want to know how far we can trust to them as indicating a serviceable knowledge of the subjects they comprise. They are the means, almost the only means, of causing young men of moderate ability and powers of application to exercise their brains; and the subjects should be chosen, and the course of Examination planned, more with the view of keeping the mind of the student in action, than with the idea of measuring his capacity, or with regard to the value of what the pupil will carry away with him. The matter acquired goes for little, in the case of the duller young men, in comparison with the importance of educating their will, and giving them the use of their brains, and the power of working when they feel disinclined. These Examinations also exercise an effect on the parents. Without them, the sons of the wealthy would often, owing to parental indulgence and indifference to educational discipline,* grow up, not only in ignorance, but in torpor of mind; the Examinations which now

* Mr. Trevelyan, *Life of Macaulay*, p. 335, observes well on this point:
"It is throwing away money to spend a thousand a year on the education of three boys, if they are to return from school only to find the older members of the family intent on amusing themselves at any cost of time and trouble."

Mr. Gladstone once observed that there was never a time when the wealthy classes in England seemed so devoted to amusement. Wealthy men, however, often work extremely hard, but their work is out of sight, it is done at the office; and the home, which alone the young people know, is the place of holiday and relaxation: thus the young are impressed with the idea that enjoyment is the business of life, from the work being put out of their sight. Parents who have little time for pleasure themselves seem to get a palpable return for their labor in the pleasures they can afford to their children.

stand at the portals of most professions do for the wealthier classes what the School Board does for the poor. But though mental exercise may be the first thing to be considered in framing a course of study, the steps of which are to be marked out by Pass Examinations, yet some kinds of this exercise will result in a little knowledge, or in a few conceptions, which enlarge the mind, or in some accomplishment which may be kept in use by the ordinary occasions of life (I am not speaking of professional knowledge), while others yield nothing beyond the exercise itself. Some of these last may give kinds of exercise so essential for growing brains that their advantage in this respect may more than counterbalance their want of utility ; this is a question for the educator. What I have here to consider is, what the knowledge or the degree of accomplishment acquired for pass examinations by young men of moderate powers is worth as an actual possession.

Some subjects of study will yield a larger residuum than others, and some modes of study will be more productive than others, both in point of knowledge and training ; there may also be methods (see p. 39), which will give small results but much mental profit, while others may enable the student to produce a considerable quantity at a given time, without his deriving any permanent good either from the process of learning, or from what he has got temporarily into his head.

The modes of learning which yield permanent knowledge are also in most cases those which confer most good as training, hence we may take the conditions which I have laid down as conducive to the durability of knowledge, pp. 268 — 271, and apply them to the case before us — recollecting always that the class of students under consideration can seldom advance far in a subject, and that they can seldom carry any considerable amount of information in their heads for long together.

The improvement produced by undergoing a course of Examinations is most seen in the increased power of catching the point of questions and in expressing the answers. "Paper work," as it is called, is burdensome to schoolmasters, and the duller pupils are therefore seldom well trained in "writing out": but they are necessarily much practiced in this when they have to be prepared for a paper Examination. This improved power of expression is likely to last because it is called into play whenever pen is put to paper.

Different subjects add to mental wealth in different ways and degrees. The advantage of Geometry lies chiefly in mental training, but in undergoing this training the dullest student can hardly help getting some clearer conceptions with regard to space, and these may continue by him through life. He may likewise retain a knowledge of Arithmetic, and possibly of Algebra, which may be considered to have value. With regard to the physical sciences, such as Mechanics, Heat, &c., their value as acquirements will depend very much on the degree in which the pupil has been trained to observe common phænomena, and apply his principles to the explanation of them. History and Geography are the subjects which offer the most frequent examples of ludicrous errors : these often shew that the pupil has been only trying to tack *words* together ; for instance, the name of a battle and its commander, a country and its capital, and a few such errors shew that the whole of the knowledge displayed is of a flimsy and worthless description: the remarks made p. 254 will apply to this case.

With regard to languages it should be observed that the preparation of "set subjects" shews no knowledge of the language worth speaking of. Such subjects are necessary for class teaching, and if properly chosen and treated so as to shew a thorough comprehension of the author, and a knowledge of what is wanted, in order to understand the book thoroughly — if, for instance, a Greek play is treated as a play of Shakespeare would be — they may be of great value as a nucleus for much improving teaching, and they supply very definite work.

But as such a subject will practically be prepared either with a "crib" or by taking down the translation given by a teacher, no confidence can be placed in a knowledge of it as shewing acquaintance with the language. I should therefore strongly urge the introduction in Pass Examinations of what are called "unseen" passages. In the case of Latin and Greek these would, in the present state of education, have to be very easy, if any considerable proportion of candidates are to pass. Rather than give up requiring the translation of such passages, I would allow the use in the Examination of an approved Lexicon. If a youth can make out a passage by this means he must have learnt the language in the way we wish him to do, and his knowledge will amount to something, though possibly to but little. With regard to the Natural Sciences I must refer to the observations made before, only I would say emphatically, that for the knowledge to be worth anything at all it must be practical.

An important point in such an Examination is the number of subjects it may contain. The " pass men " can seldom apply themselves to one subject sufficiently long at a time to occupy the hours that they might fairly be expected to give to study, neither can they go far in one thing, but they are distracted and distressed by too large a number of incongruous subjects. Hence, the proper number must be arrived at by educational considerations, and by the character of the course of study which is connected with the Examination. I consider that not more than three *distinct studies* should be comprised in one Examination, but two or three books or subjects in one study might be taken in, such as two books in a language, or two or more subjects in Mathematics.

The Examination may be made difficult in two ways ; by increasing the number of subjects in each of which it is necessary to pass, or by exacting a high standard in a few subjects.

For instance, if candidates were required to pass in each of a dozen subjects, nearly the whole of an ordinary batch would fail, and yet those who succeeded might know nothing. If a thorough proficiency even in a few subjects is exacted, weak men will not pass, whatever pains they may take, but those who do pass will have a knowledge of some value. But if we reduce the number of subjects too far, without raising the standard considerably, if, for instance, we allow candidates to take one or two subjects at a time, and require only a moderate proficiency, our series of Examinations will not serve to sift out the incapable, and will be no guarantee of the knowledge of those who pass, for some will have got through by reading only half the subject.

The real value of all Pass Examinations depends on the teaching with which it is associated. When the Examination is held up as a challenge to all comers, success in it is a very uncertain kind of criterion. If the programme contain scraps of eight or ten different subjects, in each of which the candidate must satisfy the Examiners, then the system is unwholesome in itself. Its evil effects may be mitigated by judicious teaching, but they will be intensified if the youth perceives that his teacher does not believe in his getting good from what he is learning, but is only helping him over an obstacle, which for some inscrutable reason he has to surmount.

What the passing of a qualifying Examination principally shews, besides memory, is a certain degree of moral power, and if we know nothing of the circumstances under which the youth has learned, we can judge but very imperfectly of this moral power. He may have been forced through one Examination by having been kept under the eye of a master, and out of the way of all temptation, but it does not follow that he will ever be able to pass another of no greater difficulty. He may have got too old for scholastic compulsion, and be incapable of any kind of self direction. Failures at the University come more from impotency of will than from incapacity of any other kind; next to this from *impatience.*

We have now considered the action of Examinations when employed to test knowledge. We found that when they were employed to test ability, they might lead to the hypertrophy of a certain set of faculties, or to the development of mere adroitness, or to a straining after point and profundity; so also we have seen in the present chapter that when we are in quest of knowledge an evil of another kind is engendered. When the pupil is to get credit or profit from the display of knowledge, the tutor may give him more help than is good for him ; he may do all the headwork for him, and only expect him to recollect what he is told. In both cases an unwholesome influence is exerted by Examinations being used for a purpose which does not belong to them considered as educational appliances.

The knowledge that is got by much *telling* and *shewing* on the part of the tutor is much less permanent than that which is due to good work done by the pupil himself, but while it lasts it is hardly to be distinguished from this, and it brings its possessor profit in Examinations. A man can be got over more country by being carried over every ditch — but then he never learns to leap ; so pupils go farther by having every difficulty forestalled, but they do not learn to use their brains and depend on themselves. If we only want to use the knowledge and not the man, we do not care whether he has been overhelped or not, so that he can give us the assistance we want. Society needs, however, only a few experts, for the knowledge belonging to one man may be made to serve many, but she wants as many intelligent men as she can get.

The ill effects just spoken of shew themselves most in the weakest men : strong mental constitutions soon throw off the effects of ill-judged treatment, and have energy to spare for perfecting their healthy growth. So that if the standard be fixed so high as to exclude all but really able men, the ills arising from a vicious mode of preparation will hardly appear ; but if a large proportion of candidates have to be selected, many of them will shew the effects of such evil training, and those who fail will have suffered still more.

Examinations, when used as tests, attach rewards to certain results of education which may or may not be proportional to the improvement of the pupil ; and therefore they may engender a system of education which sacrifices everything to getting these results at the time when they are wanted for exhibition. In educational legislation, results are convenient things to go by ; we can tabulate the number of boys who have arrived at this or that point, and to get them forward is, no doubt, one object, but if it be over-valued, the teacher is led to aim at pushing on, rather than at extracting all the good from each lesson.

I arrive then at the following practical conclusions. Examinations, regarded as appliances in education, should be directed, not primarily to discovering ability or knowledge, but as *sanctions* to systems of teaching. They should serve as landing-places, to portion out the course, and give an object to teachers and pupils in pursuing a definite track. So far as they are used to see that a pupil has done properly what he has been given to do, there is no drawback to their use. Examinations based on such principles may serve the purpose of selection well enough, inas-much as great nicety of discrimination is not attain-able, nor indeed is it really required. All kinds of ability, which are cognizable by Examinations at all, and knowledge of all sorts, except that which is spe-cial and recondite, may, I believe, be brought out sufficiently for our practical needs by Examinations which are adapted to educational systems ; and this affords the only prospect I see of escape from the difficulties which attend the use of Examinations.

When all the students have had the same work given them to do, the same time to do it in, and much the same kind of teaching, we can classify them as to "merit" more satisfactorily than when they may have had very different advantages; and when an educating body has the control of the Examinations, they can take precautions for preventing the evil arising from over-eagerness in competing. Hence, the performances of a pupil in a series of Examinations, connected with a definite course of instruction, afford a better criterion for judging of him, than does a display in an Examination open to all comers, and they also enable us to judge, in some degree, of moral qualities, such as application and perseverance.

Examinations counteract the desultory tendency in young men, and supply discipline by enforcing definite work; they therefore, as has been said, keep candidates in a state of pupillage. But when men have passed beyond the time for pupillage, and should be a law to themselves, it does them harm to be kept in leading-strings. Self-direction is a quality which is not expected early in life: youths, we know, even though they may be ready to apply themselves to work when it is given them, can rarely find work for themselves and set themselves to it. Examinations do this for them; they supply this direction from without, but if they be continued too late in life, they may prevent its ever coming from within; besides, they discourage spontaneity and independence of judgment. Hence, we should not continue Examinations beyond the age of twenty-two, excepting when a guarantee is wanted of Special or Professional knowledge which is to be turned to actual use, and such Examinations need not be, and should not be, of a closely competitive character.

CHAPTER VII.

PRIZE EMOLUMENTS IN EDUCATION.

WE have had occasion from time to time to glance from the mechanism of education, to which the subject we are considering belongs, to the forces which keep this train of machinery at work. The motives which lead people to study are the forces in question. These motives are much the same as those which actuate men in other courses. If a life of study supplies these for itself, that is to say, if learning brings profit or pleasure enough to remunerate the learner, then their will be no need of interference, but if it do not, and we want to have learned men, then we must supply these motives in a direct form.

I must now refer to what I have said in the second chapter, pp. 51 to 53, to shew the kind of advantages accruing to society at large from having many highly educated members.

Whether the existence of a class of cultivated persons in the country is worth what it may cost to obtain, is a question for the public. If there be no want of such cultivation, and no use for it, there is an end of the matter: but if such a cultivated class is desired, as contributing to the credit or well-being of the nation, money must be spent in order to get it. First-rate genius, it is true, will neither be forced nor suppressed; no emoluments will bribe it into existence, and no neglect will extinguish it: but of such geniuses we only see three or four in an age. There are in the country, however, many young men of

assiduity and intelligence, who may have a very considerable share of intellectual tastes, and who, though
not geniuses, may do good literary and scientific
work. The destination of these persons in life will
be determined by the ordinary considerations which
influence men, viz., by the prospects of pecuniary
profit, social position, and congenial work; under the
last head we must take into account the pleasure
which some find in the pursuit of knowledge "for its
own sake." This expression is somewhat vague, and
its exact meaning will be considered further on.

When parents have to plan out a future for their
sons, they must be governed by considerations of
prudence. The advantages of a high cultivation in
giving a young man a better use of his faculties are
not definite enough to justify a person of limited
means in incurring the outlay for his son. Even if
the student be supported at the University by Scholarships, still he must expend time and labor to get this
cultivation. During this time his contemporaries,
without doing harder work, may be making their
way to a maintenance. The parent will look to some
counterbalancing advantage; this may be offered in
the form of *the chance* of a Fellowship; for speculative returns set men to work in all lines of life, and
to aim at a Fellowship is to embark in a sort of
venture. Again, the youth himself may have a taste
for study, but still he may require a prospect of
recompense for the drudgery of learning, not as an
amateur, but in the most thorough manner possible.
Many persons find pleasure in drawing, but few will
go through a course of perspective and anatomical
studies, unless they have to earn their bread by their
pencil.

We conclude then that the highest kind of education or attainment is a sort of crop which does not remunerate the producer so directly as to make it likely that it will be grown, unless some special market for it be provided.

Society, at present, desires that such a crop should be grown, and therefore it provides remuneration in the several forms of Scholarships, Fellowships, and Government appointments, which at present offer this special market for it. The awarding of these Civil Service appointments by Competitive Examinations, makes Fellowships or some University rewards of the kind a necessity, if we do not wish the best intellect of the country to be drawn off to official employments. Moreover, these appointments are often awarded at so early an age, that candidates for them cannot have completed the full course of studies required for the highest education. Such education might therefore disappear, or become confined to a small class, if no equivalent advantages were held out at the Universities as recompenses for a prolonged and complete course of liberal mental cultivation.

In short, such liberal cultivation is, in itself, partly of the nature of a luxury; and as we cannot expect a man to accept a luxury, however much he may appreciate it, in payment for work done for our satisfaction, we must provide some solid remuneration, or at least the hope of it, if we expect such work to be performed. If we do not, it will be squeezed out of existence by pursuits which lead at once to a maintenance, that is, by mere " bread studies," which are said to be absorbing young men now, even in Germany.

Hence, we see that endowments spent on fostering learning, such as Fellowships, are not *eleemosynary*, because they are bestowed, not out of compassion, but with a view to obtaining " valuable consideration" for the expenditure: the donors meet with due return for their gift, and part of the money so spent goes not to the candidates but to the teachers (see p. 50). Scholarships are indeed eleemosynary in certain cases, as when they are appropriated to a particular class, clergymen's sons, for instance, or to a certain district. For appropriation usually implies a low standard of qualification, and the profit to society arising from giving an average youth greater opportunities than he otherwise would have had, is not appreciable. Some youths who through benefactions are led to come to the University might perhaps be more useful to society if they engaged at once in the work of life. But where we find the special ability which marks the material, out of which men of learning or science are made, and its possessor is enabled by means of an endowment to turn his peculiar gift to the use of mankind, this is not an eleemosynary application of funds, because society is enriched by the cultivation of a rare faculty which would be lost without such assistance.

A youth selected for such help who turns idle is not performing his part of a bargain. Sometimes young people regard the Scholarships, not as entrusted to them for their improvement, but as something that they have earned by past exertions; taking this view, the Scholarship goes only to stimulate work *at school*, a function which more properly belongs to school Exhibitions. If the student on obtaining a Scholarship on admission to a College conceives that his work is done and turns idle, the money is wasted, or does positive harm, so that the power of withdrawing a Scholarship when the progress of the student is unsatisfactory should always be retained and exercised on occasion.

If the candidate be in good circumstances, and would come to the University whether he got the Scholarship or not, the only good that arises from the expenditure lies in the stimulation of school work, and in the moral advantage which it is to the son of a rich parent to feel that he has earned something for himself. This, though not very tangible, is not altogether to be disregarded, because the sons of wealthy persons are sometimes injured for want of feeling the desire to do something for themselves. The awarding of Scholarships by open Examination before admission presents many difficulties. It will be considered further on.

The application of endowments to cheapen a certain sort of Professional education, that of the clergy, for instance, is of a different kind; it is not eleemosynary, because a return is got for it, namely, a larger supply of candidates for ordination, and possibly a consequent reduction in the stipends of curates. Endowments so applied are in fact given to the Church Establishment, and were often intended for this purpose. Preparation for Holy Orders being rendered less expensive, the number of qualified candidates will increase, but what the candidate saves on his education he may lose in the reduction of stipend consequent on the greater supply of curates; if so, the gain will fall to the incumbent. But the practical effect would probably be that the number of curates would be so far increased by the facility of finding suitable persons, that the stipends would not fall, and the benefit of such an application of endowments would therefore be felt in the increased efficiency of the ministrations of the Church. Similar considerations apply also to the cheapening of education for the Scholastic Profession.

College Fellowships perform various functions which will be treated of in the next chapter. Here I am only concerned with the influence they exert on the higher education. This is very great, and extends beyond those who are themselves candidates for these emoluments. Moreover, it is in the selection of candidates for Fellowships that the opposition between the two uses of Examinations, that of picking out the ablest competitor, and that of sanctioning a course of education, comes most prominently into view. Here we touch upon the mainspring of the whole system of our Higher Education. Boys at school are taught with a view to getting Scholarships at College. Youths are elected Scholars at a College because they are likely to be high Wranglers or to get First Classes, or to do well in some Special Examinations ; and students aim at these distinctions in order to be in the way for getting a Fellowship. Further, besides the competitors who have some prospect of success, we have a crowd of others, who, though they may never have had hopes of a Fellowship, follow in the wake of those who look for one : they aim at a place in the list of University Honors, and their course of study, so far as it goes, is similar to that of candidates for Fellowships.

Hence, if the course of study which is most conducive to getting first a Scholarship and then a Fellowship is not such as is most desirable in an educational point of view, the ill effects of this will be felt not only in the University, but also in the schools, which, in preparing students, are guided by the College Examinations for Scholarships, and by those for University Honors.

That we may understand how an Examination framed solely with a view to discriminating between candidates may differ from one framed for educational purposes, I will take an illustration or two from elementary subjects, as being the most familiar ones.

Examinations are conducted now chiefly by printed papers, and these papers come into the hands of the students (if we attempted to prevent this, we should only give an unfair advantage to those tutors who had contrived to secure possession of a copy): the student's reading is therefore much directed by these papers. If his teacher advised him to learn what would evidently not be set, he would not take his advice, or only do so in a half-hearted way. Hence, if we mean to influence education, our Examination paper must represent the subject as *we wish it to be learnt;* but some of the questions set with this view may be ineffective for bringing out ability, and may turn on points which would not come into use in the practical employment of the knowledge. If, therefore, we are in search of a person who is to win credit in his future career as a man of talent, or a discoverer, we must set a paper of a different character from that which we should draw up as a guide to sound study.

For instance, we will take Geometry, and suppose that we are examining youths for a mathematical Scholarship before admission at College. The demonstrations of the known theorems will be equally well done by many of the competitors ; they will therefore be useless for the Examiner who wants to find out the most promising candidate. The writing of them out is wearisome, it takes up time, and withdraws attention from those questions which are designed to bring out ability, so that for the immediate purpose of the Examiner questions on these theorems had better not be set ; but if it becomes the practice to set no simple propositions, propositions will no longer be learned, at least, not for production, and yet even the best candidates derive profit from being forced to learn them, while the inferior ones would get no good, worth considering, from the subject if they did not do so. If then those questions only are set which help to bring out promising men ; — those questions, that is, which serve best for selection — then the influence of this Examination upon education may be a mischievous one.

Let us take an actual case. An Examiner who was asked to set a classical paper for the University Local Examinations, the primary object of which is educational, once remonstrated at being directed to set grammatical questions. These, he said, were often answered best by dull boys; they took up much of the time allowed for the papers, and gave the Examiner useless trouble. His experience, he added, was that a few well chosen pieces for translation, without any questions, effected the purpose better; he had been in the habit of setting papers for Government Examinations, in which right selection only was aimed at. Taking his own view, he was no doubt right ; but as we wish boys to learn grammar, it is necessary that they should find questions on grammar in the papers which are set them.

Moreover, in an educational Examination "marks"

are given according to regular rules, a kind of understanding is implied, that the pupil will obtain a fair return for every portion of his work, and an Examiner in a set subject aims at making an exhaustive paper upon it, so that a pupil may find opportunity for shewing what knowledge he has acquired. As has been said (p. 255), credit must then be given even for imperfect knowledge, because it is not supposed to have reached its final state : we are valuing the crop while it is still growing.

But in Examinations used to test ability, the Examiner should not be fettered by any such implied contract, he must be free to be guided by *impression;* for he wants to find out, not what the man has *learned,* but what he has *become* by the process of learning, and he may judge best by symptoms casually disclosed (see Chap. IX.). If we wanted to pick out a classical scholar, a piece of Latin Prose Composition, grammatically correct, but wholly wanting in spirit and in idiom, might go absolutely for nothing, but it would be unjust and inconsistent with our purpose if we gave it no credit in the annual Examination of a School or College.

Examinations of Schools present a particular case, for in them a chief object is to see whether the masters have taught what they should have done. The Examiner sets questions to find out whether boys are familiar with a certain construction in syntax, or a certain artifice in solving equations, because a teacher ought to have given this knowledge to his pupils. This differs from the course that would be followed in examining for a Scholarship, where the Examiner wants to see what there is in the candidate, and avoids questions which only shew whether his attention has been called to some particular point. Thus the Examiner who wants to select the ablest youth for an open Scholarship, for instance, acts almost in opposition to the teacher; the one appears to be trying to baffle the other. The youth is trained to make a show, and the Examiner mentally tries to clear away the effects of training. Of two boys who get equal marks, one having been well taught, and the other ill taught, the Examiner would not hesitate to choose the last. One may be as good as he ever will be; the other is pretty sure to improve.

This may seem discouraging to teachers, for the better the teaching the greater is the deduction mentally made by the Examiner, who has to judge, not about the actual knowledge possessed, but the promise of performance three years later. This hardship belongs to the "open Scholarship" system, and is inseparable from it. Exhibitions given away at School operate more satisfactorily, because they are awarded to those who do best in the aggregate work of the school. A diligent boy may hereby surpass a cleverer one, but the School does not want to find where the greatest natural ability lies, but to reward steadiness and intelligence: in this case, good and careful teaching meets with the recognition it deserves.

The points of contrast here brought out between examinations used in selection and those used for education, may be noted also in the higher examinations, but they are much less marked; because, in an examination of great extent, subjects are treated in such a complete manner that acquaintance with a few special points goes for very little, and Examiners may take it for granted that all candidates have been properly taught. Moreover, as education proceeds the more nearly it approaches to self-education, and the more, therefore, we see of the man himself in the quality of his work.

In a comprehensive examination, originality will come out somewhere, and general strength is sure to make its mark ; so that an Examination at the end of a long educational course will be a good guarantee that one who gains distinction in it is an able, as well as a highly instructed man, though it may not serve to pick out the very *ablest* from among half a dozen talented competitors. I have shewn, however, in the fourth Chapter, that it is hardly possible to effect this at all in a way that shall be quite satisfactory. Examiners vary much as to what they mean by ability, and as to how they judge of the indications of it ; and if the object is to select those who are most likely to make a figure in life, as it sometimes is in the case of Fellowships, physical causes and moral qualities will operate with such force as often to falsify our prognostications. But if we are guided by Examinations connected with a sound educational course of considerable length, the mere fact that a young man has steadily followed it throughout, and has not flinched from the drudgery it involves, affords us a *moral index* which compensates in a degree for the examination being less suited than a special one might be for "bringing out the cleverest man."

I dwell upon this point because, as I have said, the possibility of finding a satisfactory solution to the difficulties connected with our subject depends upon whether educational examinations can be used for the selection of candidates for appointments, and the like.

If they can give results accurate enough to serve as a guide in the dispensing of patronage, then, what in the first Chapter I have called the *antagonism* of the two purposes of examinations will disappear, and the tutor will no longer be distracted by seeing that one course is best for the good of the pupil, and a different one is most conducive to his success in Examination. When this comes about, the patronage disposed of by competition will, in fact, become so much capital, applicable to providing a healthy stimulus for education.

At present it often leads to a special kind of preparation, very effective for its end, and to young and plastic minds not quite so injurious as is commonly supposed, but still far from what we should desire, and which is very expensive. Many boys leave school directly they catch sight of the army examination : they take their fill of sports and enjoyments at school as a kind of a carnival before the season of training for competition. This disposable patronage is like a head of water-power : every drop is wanted, in these days of easy going, to drive the School Mill, but a great part is now diverted to little sets of works elsewhere, which it drives briskly enough. Here we have needless waste and conflict.

The freedom and diversity of Education in England (see pp. 49, 148) afford difficulties in the way of employing the school examinations, which are educational, for disposing of patronage. Some classes or districts or interests may gain or lose an advantage by such a plan ; and it will be said that they do so, whether it be the fact or not. Moreover, this freedom of the higher education has some deep-lying advantages which make up in part for the want of regular system and the inconveniences which come of it, and this absence of uniformity is quite English and dear to many Englishmen.

I have hopes, however, that attention will be called to the subject of the consolidation of examinations, because I foresee that the *money* question will shortly become serious, and on this point the public is not deaf. The cost of examinations is now becoming very great, both to the Government, who pay for the competitions, and to the schools, or in fact the parents, who pay for educational examinations. By combining the two examinations, each party would save half the cost, one set of machinery would do instead of two, and boys would not be led to suppose that they are to play at school, and go to a tutor's to learn. Not only is the amount of examining which now goes on very expensive in money, but it consumes the time and energy of men whom the country wants for better things. The periods during which our learned men and teachers are set free from their stated occupations, and of which they want every moment, either to recruit their brains, or to keep themselves abreast of the progress of their department of thought, are often mis-spent in conducting examinations and looking over papers.

The solution of our difficulties must be sought in some system of examination of schools. That now carried on by the Joint University Board may serve as a specimen. A good Examination at the Universities in disciplinary subjects, affording room for distinction after a few terms of study, but giving no *title**, like Moderations at Oxford, might work well

* Titles mislead, and come to be coveted for themselves, not as tokens of education: they obtain a market value, and then a demand is made for a description cheaper in point of the time and attainments required. In Germany three years of

in conjunction with this plan. Those candidates
only should be allowed to compete for the better
class of appointments who had reached a good position in some such examination ; and further discrimination might be effected by a brief examination in a
restricted number of subjects of the "Arts" class.
The marks would have to be allotted on some system
which would give weight to excellence in a single
branch (see Chap. ix.). In the case of University
rewards, the emoluments are in the hands of the
academical bodies themselves, and they can set the
example of a system of selection, which, so far as it
depends on examinations, shall be based on those
which are framed as supports to the highest education.

study is required, but no first Degree is given. Our B.A. is historical, and itserves
instead of such State requirements to attract students. Fresh Titles would bring
in money, but would intensify the notion that a person must be paid for anything he
learns.

CHAPTER VIII.

EXAMINATIONS FOR COLLEGE FELLOWSHIPS AND SCHOLARSHIPS.

IT must not be supposed, from the heading of this Chapter, that I intend it as a pamphlet on the reorganization of Colleges. I may make general suggestions, and I shall refer to a scheme traced in outline in the Third Report of the Royal Commission on Scientific Instruction, but I cannot enter on the points of celibacy, tenure, pay, and retiring pensions; and yet it is on the way in which these matters are dealt with that the success of legislation on the subject must depend.

Fellowships fulfil at present very complex functions.

I. They constitute the pay for years of systematic study. All diligent students cannot indeed get Fellowships, but the class is remunerated by the possibility of some among them attaining large rewards.

II. Moreover, Fellowships fulfil certain social and political purposes (see p. 50). They serve as "ladders" or shafts, whereby access to the surface is opened to the lower-lying strata of society; but this function is disconnected with academical ends; it has nothing to do with the advancement of learning, it is accidentally fulfilled by Fellowships, now that they have come to be annuities dissociated from duties, but it might, as far as logical considerations go, be discharged by pensions from the Civil List, for it touches the State rather than the University. The present condition of things has, however, a great advantage, because the Universities and Colleges are, of all bodies in England, the most free from political feeling and the chance of jobbery.

III. Fellowships also assist in making up the income of the tutorial staff, though this effect is much impaired by the allowing of non-residence, because a resident Fellow will not reckon his dividend as pay for work done, if he can receive the same sum without doing work at all.

IV. Further, these Fellows, or the Seniors of them, but very commonly the whole body, have the government of the College in their hands.

It will be seen that these functions may be incongruous. A youth may have attained a certain proficiency, and have a right to the wages of his work, but he may be unsuited in point of temper, or from want of power of keeping order or of commanding attention for taking part in College work, and he may be as far as possible from being the sort of person who would be selected to be put on the Governing Body of a place of the higher education.

It seems to me that our difficulties, which arise from a Fellowship having two or more functions to fulfil, will be best met by having two or three classes of Fellowships — call the lowest of them Studentships, or what you will — and by separating these functions, assigning some to one class of Fellowships, and some to another. The view taken by the Royal Commission on Scientific Instruction of 1873 agrees in most respects with mine. I shall give in an Appendix to this book that part of their Report which treats of Fellowships, with a few remarks. This will furnish the reader with a scheme of reconstruction, based on the principles which I proceed to explain. I must say a few words to shew how Fellowships came to be what they are.

The middle ages developed many forms of corporate life; one of these was the Academical College, a brotherhood banded together for quiet study. A few scholars might receive instruction, but it was not founded as a school : authority would have been more concentrated if it had been so. The idea that lay at the root of it was that of a Family, and a new Fellow was adopted into it, being chosen apparently from the knowledge that the others had of him. University distinction could not have been considered, as candidates were elected before they were of standing for the complete Degree, and it was for this that the most important Disputations took place. Even in the few cases in which the Fellows could be laymen, celibacy was made essential, not, as it seems to me, from monastic notions, but because it was essential to the contemplated kind of common life. Fellows received no money from the College, but only shelter and humble fare; and they were bound to reside in College during nearly the whole year, unless they had leave of absence; thus a Fellowship was valueless to a married man. When we approach the Reformation, we find, from the statutes of the foundations of that period, that the Colleges had come to be regarded as places of education; for stipends are attached to educational offices, and provision is made for College discipline. It was not till the end of the 17th century that the surplus of funds beyond the household expenses was divided among the Fellows: this changed the nature of the institution altogether. After this, a Fellowship had attractions for a non-resident. The idea of Family was weakened, and the "ladder" theory then became applicable, for a non-resident used his Fellowship to push his way in a profession. Further, when Examinations for University Honors were introduced, and these, or Special Examinations in the subjects of University study, were used as the modes of selecting persons for Fellowships, then, these emoluments began to act as a recompense for diligence and intellectual distinction. The new Statutes given to the Colleges in 1857 — 1860, upheld in the main the existing practices, and under these Statutes Fellowships are now held under various kinds of tenure — sometimes for life, sometimes for a term of years, sometimes with, sometimes without, restriction as to celibacy and the taking of Holy Orders ; but, in general, a Fellow of a College is simply an annuitant, receiving from £225 to £350 per annum. In many cases he is one of the Governing Body of the College, and is bound to attend College meetings, but has no other duties to perform *quâ* Fellow, though the Tutors and College officers are almost always taken from among the Fellows.

These Fellowships are bestowed, *speaking roughly*, either by special Examination open to the University, or with reference to the place obtained in the lists of University Honors. When Special Examinations were relied upon altogether, it would sometimes occur to candidates to avoid the Honor Schools altogether, and to read directly for the kind of Examination by which the Fellowship was bestowed. This tended to lessen both the glory of the College to which an aspirant belonged, and also the *prestige* of University Honors. Steps were taken to discourage it, and at Oxford, where Special Examinations had been, and are still, generally employed, a provision was made by many of the College Statutes of twenty years ago, that no one should be elected to a Fellowship unless he had obtained a place in the first class of one of the Honor Schools.

At Cambridge, the Colleges, with the exception of Trinity College, were formerly guided in awarding Fellowships by the result of the Mathematical Tripos, and by the other kinds of University distinction, prizes, and the like, obtained by the candidates. Classics were scantily represented, compared with Mathematics, until about 1825, when the Classical Tripos was instituted. Other Triposes have since been taken into account.

The Examination at Trinity College, which was confined to the Bachelor Scholars of the College, was in some degree educational; it afforded scope for distinction in Classics, and, in fact, kept that study alive in the University in old times.

Here we must mark how these different modes of testing qualifications for Fellowships act with reference to the leading purposes which they have in view.

The system of Open Special Examinations appears to be most directly suited to securing the ablest men for a *particular College*, while by adopting the University Examinations as a guide, the Fellowships supply inducements to study for University Honors. In Cambridge phrase, they "keep up the Triposes."

The respective advantages of the two plans, viewed in the interests of the Colleges and of the Fellows themselves, were closely canvassed when the change of College Statutes took place (see p. 14), and is discussed in the Report of the Royal Commission on Scientific Instruction given in the Appendix. The first plan may act best for *selection*, in certain cases. The College that has the first choice out of a batch of candidates does better, and that which has the last choice comes off worse, than each would under the other plan. The system may lead to a little manœuvring in order to get the first choice. So far as rewarding merit goes, one system answers as well as the other. Under both systems, the same persons would get Fellowships in nineteen cases out of twenty, and in the twentieth case it would probably be an open question whether the person elected under one system or the other was most deserving : hence, it is only a question of the *distribution* of able men among the Colleges. We should hear complaints soon enough if deserving persons went unrewarded, and no such complaints arise. A College, however, may prefer judging of candidates for itself to accepting the award of the University, for persons commonly have confidence in their own powers of discrimination, and think that, as being the best judges, they will get the best bargains.

Economical considerations are all on the side of adopting the Degree Examinations as a criterion. For if a candidate for a Fellowship has to wait for two or three years, and during this time has to keep his knowledge in a state fit for production, this amounts to his risking much more on the venture, and he will require a larger prize in proportion to what he is called upon to stake. This, according to my view, as will be seen presently, is important, for since with the multiplication of branches of study

we require more *numerous* rewards, the demand on
our resources will be heavy. It is therefore important to keep down the amounts to the lowest point at
which they will effect what we want, and this point
is lower under the latter scheme than under the
former. I think that the prospect of from £120 to
£200 for from five to seven years would furnish
sufficient stimulus, and that in fact the students
would work as hard for these emoluments as they do
now for nearly twice that amount; but then they
must be set free from Examinations as soon as they
have got their Degrees.

Society is chiefly interested in the influences exerted on education by these different ways of bestowing Fellowships. If one way does more good than
another, it will tend to a larger *production* of the class
of men for the sake of whom *reward* Fellowships
exist. The system of Special Examinations for each
College held as occasions arise, is ill adapted to
fostering a spirit of " research." The candidate who
has taken his Degree should read in a spirit different
from that of one looking to an Examination; he should
no more burden himself with matter merely for production, than a person would who was reading with a
view to literary work. But the possibility of a call to
display his cleverness at any moment keeps him
always on the strain; the bow is always to be ready
for discharge; and so every passage that he reads is
considered with the view of being turned to account,
in answering a question or in an essay. So much is
this the case, that I have been told by candidates,
that, when after a long course they had ceased reading
for Fellowships, and this artificial stimulus had been
removed, all reading seemed to them for a time to
have lost its interest.

It is well, indeed, that a man should go on studying after his degree, but then he should study as a man studies; and study which is subordinated to an impending Examination is *pupil* study : it is directed to learning, not to judging. The *pupil* has to keep up *skill* of certain sorts, to accumulate knowledge, and to hold it by him in a fit state for production on demand. The constant anxiety lest some of this information should slip away engenders a feverish habit of mind. These evils are pointed out by Mr. Sayce, in the article so often quoted, with reference to Oxford. The Cambridge system has produced evils of another kind. Educational machinery was used to effect a nice sifting and sorting; it was modified to effect this object the better, and thereby served its proper function the worse. The range of the University Honor Examinations has been widened to include the subjects which belong to the professed *savant*, because the Colleges wanted to find out who were great Classics or great Mathematicians. Such persons would give *éclat* to the College as Tutors, and would add to the intellectual character of the Society. The result is, that the special course has become too extensive for the period of residence, that general education is sacrificed to make time for it, that study is hurried and strained, and what the Germans call "tumultuous," and that excessive attention is drawn to the points which mark ascertainable differences between men : in consequence of which the qualities which produce these differences, such as ingenuity and powers of imitation, are cultivated to an undue extent.

I will now lay down the general outline of a plan which would, I think, answer the ends in view.

We want to fulfil two purposes above all ; first, to induce able young men to pursue some kinds of study farther and more systematically than they will do without a prospect of recompense. The Government offers such prospects in the way of Indian and other appointments, which are open to competition, and the Universities must offer like advantages or lose the able men. Secondly, we want to select for the Colleges the fittest and ablest men for their staff and Governing Body. We have hitherto been trying to effect these two purposes with one set of machinery, and we have met with imperfect success. It seems an obvious expedient to have different sets of machinery for the different objects.

We must recompense young men for applying to study which is not remunerative, instead of taking to a business which will yield them an income, but we need not give them more than will bring us the men we want. At present our rewards, though not too numerous, are unnecessarily large ; we could obtain what we want for a smaller outlay.

To supply *rewards* " pure and simple " the Colleges might turn some Fellowships into Studentships of two grades of value, tenable for a short period after degree, free from all restrictions and all duties, but not conferring any authority whatever. They probably would be called Junior Fellowships, but I call them here Studentships, to avoid confusion of terms. To get a clear conception we may suppose that the lower class would be worth £120 and the higher £180 per annum, tenable for five years ; or a smaller sum might be given, and the period of tenure be lengthened.

The advantage of having two classes of Studentships would be of the same kind as that of having two or more classes of Scholarships — we might adapt the recompense to the work done.

I have said that I think that these Studentships should be bestowed according to the result of the Educational Examinations of the University. But we have also to consider the Further Examinations, as for shortness' sake I will call them ; these would embrace the highest branches of knowledge treated in the way required by the professional *savant.* They would therefore carry weight as affording recommendation for Professorships and College Lectureships, to some of which Fellowships might be attached. But these Further Examinations may possibly require more direct support than this. The Studentships might sometimes be given for the Further Examination taken in addition to the Educational one; or a person who had obtained a Studentship of smaller value might be promoted to one of greater value on obtaining distinction in the Further Examination. There would probably be some branches of learning in which the division into educational and scientific departments, with Examinations for each, could not at present be made, and emoluments would be given for these by a single Examination as now.

Besides these Studentships a certain number of Fellowships would be retained. The Governing Body would consist of the Head and the Fellows. The chief College offices should be annexed to Fellowships, which would become endowments of these offices and be vacated with them, like Professorships. In addition to these Fellowships attached to College offices there might be as many more as the funds will supply ; these should be held for a term of years, or possibly for life, by persons who had attained distinction in science or learning, or who had done specially good work in education or literature. These Fellows would strengthen the Governing Body.

The Studentships, being intended solely as a support to the Honor Schools, should be awarded mainly with regard to distinctions obtained in them, but any College or University Prizes, and indeed all that a student had done in his Academical career, might be taken into account, and allowance be made in cases of illness. The bugbear of jobbery, which was at one time always before the eyes of University Reformers, need not make us afraid of leaving room for discretion : public opinion is so strong that there is no fear of favor. There is more fear that electors will be afraid of acting on their private convictions when they think that a candidate deserves a Studentship, but where circumstances have prevented his getting the full amount of distinction to shew. An electoral body should have a wide discretion, and as the student elected would have no voice in the government, and therefore no party or political feeling need intrude, the Fellows might be as thoroughly trusted to dispose of Studentships, as they now are to give away Scholarships.

The Fellows *proper* should not be chosen with sole reference to Examinations ; but with a view, in the case of the College officers, to their fitness for their post ; and, in the case of the others, to the literary, or scientific, or educational, work which they have done : these last should be chosen on the same grounds that Professors would be appointed.

The Fellowships would serve as inducements for the holders of Studentships to apply themselves to earnest study. At present Fellows are elected because they have laid in an extensive apparatus with which they *may* do something if they like, but they have become habituated to look to advancement as their motive, and after being elected such motives are suddenly withdrawn. To have an assured maintenance, and to live among a critical society, may prove adverse to laborious investigation and to publication. If an Examination is needed for choosing Fellows, it should turn greatly on Dissertations (see p. 208); but most weight should be given to what the candidate has done after reaching manhood, in the way of writing, lecturing, or scientific work; the prospect of meeting with persons likely to work in earnest will be much improved by selecting those who have already embarked in independent study. The surest way of getting what we want, be it " research," or learned books, or what not, is to offer high rewards for good performances when they appear.

In electing to a Fellowship the distinction gained by the individual at his Degree, and more particularly in the Further Examination, supposing that there should be one in his line of study, might be taken into some account, as vouchers for the possession of knowledge, as they would be in electing a Professor. There should be no limits as to the age or *standing* of candidates for Fellowships, though there might be such in the case of Studentships.

Again, in distributing rewards, account must be taken of the need there is for them. Unnecessary rewards, like bounties on a manufacture, do harm. If study were in itself remunerative, we should want no recompense for it, and the funds expended in this way would become applicable to other purposes.

Hence, the more nearly a kind of study approaches to a Professional training, the less it will be necessary to bestow in order to keep it going; for professional study provides its own remuneration; the skill acquired is in itself a valuable possession. A study, however, which, like Law, is not carried on in a strictly professional way at the University, would not be pursued there in consequence of this margin of difference, unless it carried some rewards, or was supported by being accepted as part of a professional course in the Examination. But smaller rewards, the £120 Studentships, for instance, would suffice for the branches of study which are connected with Professions. The broader the margin above spoken of, the more will have to be given.

It would, however, be no gain to education that the whole force of College advantages should be expended in support of the University course, unless this University course were a good and complete one. I have said that I propose to devote the Studentships entirely to the support of the University Honors, in order to induce the promising young men to provide themselves with a high and complete education. This makes it imperative on the University to lay down courses of education proper for persons of various turns of mind, not unduly fostering particular kinds of talent, by framing Examinations with a view to finding out the persons of most brain power, but recognizing the need of *Supplementary Studies* (see pp. 225, 235), in combination with those which bring only particular sets of faculties into play. Hitherto, in recasting the Honor Examinations at Cambridge, the Fellowships have sometimes proved an impediment. The question has arisen, How, if we reduce the efficacy of our Examinations as means of discrimination, are we to give away the Fellowships? How shall we secure that they will fall to men of real power? Thus the Examination has been made subservient to the disposing of emoluments, the *raison d'être* of which emoluments is, or should be, to lend support to the education that is represented by these Examinations.

Inasmuch as excellence in one branch has been found to be the best criterion of power, each branch of study has been carried further and further, in order to afford more scope for the display of special powers. The old College courses of study in Cambridge were often wide and liberal, and the pupils looked to the College Examination at the end of the year, which involved well-chosen subjects of different descriptions; but of late persons have become impatient of everything that draws them from the course in which they are to run for their great prize. Moreover, the public rates the success of a College, not by the good done to the average student— for of this it knows nothing —but by the distinction won in Honors. This urges teachers in a direction which they are often inclined to follow, for those who have just won renown in one of these special arenas, feel a keen interest in these conflicts, they desire to fight their battles over again in the persons of their pupils. This state of things may be altered by disposing of the Fellowships (as opposed to Studentships) by means which turn only in a small degree on the result of Examinations. The College will not feel that its credit depends on those who hold mere *Studentships :* and it will not be intent on securing men of *power* for them. For unless the Student become a Lecturer he will have little connection with the College, or opportunity of conferring credit upon it. Studentships should be the more numerous because the Educational Examinations by which they ought to be awarded may be a less exact criterion of merit than those now in use. The Educational Examinations will be *discriminating enough*, provided we have plenty of prizes to give away; if prizes were few we could not be sure of awarding them rightly. The Examination for the Indian Civil Service (see p. 236) answers its purpose because so many candidates are accepted, that *all* the able men may be taken.

Having got rid of the causes which lead people to overvalue prodigious and precocious knowledge of one sort, we may arrive at a sound and philosophical University course for the higher men.*

The first requisite, as I have said, is to bring the range of the Educational Examinations for Honors within such limits that a youth of ability, with a good school education, may cover it within the duration of his University course. University Honors should depend mainly on University work. If the course be too heavy for the time allowed, or if it require long previous training, some youths will be taken off their general work at school, and be put into a narrow groove at a time when their minds particularly require general expansion; or else they will defer coming to the University. If we reduced our course in point of time, retaining a creditable standard, the only effect

---

* The course for the Ordinary Degree at present is fairly enough suited to the wants and capacities of the class of men who engage in it, both at Oxford and Cambridge. At Oxford the general education of the Candidates for Honors is well provided for by Moderations, but at Cambridge it is at present (1877) represented by a wholly inadequate Examination. A scheme was brought forward some years ago, but the best part of it was thrown out, and the present transitory condition is most unsatisfactory.

would be to drive the able youths to a special trainer for a year before coming up, and some might be incapacitated or discouraged from competing, owing to finding themselves at a disadvantage from bad schooling, or from their parents having been uncertain about their destination. It is well that persons should have a chance of repairing such injuries by their own exertions. This is a strong argument against shortening the University course; it would not leave room for recovering lost ground, and so would practically confine University Honors to those who had had judicious parents. The Vacations afford no room for extra work, as the Honor men already use them for study. At Cambridge there is in fact a Vacation Term during July and August.

Secondly, the three years from eighteen to twenty-one, the proper season for University residence, should, as I have already said, not be devoted entirely to a single branch of study. For all but very strong and precocious minds it is too early to turn the whole mental energy into one channel, and there is not one student in twenty who has been sufficiently educated "all round," when he comes to the University, to be properly remitted to a special study. I conceive that the first year or year and a quarter should be given to a course comprising at least two branches of study, which should be *supplementary* in some measure to each other: but one or both of these might bear on the courses in which the Student ultimately aims at Honors.

By restricting the range of these Honor Schools, and putting those abstruser parts of the studies, which concern the man of learning only, into a Further Examination, we should enable some to take double

Honors, which have become rare.   Strong men, who can reach excellence in a single branch, had best concentrate their efforts on this; but some minds will thrive best on a more varied diet.   The Further Examinations should be held of course subsequently to the Educational Examination which should give the Degree; and I contemplate that the results of these Further Examinations, for which the Candidates in each branch would be few, should appear in a class list containing three or four classes with the names alphabetically arranged.   In the Educational Examination I would place the names as nearly in order of merit as the case admits; when the subjects are difficult to compare, as in Natural Science, we must be content with a rough classification.   Electors to Studentships might, if they wanted more guidance, require testimonials from Examiners, or obtain access to the marks (see Chap. ix.).

The interval between the two Examinations might be left undefined.   I do not see why a person should be excluded by reason of his standing from engaging in the Further Examination, as the distinction of one person in it would not involve the depression of another; at least the superior limit of age might be placed high.

I have referred in p. 51 to the *proper proportions* of the funds to be spent in rewards and in other ways.

Distinctions and recompense are not the only ways of supporting education; we may cheapen it as well as reward it.   How much should we do in one direction, and how much in the other?   Let us consider the effect that would be produced by expending all our College funds in providing gratuitous instruction.

That is to say, in paying the Tutors as the Deans are now paid, out of corporate revenues; or, as this would make but a very trifling difference in the whole expense of a student's maintenance, let us suppose that we provide gratuitous lodging also, but give no rewards for attainments. In the case of the well-to-do classes, education would not be affected; the same persons would come to the University who come now. We might attract by reason of cheapness some poorer men of moderate capacity, but the abler ones would lose more by not having Scholarships and Fellowships to look to than they would gain from the smaller cost of instruction. In fact, the advantage would be to the stupid at the expense of the abler. When this point was debated on the occasion of the last University Commission, it was thought preferable to spend the funds that were available in increasing Scholarships, whereby the abler men would get the means of paying tutors, rather than to give instruction or maintenance below cost-price. The question of the way of disposing of Scholarships is an important one, and will come before us presently.

If we are right in concluding that without rewards we can not look for high proficiency, the conversion of the prize emoluments into gratuitous instruction would take off all our high class students except those who had an innate love, not merely for intellectual pursuits, but also for following them in a strictly regular way. Hence, Society would not get the cultivated class we have supposed her to require, but a largess would be conferred on parents throughout the country.

With regard to men of moderate abilities and industry, I doubt whether it matters much to the country whether they come to the University or not. Some are the better and a few the worse for so doing, but the benefit is more to the *man* in " social advantages," than to society at large. If professional education be cheapened, I have shewn how it would operate in the case of the Clergy and Schoolmasters. In Law and Medicine, an increase in the number of practitioners must reduce the average income of the individual, and as the fees are fixed by professional rule, the public would gain nothing. But then, other walks of life — those which the young men would have entered upon if they had not, by increased facilities of instruction, been induced to become lawyers or medical men — would benefit by being relieved of pressure. Thus, theoretically speaking, the salaries of clerks in offices might be raised by the Universities offering gratuitous instruction in Law and Medicine.

Now let us look at the other side of the question. The students who want instruction in the very highest branches of learning or in abstruse sciences are few. In some kinds of learning there are not enough pupils in all England wanting instruction to support a teacher, unless the rate of payment were so high as to be prohibitive. The student, who turns towards such recondite studies, designs to put himself in a position in which he will be fitted to render exceptional services to Society; and Society, besides inducing him so to do, by offering him a reward for his learning when he has got it, may very properly help him in obtaining it. If, however, we establish our advanced teacher without providing any emoluments to be got by the learning he gives, the teacher would be almost without pupils, for though we may pay the teacher, the pupil has to find head work, and this he will not give for nothing. Hence, we must first provide inducements to work, and then subsidize teachers for advanced study, especially for liberal studies, which are not remunerative in themselves, or for recondite matters, such as languages which are little cultivated; but to cheapen by means of endowments an ordinary liberal education, such as is commonly wanted for the upper middle class, amounts to this, that the state, or some endowed body, hereby gives a largess to a section of the people by presenting them with what they would otherwise provide for themselves.

This brings me to a point on which I must say a few words. I feel that the sentiment which exists against the "mercenary spirit," as it is called, of Political Economy, may be excited by my supposing teaching and learning to be subject to the laws of that science. I am dealing with things in the mass, and have to consider the motives which actuate the majority. Many members of every class or profession will be actuated by the highest and most disinterested motives, but the action of the class, as a body, is usually determined by class interests (see p. 20). Some individuals will pursue learning "for its own sake," but by the mass of students and their parents study will be mostly regarded in the same light as professional pursuits, namely, for what is to come of it, and it is *for this mass* that Institutions are framed.

The expression "the love of learning for its own sake" requires consideration. We do not mean by it, I think, that *nothing* is to come of the learning. There are some people indeed who like to accumulate knowledge as a collector does curiosities, and who then throw it by, satisfied with possessing it; but these are not the kind of people we want. We suppose then that the learning is to be used somehow, and if used, why not used in an Examination as well as in writing a book or a " Programm*," which is what the German student looks to doing? It seems to me that the difference lies chiefly in the Examination use of knowledge being *immediate* and *direct:* the knowledge is delivered to the Examiner much as it is received from the teacher. A German student works up his learning into a great book : this, it is true, is his way of getting consideration for it, and answers to the Examination use of it; for the book may be simply an incumbrance to literature, and be written solely with a view to what a German student calls his "vorkommen," that is, his advancement; but still what he has learnt undergoes some transmutation in his mind.

Again, when a student learns what is necessary for the thorough and intelligent exercise of his profession, in the way that a Civil Engineer will sometimes learn mathematics, then he has a genuine healthy interest in his subject, and is usually a satisfactory pupil. If he analyzed his motives — a process which people are seldom the better or wiser for — he would find, I dare say, that he did not love mathematics for *themselves,* but because they would be of service to him ; but, in fact, he really meant to *possess* himself of them, and he would not, therefore, be satisfied with anything short of a thorough comprehension of each step of reasoning, and of the mode of using what he had learnt (see p. 260).

* On the taking of Degrees, on School Anniversaries and the like, Germans are expected to produce a Dissertation, called a " Programm;" this serves for something to shew when they seek promotion.

If, therefore, by inducing people to "pursue knowledge for its own sake," we mean, leading them to learn it for their own use, and not in order to dispose of it, when acquired, we get a definite meaning for the phrase. Examinations offer a market ready to hand, and lead people to look for "too quick returns," and in too direct a form : this is the evil to be combated.

Let us now consider how the present Fellowship system works. A young man gets his Fellowship at twenty-three, and has then to take to a Profession. His learning has served its turn by being produced in the Examination, and is likely to be thrown aside. To avoid this, we must pay, not only for the knowledge being acquired, but for its being employed in the way we wish ; that is to say, we must hold out the prospect of further reward, for putting the acquired apparatus to good use. At present our whole reward is given for laying up the apparatus ; some recompense, as we have seen, is required for this, but we need not give more than is necessary, and we should keep the Fellowships in reserve as rewards for the use made of the training and knowledge.

The view of the Fellowship as a "ladder" to a position in life, hardly comes before me now, but the Studentships would perform the "ladder" function to a certain extent, as well, for instance, as Fellowships did in the early part of the century, when they were of about the same value, relatively to prices, that I propose for the Studentships. This, as it appears, was a time when an unusual number of able young men from the Universities raised themselves by these "ladders" to leading positions in life. Overmuch pecuniary reward generates over-expectation and excessive wants, and if our young men are given such good incomes at starting that they are led to believe themselves entitled to live on a higher and a more luxurious scale than their contemporaries, we are doing the very reverse of assisting either them or the cause of science. The great advantage of Germany as regards learning lies in its simplicity of ways of living. A large income is, or was, much less a social necessity there than it is with us.

I will here, as I have promised (p. 49), glance at the way in which the problems that have occupied us have been dealt with in Germany.

When writers find something wrong in their own neighborhood, they will often indulge in the belief that things must be as they ought to be somewhere else; and educational writers turn to Germany as their happy land. Germany *had* many advantages as a cradle of cultivation, and has some still. They spring from the homely life of her middle class, and the absence of straining after social position. I hear that there are changes for the worse in these respects; still she is free from the mass of idlers, who in England are brought up to live on realized property. Parents there are on the side of education, and hard devoted work is still part of the religion of the land. Yet, while we are pointing to Germany, while our writers are talking of the "crowded lecture rooms of German Professors," and asking why we should want endowments when Germany does without them, German Professors of liberal "Arts" are complaining that though they may get an average audience of a dozen, the same students seldom drop in two days running; they cry out that the "Brodwissenschaften," that is to say, professional studies, carry off the students, that liberal education is on the decline, and that even those who pursue it follow it with a view to the scholastic profession ; they tell us that endowments like English Fellowships are wanted for keeping the Higher Cultivation alive.

It must not be supposed because there is no B.A. Degree that there are no Examinations in German Universities.   Youths go to them commonly at twenty, that is two years later than they do with us, and their general education is pretty well vouched for by the Examinations on leaving school.   There was formerly an Arts Examination in most Universities ; this is now dropped, and I have heard the expediency of the step questioned ; but the Doctor's Degree, which answers to our Honors, is only conferred after a *" rigorosum Examen,"* and the diploma *"pro facultate docendi"* is given by the result of an Examination of high standard in what we should call " Arts," and the candidates are placed in four classes.   Position in these classes leads to income, for in Germany teaching and learning form perhaps a more lucrative profession *absolutely*, and far more so, relatively to what is made in other walks of life, than they do with us.   There are in German-speaking countries one thousand Professors, two-thirds of whom receive stipends besides fees, and in many cases the emolument is as good as is got in our own Universities. The German Professor is a person *retained* for the service of learning.   He is kept free from worrying duties, which are inconsistent with study.   He has no discipline to enforce.   He does not pretend to *teach*, that is to say, to see that any one learns ; he delivers what he has to say, as a preacher does ; those come who like, and at the end of his three-quarters of an hour's address any pupil who has anything to ask him will find him happy to answer him; but he has no anxiety, no responsibilities to parents, no collision with pupils; so that his position is a good one for a person of a studious turn, and the German governments, who are acute on points of economy, act on the principle that a *savant* may be secured for a moderate payment, because the market for *savants* is limited; but when they want a man of administrative energy, for the management of a scientific department, or for maintaining discipline in a place of education, they know that they must pay more, because this kind of ability has a ready market, and can secure its price. Hence, though the enthusiasm for knowledge is, I believe, stronger in Germany than in England, still the position of equilibrium of the whole system is determined, as it is with us, by forces of the character of those we meet with in economical science.

The inducements to laborious study are more productive in Germany, because they are given for the fruit, or at the right season for fruit, while ours are like a prize given for the fullest blossom. Our Fellowships stimulate the University student, they reward *student work*, and this no doubt they call out in abundance and of high excellence.

One advantage of Germany lies in the continuance of study beyond the student course. This study is independent of the University; it is often carried on away from it, under penury, which to an Englishman would be intolerable, brightened by devotion to study and the hope of distinction. The reward most commonly looked for is a Professorship. This, as I have said, does not mean a position in which composure may be ruffled by conflict with boobies, or exhaustion caused by attempting to enliven the heavy by a transfusion of energy: the German Professor has not to do the work of a French one at a Lyceum. Such a position would be no boon to the *savant.* But the Professorship offers leisure for the further prosecution of study, to which the Professor is also stimulated by the prospect of a better post : and if a Professor writes a book, the sale of enough copies to pay expenses is practically ensured.

Thus Germany applies a graduated stimulus through life, with a view of producing the most effective set of *experts.* We may note that absolute governments regard education in the first place as a means of manufacturing *experts* for government use, while popular ones view it rather as a means for the rearing of useful *citizens;* and in all comparisons of systems of education, this should be kept in mind.

The credit of an English University rests on the character of the students it turns out. As Dr. Pusey is reported to have said to a German Professor, "We make not books but men." It is on the self-reliance and intelligence of the graduates, as shewn in life, that the good name of the University depends. A German student, eager for the honor of his University, enumerates its chief Professors and their works; an English undergraduate might hardly know the names of the Professors, or of any Lecturers but those at his own College, and as to these he would care little whether they had written anything or not. The University with him means the "men," while with the German it means the Professors, and these are regarded less as teachers, than as writers. Advancement is sought in Germany by writing on every possible occasion, and this is nearly as objectionable as our Examinations would be for grown men. It leads to writing for writing's sake, and the upholding of paradoxes in order to find something to say. Now and then, no doubt, a man of talent by being forced to fix his attention on a point, in order to produce a Dissertation for some special occasion, hits on something he might not otherwise have found, but this case is one in a thousand.

The waste caused with us by giving excessive rewards too early would be obviated by giving the Fellowships later and for *performances*. They would then fulfil the function of the German Professorship. They would stimulate work, and give support during a career of study.

I must now deal briefly with the subject of College Scholarships. These may be viewed in two lights, as follows:

I. They are the prizes, which give life to the whole system of instruction in a College. A Scholarship carries a status with it which is much coveted, hence this gives us a reward the value of which does not wholly depend on *money worth*, and the action of which is thereby the more wholesome.

Scholarships which are intended to act in this way are usually awarded, among the Students of the College, according to an Examination in the work of the year; they may be augmented or withdrawn according to the result of the Examination in subsequent years. Thus used, Scholarships are purely *educational* appliances, used to supply interest and concentrate attention on the College course. This was the old Cambridge plan.

II. But these emoluments may be regarded as means of "securing good men for the College." In this case the Examination cannot be in connection with the College course, the subjects must be chosen with reference to the coming Honor Schools, in which distinction is expected. Here we find two varieties, for the Examination may be open (1) to all undergraduates in the University, which is a plan commonly adopted at Oxford, or (2) to candidates from the Schools under 19 or 20 years of age. This plan originated at Oxford, but is now in use at both Universities.

The action of Scholarships regarded in the way (I.) is unexceptionable, and often very useful. There are subjects—English Literature and Mental Philosophy for instance—which are ill suited to be the subjects of a general competitive Examination, but which may be taught with great advantage by a College Lecturer to a class round his table. But if permanent good is to be got, pupils must not only listen and take part in the discussions that arise; they must also condense their thoughts into a shape fit for expression, and must gather up the whole subject at once. This they will not do unless for some special occasion; some object will be wanted, and an Examination, backed by the possibility of gaining a Scholarship, answers this purpose admirably.

The use of Scholarships in the way (II.), as means of securing good men, may be looked at with a view to the good of the College, or to helping the scholar. A College no doubt benefits by the presence in it of able men ; the tone of the society, and the standard of attainment, is raised thereby. It may not indeed be well for a College to consist exclusively of what are called "high men." A clique of clever young men living by themselves get a false view of life.

They fancy everything is to be done by cleverness, and are amazed, when they come to practical work, at the great power of stupidity; but without a fair sprinkling of ability worse evils arise, for men seeing nothing better acquiesce contentedly in their own mediocrity; one who is a shade better than the rest passes for a prodigy, and, as young people must have an aristocracy of their own, they will, if they cannot get one of ability, make up one out of social pretension, or of preeminence in sports : so that, though the Head or Tutor of a College may have got past setting his heart on having high Degrees to boast of, still, from the most legitimate motives, he will wish to get an accession of able students.

The Examination employed in case (II.), both for varieties (1) and (2), would be a sort of anticipation of the Examination for Honors, and the Examiner would regard the doings of candidates with a view to the Degrees they were likely to take.

A different view of Scholarships may, however, be taken. They may be regarded as helps for "deserving young men." Supposing, as in case (I.), that the Scholarships are confined to undergraduates who have commenced residence, it would make little difference as to the persons chosen, on the whole, throughout the University, whether each College disposed of its Scholarships by its own educational Examination, or by an Examination open to the whole University, always supposing, what is practically the case, that the supply of Scholarships at each College is adequate to rewarding those who may properly look for reward.

As a matter of fact, under either system, matters so adjust themselves that no deserving person goes unrewarded. At Oxford the College Scholarships are commonly open to competition in the University. At Cambridge the system of giving the Scholarships in the College is the common one, but a student of another College can migrate, and obtain a Scholarship, and when a College is known to have few promising men in a particular year, this commonly happens.

When the plan (2) is adopted, the Examinations can have no reference to the instruction given in a particular College, but *testing* Examinations must then be employed. Preparing for these Examinations causes distraction from the educational course. There is besides a waste of money in moving from College to College, and also a loss in the "break of gauge" in changing one set of instructors for another; the interest, moreover, of a College Tutor in his men is weakened by the idea that by teaching them well he is only giving them wings to fly away.

I now come to a matter which many of us regard as the source of much evil, the "Open Scholarships," given by competitive Examination before admission to the College.

Twenty years ago there were a few only so given. These were at Oxford; to obtain one of them conferred great credit, and the plan attracted very able men to the particular Colleges. The system had been considered in some Colleges at Cambridge, but the objections to it were thought to outweigh the advantages, and it was not adopted until after the change of Statutes in 1860, when circumstances made it necessary. The Oxford Statutes had been altered a few years before. The Oxford Colleges, seeing the high repute attained by Balliol and other

Societies which had long given Open Scholarships, threw open their Scholarships to competition before entrance. This gave a great stimulus to the schools. The clever boys were drawn to Oxford in large numbers, and Cambridge was forced to follow in the track. Soon the competition of College with College raised the prices from £50 to £70, and eventually to £120. Schoolmasters found that a clever boy was a valuable article, which by proper management might be made to fetch a considerable sum. The schoolmaster not only wished to do well for his scholar, but to get due credit for his school in the newspapers. "I cannot afford," wrote a schoolmaster to me, about 1858, when we were suffering at Cambridge from the drain of ability to Oxford, "to send boys to Cambridge, though I should like to do so. They may indeed get Scholarships at the end of the year, but no one knows what schools they come from; while my boys who go up to Oxford and get Open Scholarships spread my credit all over the country." When the advantage of the parent and of the schoolmaster pulled in the same direction, the force was irresistible. Soon the public came to measure the efficiency of a School by the number of these prizes it carried off. This has been most mischievous, as many schoolmasters feel. It leads to the able being overtaught and the duller neglected.

Mr. J. M. Wilson, of Rugby, writes as follows to the *Journal of Education* in Nov. 1876:

"Twenty years ago, more or less, the Colleges generally threw open their Scholarships to be competed for by boys at school. It seemed as if much was to be said for the change; it seemed to open the endowments of the Universities to boys of talent of all ranks; it seemed even to benefit the Colleges; and while only a few Colleges were then open, they were the gainers; but when all offer Scholarships it becomes a contest among them. They bid, and try to outbid one another, for clever boys. It alters the distribution of the clever boys among the Colleges to some extent, and that is all.

But the effect on schools is much greater and more serious. For the winning of these Scholarships has become the great object of many if not most schools. Boys go up and try at one College after another, under the advice of judicious men, who know the probable standard at each College. Scholarship classes are formed at school, examination papers are studied, regular education is laid aside for special preparation, the boy is cleverly steered, and the cleverest boy and cleverest jockey jointly win the prize, and divide the applause; the honor is duly paraded at the speech-day by the smiling head-master to smiling boys, applause follows, which lasts for several moments, and care is taken to have the success announced in all the papers.

I do not hesitate to say, after a good many years' experience, that the effect of these Scholarships on Schools is almost unredeemedly bad. They are not necessary as a stimulus; they are totally inadequate and misleading as a means of comparing school with school; and they do a good deal in some cases to degrade the work of masters and boys alike.

There would be nothing but gain to the great schools, and to the cause of higher education in England, if all the Colleges at Oxford and Cambridge announced that in future Scholarships would only be awarded to men in actual residence; and the Colleges themselves would be no losers on the whole. But if it is thought by the majority of those who have the best means of judging that any considerable number of boys who now go to the Universities as Scholars would not go at all, but for the diminution of expense and the prospect of ultimate success that winning a Scholarship affords, it would not be impossible to make the Certificate Examination serve the purpose of a Common School Examination for both Universities."

When the system was first introduced some Colleges endeavored to frame their Examinations for Open Scholarships educationally, and to take account of Classics, Mathematics, and English, all together. But very soon the schoolmasters found that their ablest boys were needed for the special Scholarships, while second-rate boys could be prepared to carry off those which were given for general proficiency; hence, College after College has been driven to "specialize" the Scholarships, which are now almost always given for excellence in one department. This is most injurious. Moreover, a very mischievous "special preparation" may be given in certain subjects, Mathematics especially. For, the range being limited, much may turn on adroitness in solving certain classes of problems, and this kind of cleverness may be stimulated to the injury of the student. Examination papers are carefully studied by tutors and pupils, and some competitors read with tutors at the University to get "University style," a good thing enough in due time, but it should not be consciously aimed at by boys of seventeen. Parents expect the Schoolmasters to watch for openings in the Colleges, and to dispose of their sons to the best advantage. But the greatest evil lies in the mercenary spirit which is called out by the prominence too early given to making money. "I will not take less than £100 a year for that boy," writes a master; "but I have another, a good, useful lad, whom you can have for £70." One boy, too, feels aggrieved if a schoolfellow have fetched more than he has. And when a youth has obtained a Scholarship I have heard of his master writing for leave for him to go in for another elsewhere, which might be worth £10 more. By two victories the master would get double credit. Boys who are "run" for Scholarships at an early age are sometimes not allowed to take them if they win, in order that they may achieve a larger Scholarship and more *éclat* for their school in the following year. In such a state of things, when boys are run for "plates" like race-horses, can we wonder at complaints that young men are actuated, not by a romantic love for learning, not by regard to their teachers or their College, but entirely by sordid considerations, and that, in the

words of a Cambridge tutor, they think that their
relations with the rest of the world are shaped by
" rights and not by duties."

A parent not needing pecuniary help would do
better to pick out a College, and take his chance of
his son getting a Scholarship there, than to send him
round trying at one College after another, and thus
breaking up his school-time. The holiday at the
University with old schoolfellows may be pleasant,
but it is costly and distracting.

It was an old objection· to the plan, that early
successes, over-much valued, would make youths conceited, and that disappointment would follow. A
return of the careers of the winners of Open Scholarships would furnish instances of this, especially in the
case of the lower prizes. Many young men will work
hard under pressure, striving for what they are eager
to get, but having no interest in learning, and some
of these will indemnify themselves afterwards by
basking in their glory, and taking their fill of pleasure.

One difficulty of the question arises from the fact
that there are a few young men who, without such
help, would not come to the University, and who
quite justify the outlay on their behalf. There are,
on the other hand, many who are lured to the University by such means, who yield society no return for
having given them a high education, and who, after
spending three years and getting a second-rate degree,
which will bring no emolument, are worse off than if
they had gone into business at first, and who, owing
to the spirit in which they have worked, have no compensation in the way of enlarged capacities for usefulness or for intellectual pleasure.

Another practical difficulty in dealing with these

Scholarships is this. No one College can act for itself. Hardly a person likely to get a good degree in Honors now comes to the University without a Scholarship, so that for a College to say that it will give no Scholarships, or only give them under less attractive conditions than other Colleges, is equivalent to giving up having candidates for Honors. Here then is a case for legislative interference, because Colleges, owing to their isolation, cannot abandon what all, I believe, at Cambridge hold to be mischievous. Common action is necessary for all the Colleges at Oxford and Cambridge, because if one or two retained the system these would secure the ablest men. By offering a Scholarship of £200 a year, a College might make almost sure of obtaining a Scholar who would gain high distinction : thus the credit which a College is supposed to derive from the high degrees of its students may be greatly due to its purchasing power. I am not without hope that the expected University legislation may help in this matter.

I agree with Mr. Wilson, that Scholarships might properly be offered to those who had done well in the Local Examinations, or in those of the Joint University Board, and this I think would meet the needs of the case. If we cannot free ourselves from this pernicious system altogether, in the way proposed, the evils might be reduced by so diminishing the number of Scholarships as to confine them to able men. Colleges sometimes give away several Exhibitions of £30 or £40 to youths, some of whom profit little by being drawn to the University, and thus a great waste of money is incurred. Scholarships should be limited to certain values, say £80 and £50, to prevent the bidding of College against College. The Examinations should also take place at fixed periods ; the boys should be under nineteen years of age ; and these Open Scholarships should only be tenable until an opportunity offered for obtaining a Foundation Scholarship.*

* The system will be hard to overthrow, because it scatters bounties. Help, as I have said, given to a lad of marked ability and small means, is not eleemosynary, because Society gets its *quid pro quo*. But if the youth be only of fair industry and intelligence, it is doubtful whether his usefulness to Society is increased enough by his having a higher education to make it worth while to take him out of his own walk of life. In this case there is hardly more reason why we should provide such persons gratuitously with higher education than with better clothes or maintenance. If we give help professedly as charity, we ought to inquire into the means of the recipients. This is not an easy or pleasant task. The City Companies effect this in some degree, and their Exhibitions, as far as my observation has gone, have been bestowed with excellent judgment, and have given help just where it was well justified.

Sizarships effect a similar purpose. Persons of much social pretension will not send their sons to College as Sizars, and this preserves sizarships for the class they are intended for. They are peculiar to Cambridge, and are given away like Scholarships. (See p. 338, head I.)

Some persons cannot venture on a University course unless they first secure assistance. These might come to the University as Unattached Students. They might easily arrange with a College to attend its course of lectures, and to compete with the Students of that College for a Scholarship at the end of the first Academical year. If they should fail, they would then have incurred no expense beyond the difference between their maintenance in the University town and at their own homes.

I fear that boys at school are getting the idea, that if they are unlikely to get an open Scholarship there is " no good " in their working. This comes of making too much of bribes as compared with duty and authority.

CHAPTER IX.

ON MARKING AND CLASSING.

PERSONS not practically acquainted with Examinations may require to know something of the machinery by which the Examiner gives effect to his judgment. I propose therefore to give some account of the mechanism employed, avoiding all technical details, and confining myself to what is required for a good comprehension of the general action of Examinations.

Two modes of proceeding come under our notice; one is called deciding "by marks," and the other "judging by impression." These processes are not distinct in their nature, for marks are, in fact, only the record of particular impressions; but besides these particular impressions produced by each answer, the Examiner sometimes receives a general impression from the *ensemble* of a candidate's work which is too indefinite to be estimated numerically, and weighed against a piece of translation, or a proposition in mathematics, but which may still help us to judge of his qualifications. These processes will be best understood by a glimpse at the mechanism when it is at work.

It makes a difference whether the Examiner, as commonly happens, is acting in concert with others, and has only a portion of a branch of the Examination entrusted to him, so that his results have to be weighed along with those of other Examiners, or whether, like an elector to a Scholarship or Fellowship, he have only to make up his own mind, state his opinions, and give his vote. In the first case, it is hardly possible to arrive at a result except by marks, if anything like an order of merit be required; but if it were only necessary to place candidates in three or four classes, this might be done by voting, in the case of each candidate, whether he should be in the first class or lower, and so on for each class : some remarks on this mode of proceeding will be made presently. If marks be used, each subject must have a definite value assigned to it. I have discussed the principles on which these values should be determined, pp. 279—283. It is moreover necessary that Exam- iners should have some common understanding as to the degree of perfection corresponding to certain pro- portions of marks ; for, supposing the Mathematical Examiner to be rigorous, and the Italian Exam- iner to be easily pleased, the mathematician will suffer in comparison with the Italian scholar. This difficulty, which is analogous to what is called the "personal equation" of two astronomical observers, is a considerable one, and is greater the more various the subjects are. Even the same Examiner judges differently, according as he is fresh or wearied.

If an Examiner have merely to give his vote and state his opinion he need use no marks, and if he does, they are to him merely notes of passing impres- sions and are equivalent to *words*, such as "excellent," "fair," "indifferent," &c. There is an intermediate case, in which an Examiner has the absolute control of one subject, but the number of marks allotted to his subject is fixed. In this case the Examiner may judge of the merits of the papers handed to him in any way he likes, provided that he arrives at numerical results in proper relation to the maximum assigned for perfection. He may use marks if he pleases to register his impressions, and he may give additional marks where an answer strikes his fancy, or for general style, or take off marks beyond those assigned to the particular questions for a blunder which reveals an abyss of misapprehension. But he must translate his results into the scale which has been agreed on.

When an Examination is conducted by marks, the order of merit is determined by the addition of these marks, however they are obtained. Candidates often have an idea that it will "go against them" to have got their marks in one way or another, as though some impression were derived from their performance viewed as a whole. Such an impression no doubt might be drawn from seeing how the marks are obtained. When we cast our eyes down the list of the marks of candidates in the Indian Civil Service Examination, we involuntarily do form some such judgment; but, as a fact, when notice has been given of the marks assigned to each subject, no consideration is paid to anything but the aggregate of marks, and the places are determined simply by addition. It is only when the list has to be divided into classes that there is room for discussion; then the question, "Where are we to draw the line?" often gives room to debate, and the character of the work of the candidates on the debateable ground may then be canvassed in some degree.

In the case of an election for a Fellowship or for some single prize, the Examiners, as I have said, often *vote* according to the impression each gets from his own paper, or from the statements of the other electors. This mode of proceeding has the advantage that it gives full scope to impression, so that if the Examiners are keen-sighted and have an eye for ability, they will probably judge well for their purpose: but, on the other hand, an Examiner who is not used to discriminate, or who has some crotchet, may do much harm; for it is the weak point of this system that a vote doubtfully given may counteract one given in the strongest possible conviction. Two Examiners, for instance, may feel no doubt that *A* is much better than *B*, and three others may be uncertain, but finally decide to vote for *B*, who is thereby elected; whereas, if the matter had been decided by the addition of the marks, furnished by all the Examiners, *A* might have been the successful candidate. Under this system, also, an Examiner of strong will and positive manner will sometimes obtain a preponderance which is not justified by his soundness of judgment.

I must now return to speak of the way in which marks are given. The system of numerical marking, as has been said above, came into use in Mathematical Examinations, where it was found to work well. There is no subject in which marks can be allotted with such precision as in Mathematics.

The various elements of Examination value, that is to say, the relative difficulty and importance of questions, the amount of previous reading needed to answer them, and, what we shall presently have to touch upon, the time requisite to write out the answers, can be all more readily estimated and allowed for in subjects which can be treated mathematically than in most others.

In Mathematics, something has usually to be

proved; if the proof holds, full marks are commonly given, and if it fails, few or none are allowed. Hence, the discretion of the Examiner only comes into play in dealing with partial solutions, or in the explanation of principles and description of experiments, instruments, &c.: the consequence is that two Mathematical Examiners, independently marking a set of papers, will usually agree within a few marks. But with Languages, especially as regards Composition, and also with Historical and speculative subjects, the case is different. The class of questions which begin with, "Give a short account of," "Discuss the question," or "Examine the principle," cannot be marked on generally accepted rules: one Examiner may have one view and one another as to the proper starting-point for the answer and the range it ought to cover. In the Universities some kind of understanding prevails on this point, and candidates are practiced in answering in the expected form; but when candidates from various quarters are set down to answer a paper involving such questions, various elements of uncertainty present themselves, and these operate to a greater extent if the time allowed for doing the paper be short. For instance, some candidates will spend too great a proportion of their time over a few questions, and others will attempt too many, and send up scanty answers.* Sometimes Examiners can use their dis-

---

* Here we see one source of the advantage gained by those candidates who have been directly trained for displaying their knowledge in an Examination. A pupil who has had such assistance understands what the Examiner means him to do, and also how he may best employ his time upon a paper of questions. Hence preparing for Examinations differs from teaching, properly so called, in this, that, besides putting knowledge *into* the pupil and giving him the use of his brains, he must be made acquainted with the *conventions* of Examinations and taught to put *out* his knowledge to the best advantage. The proper business of a school is *teaching*, but when pupils are looking to competition outside the school, they must be " prepared " for such contests. If this is done in the school, it necessitates the withdrawal of pupils from some of the

cretion and give extra marks for a question which is
answered more thoroughly than may be quite necessary, but frequently the conditions of the Examination or the understanding that exists among the candidates may render it improper to do so. Moreover,
if a discursive mode of dealing with a paper were encouraged, the difficulty of Examining would be increased.

The Examiner is usually left free to distribute the
marks allowed for his paper among his questions, and
he may find it desirable to alter this distribution in
the course of examining. If, for instance, he finds
that some question is commonly answered, nearly in
the same terms, he will conclude that he has lighted
on something contained in a manual in common use,
and this may affect his view of the value of his question. When the object is only to pick out a few candidates from a mass, the Examiner should be left, as I
have said before, as free as possible to exercise his
judgment, unfettered by the notion of being under a
covenant with the candidate to give marks for all
that is correct; but where such an understanding
exists, or where a large number of Examiners are
employed, some of whom may be inexperienced, it is
desirable that definite marks should be allotted to
each question, and that a list of the marks given should
be produced; this affords a guarantee that every answer has been properly considered, and also a means

ordinary work, and the setting up of a "special preparation" department; if it be not
done, pupils will go to an establishment which makes such preparation its particular
business. The drilling for Examinations is not without its use in *its proper time*—it
gives precision and self-knowledge; but the matter should be well assimilated before it
has to be displayed, otherwise we get what is called "cram." If the Examination be
confined to the school, all the pupils are similarly circumstanced, and the regular
school-work need not be interrupted. The subjects will, of course, be reviewed; but
this falls in with legitimate teaching. In examining a school, a knowledge of school-
methods is of course requisite, as well as good judgment and an understanding of boys.

of investigating complaints of the loss of papers, or the like.

I have said that the result of the marks given and that of the impression received do not always correspond; on this point there is something to observe. Impression is made up of many elements, some of which belong to the Examiner's particular taste, and others to the pupil's style of work. But this discrepancy may arise from a more complete view being taken of the entire work, when we judge by impression, than when we judge by the aggregate of the marks allowed for each scrap or clause of a question which is rightly answered. For instance, a candidate who sends up a number of answers, and gets credit for parts of each, but does no one question thoroughly well, may get an aggregate of marks which will surprise the Examiner, who may lay down his papers with but a poor opinion of him. It may be said that the Examiner in this case has not marked the answers with proper judgment, but such a discrepancy is sometimes hard to avoid. The difficulty arises from the multiplicity of the objects which the Examination is meant to effect. The Examiner is expected to pronounce both on the ability and knowledge of the candidate, while he must set his questions with a view to some educational programme; possibly too the Examination may be a mere qualifying Examination for some of the candidates, and so he may have to fix a standard for "passing," and act as considerately in some cases as if he were administering criminal law. He must therefore look with different eyes on the performances of the best and the worst; he adapts his vision to detect shades of difference between the abler; but if he looked half as closely into the work of the worst that he does into that of the best candidates, the slaughter would be disastrous.

Another cause of the difference between the impression given and the score obtained is that negative marks are not employed. The Examiner, according to usage, can at most withhold all marks from the question in which a bad blunder occurs, although the ill impression conveyed to him may be inadequately represented by this penalty. These understood modes of proceeding have not however been adopted without good grounds. An Examiner has in all cases a notion of the answer he wishes to receive, to this he gives full marks, and there is a difficulty in giving more marks for a very thorough answer, because possibly other men might have answered more at length if they had understood that the Examiner wished them to do so. Again, an Examiner may occasionally be struck by a remark, which is rather beside the question, but if he gave marks for it, candidates would bring in brilliant observations taken out of their tutor's " Note-book of Original Thoughts." There is also this objection to the employment of negative marks. A nervous student, fearing to damage himself by a bad blunder, may be prevented from attempting questions in which he might shew himself to advantage, and this terror might have a depressing effect : an Examiner wishes to see a man at his best, and he does best when he works fearlessly. Still, bad spelling, bad grammar, or guesses which shew utter ignorance, ought to involve some positive loss.

The general character of the question selected by the candidate influences impression, but may have little effect on the marking. Some candidates will steadily decline all questions which touch on points of difficulty, such points, for example, as are scantily explained in the common text-books, or which require nicety of conception and clearness of head. Lastly, the general style of expression and of arrangement conveys important information to a practised Examiner as to the capabilities of a candidate. Of course in some cases, as in translation, style is definitely considered in the marking; but in other subjects it can scarcely be taken account of question by question, though it makes itself felt in the whole.

The practical conclusion would therefore be, that when the Examiner has merely to decide on the fittest candidate for the purpose in view, he may act freely on impression, *translating* this impression into marks, if he thinks fit, in order to assist his memory, or to enable him to compare his results with those of other Examiners; but when he is examining what has been prepared by the pupil, on a certain understanding, it is more important to keep up the pupil's confidence in the absolute good faith maintained in the Examination than to arrive at a slightly more accurate result.

The following course is applicable in many Examinations in which two or three objects are aimed at at once; as, for instance, to guide the student's reading, and at the same time to give consideration to extent of knowledge and to furnish a criterion of ability. It is to distribute three quarters of the marks assigned to the paper among the questions, and to reserve the other quarter to be assigned by impression. It would be well, only it takes time, and time is, in heavy Examinations, very costly, for the Examiner first to *mark* all the papers sent up, and then read them over a second time and assign the marks due to impression. By this means he will know how to pitch his expectations before he begins to give the marks for impression.

I have observed that in assigning marks to a particular question, it is necessary to consider the time required for answering it; this is of course on the supposition that a limited time is allowed for answering the whole paper.

Something must be said on this subject of *time*. If we only want to find out the cleverest man, or the man of most matured knowledge, we may get rid of this disturbing element by letting candidates work at the paper as long as they like. But in educational Examinations the time that can be allowed is practically limited by external arrangements, as so many papers must be set within so many days.

The Examiner is paid in proportion to the work and the time, and during many Examinations pupils are being maintained away from their homes, so that time must be economized. Hence, the time allowed for an Examination is often scanty compared with the number of subjects comprised. This leads to setting short papers, and to affording the minimum of time for doing them. Of course a short Examination is less effective than a long one : it gives more room for luck. When an important subject is disposed of in a single paper, the questions may be suitable or unsuitable for a particular person, or a candidate may be a little unwell. These sources of error are eliminated in a long Examination.

Again, when scanty time is allowed, practice in writing out becomes so important, that a schoolboy is sometimes taken off his regular work for some weeks before an Examination, in order to get practice and dexterity in " serving up " his knowledge neatly and rapidly ; thus by allowing too short a time for a paper we put those who are not specially trained at a disadvantage. On the other hand, it is said that rapidity and readiness are qualities of great service in life, and that they should be rewarded as much as any others. But this argument implies a comparing of things not of the same kind. It may be well to judge of readiness, if the candidates know they are to compete in a display of this quality, and a proper means of shewing it be devised; but if we hurry a student we cannot tell whether he can *think* or not, and we cannot say what comes from quick writing and what from superior knowledge.

A pupil who knows his work thoroughly will be able to answer questions much more readily than one who has to hammer out his replies. This in a strictly educational Examination justly brings him a reward, but if we were looking for the ablest man we should think as well of one who got the same questions answered in four hours by using his brains that another did in three hours by greater help from his memory.

The received general rule, when we want to judge of ability, knowledge and diligence all at once — and I have no better to offer — is that the paper should not be longer than a thoroughly well prepared and able student can answer in the time.

If the paper be too long in proportion to the time allowed, the effect is the same as if separate candidates had separate papers, for each will make his own choice of questions. An element of uncertainty is hereby introduced. The man who knows where his own strength lies, and who can see at a glance what he can do and what he cannot, and can invest his time with the greatest judgment, derives an advantage. This, it may be said, he fully deserves, but there is a difficulty in setting off this quality against superior ingenuity or power of rendering an author; sometimes mere quickness of writing may produce a difference. I have known long and exhaustive papers produce results which were at variance with the rest of the Examination, and which were not confirmed by subsequent trials. Moreover, a paper that is too long enables a candidate to avoid the very questions that we most depend upon for judging of the correctness of his apprehension of the subject.

On the other hand, a paper that is too short may answer educational purposes well enough, but it may fail to discriminate between two or three men, each of whom will answer all the questions.

A Mathematical Problem paper offers a special case. No one is expected to solve all the problems, a certain choice is intentionally offered. An element of disturbance is hereby introduced; when there are two or three such papers, the disturbances may neutralize each other; but a single problem paper in a Mathematical Examination may cause an erroneous result. The harder the problems are, the more mischief the paper may do; for, if no one can solve more than two or three, a single problem will be very important, and a candidate may hit on a solution by some chance thought. If the problem paper be very long, it denotes a vast expenditure of thought in the making on the part of a man who might have been doing something better, and it adds to the uncertainty in a still greater degree. For a candidate can hardly spare time to consider each problem, and he therefore decides hastily as to which he should attack, while much depends on his judgment in so doing: twelve problems for three hours is the common rule.

Questions that are too hard may cause a ruinous loss of time; the Examiners should therefore know the general calibre of the candidates.

Sometimes an Examiner must test a very wide range of knowledge by a single paper; the result in this case can only be regarded as a rough approximation, but the plan adopted in some Government Examinations under these circumstances is a good one, viz. to subjoin a few questions in the higher parts of the subject and allow any of them to be substituted for any of the others. Another useful plan in such cases, especially with subjects like English Literature or Classical Antiquities, is to set a number of questions, perhaps a dozen, and only to allow the candidate to do four or five of them. This leads him to possess himself of certain points thoroughly, and enables him to shew whether he has got beyond the outside of the subject.

We now suppose that the score of each candidate in each paper is settled, and we arrive at the question, How are these particular scores to be combined? If we simply add them together, experience shews that many-sided mediocrity will get more than its deserts. It is with learning as with the boring a shaft for a mine, the labor of advancing, and, possibly, also the value of the returns, vary with the square of the depth, or even in a higher ratio. Hence the reward should vary in the same proportion. Unless the total of the marks assigned to a paper be made inconveniently large, it will be difficult to mark the higher questions adequately, in relation to the lower ones, without so reducing the marks of the latter, as to leave insufficient scope for marking differences in the answers. The result is that excellence is insufficiently rewarded, and this leads candidates to read a single subject too diffusely, and, when several subjects may be taken in at once, to enter upon too many. I have hinted at a plan (p. 173) of squaring the marks, which in certain cases would fairly express the relative degrees of excellence; for a person who gets half marks is not more than a quarter as good as one who gets full marks, but this plan would be troublesome if the marks were numerically high. The simple plan adopted in the Indian Civil Service Examinations, though not continuous in its operation, is far easier to apply. It consists in deducting a fixed number from each score in the particular subjects, and adding the remainders thus obtained in each subject, in order to arrive at the ultimate total score of the competitor. The number deducted may be the same for all subjects, or a proportion of the whole number allotted to each subject. This system prevents an undue reward being given to smatterings, but it does not equally well answer the purpose of largely rewarding high excellence.

The plan would be more complete if the excess of each score above half marks, if such there were, were added to it, and then one quarter of the whole number of marks assigned to the paper were deducted, so that if the paper gave 500 marks we should have the following results:

A obtains full marks 500 and is credited with
$$500 + 250 - 125 = 625,$$
B obtains 400 and is credited with
$$400 + 150 - 125 = 425,$$
C obtains 300 and is credited with
$$300 + 50 - 125 = 225,$$
D obtains 200 and is credited with $200 - 125 = 75$,
E obtains 125 and is credited with $125 - 125 = 0$.

This plan it will be seen would enable a competitor to get more marks than the total put down for the subject, but as all the subjects would be affected in the same way, their relative value would be unaltered.

The subjects for the Mathematical Tripos at Cambridge (see p.135) are now distributed into groups, and a certain number of marks are assigned to each group; this was done with the view of inducing students to read a few branches of Mathematics and Natural Philosophy with completeness, instead of roving over a large surface and selecting the portions which they could most easily handle. No change, however, in the mode of study was effected by this step, because the old course continued to be the most profitable; people found a little of many things more remunerative than much of one thing; but if the marks allotted to each group were dealt with by some mode similar to the above, candidates and their tutors would find the plan of reading, which it is desired to encourage, to be also the most remunerative in point of marks, and it would be generally adopted.

It may seem degrading to have so often to appeal to apparently mercenary considerations, but, as I have before said, we want such considerations with *youths*, to supply the place of the motives for professional exertion in men; a boy who will do nothing at school, because he does not "see the good of it," will often work hard enough when he sees that exertion and application will bring him what he wants to obtain, and this demand for definite returns is now greater than ever. The young people at any period naturally reproduce the views prevalent at the time among their parents. Grown men do not require such artificial stimulants, because duties which are imperative supply their place with the many, while the pursuit of knowledge, or of some object which furnishes the interest and occupation of life, does the like for a few. This brings me to the most important part of this chapter, the question of the conflicting advantages of an alphabetical arrangement and of one in order of merit.

We are here regarding Examinations primarily as modes of discovering the relative qualifications of certain persons for some purpose which the Examiner has in view, or on which the public wants to have means of judging. The more therefore that Examinations can honestly tell us, as to such relative qualifications, the better they effect their end. If we have little confidence in the readings of our instruments, we must not pretend to register very nice observations, but we may, unless there are other reasons to the contrary, publish such an estimate as we believe to be trustworthy as far as it goes. If our observation is only true to minutes we must not pretend to give it in seconds; but there is no reason why we should confine ourselves to hours.

When there are only a few emoluments or places to be given away, we are forced to make a selection. Now an Examination held especially for making such a selection generally does *some* educational harm. If, then, by arranging the competitors in educational Examinations like those for Honors in the Universities, in as close an order of merit as we can, we are able to do without special Examinations, we are so far doing good service to education by adopting this mode of arrangement, unless we have to do with persons so sensitive, or with a mode of preparation so prone to produce artificial learning, that more would be lost in this way than by holding special Examinations.

At Oxford the classes are arranged alphabetically, and, looking to the character of the studies in their most important school, I do not think that any other arrangement could be adopted; but in consequence of this mode of classification it is necessary to hold Examinations for Fellowships after Degree, a plan which is open to objections *a priori* (see p. 14), and of the operation of which at Oxford Mr. Sayce, in the pamphlet above quoted, speaks unfavorably.

I hold that it is desirable to use our educational Examinations as means of disposing of our emoluments, and in order that these Examinations may be so used, their results should tell us as much as the Examiner can confidently state about the candidates.

When the subjects of Examination are not homogeneous, or when they comprise matters of taste or opinion, or when an extensive subject has to be dealt with in an insufficient time, then there must be much uncertainty as to the order of merit. The more free the Examination is from these causes of incertitude, the more closely may we place the names in such an order. This incertitude will vary for each *subject* in a given Examination, and it may also vary from special circumstances affecting the whole *Examination;* the more multifarious the subjects the greater it will be. It is measured by the percentage of the marks of candidates within which it is requisite to "bracket" them as equal, considering each subject by itself. To determine this percentage practically, we should require to have the same sets of answers in various subjects, marked by different Examiners: we should find that in certain subjects the lists nearly coincided, but that in others they varied more or less, and we might fix our percentage accordingly.

We might find, for instance, that if we "bracketed" in Mathematics all those who are within three per cent. of each other, the same list would result from the marks of each set of Examiners; but that in the case of Classical translation we should have to bracket those whose marks were within five or six per cent. to get the same list from both sets; if we took Classical composition the percentage required would be higher. This percentage I propose to call the *index of indeterminateness* for the subject in question. When the subjects are of various kinds, or when all the candidates do not do the same papers, but performances in one thing have to be set off against performances in another, this increases the *index of indeterminateness* for that Examination. For instance, the index in a single Mathematical subject may be taken at two per cent., which was the rate formerly fixed in the Mathematical Tripos. Thus persons scoring 5000 and 5099 would have been bracketed equal, but one who obtained 5100 would have escaped being bracketed. But since the range of the Examinations has been extended, so that many candidates take different selections of subjects, our index above spoken of has been increased, and candidates are now bracketed where the difference of marks is within three per cent.

Mathematics and those branches of Physics which can be treated mathematically give the most definite results. Chemistry, with its allied sciences, would perhaps stand next, and then Roman Law.

With regard to Classics, we find that Examiners usually agree pretty well about translation, but that prose composition affords room for some difference of opinion, and verse composition gives much more.

When in a Classical Examination we have set subjects, together with History, Philosophy, and Philology, the Examination ceases to be homogeneous. Some candidates may pay no attention to one of these branches, but may concentrate their strength on another; this increases the indeterminateness of the result; and the degree of confidence that can be placed in it must depend on the *system of mechanism* adopted for combining the marks (see pp. 356 and 361).

When several subjects are grouped together which are dissimilar, and are not all taken up by each student, as in Natural Science, great uncertainty must result. A student may do very well in one branch, and yet so poorly in others as to come out very low in a general list. But if separate lists are drawn out for the separate subjects, the credit of the Examination is lessened, because fewer names appear in each, and a scanty list carries small weight with the public: besides, the public is bewildered by a multiplicity of lists, and is found to pay little attention to Honors which appear in this form. The "index of indeterminateness" might be so high, that the "brackets" would be large enough to form separate classes, in which case we come to an alphabetical arrangement in classes of moderate size, and this may be the closest classification which the case admits of.

It has been proposed to note by "asterisks" those who are distinguished in particular branches, but a difficulty occurs; we must here trust a single Examiner: there may be a want of uniformity of view as to what constitutes excellence. The more abstruse the subject, the more necessary it will be to have for Examiners persons who are rather *savants* than teachers. Such persons may not understand the mode in which a pupil's mind acts, as an Examiner ought to do, in order to mark ability and distinguish first-rate work. The mode by which the results of a Natural Science School or Tripos can be best used for the awarding of College Endowments, appears to me to be to allow the College authorities access to the actual marks obtained by the candidates: this is a possible expedient. The case of Moral Science is not very different. The subjects comprised are less diverse, and are more commonly studied all together; but there is much that is speculative, and therefore there is much room for difference of opinion between Examiners.

Thus far we have spoken of a *relative* measure of proficiency, but in some cases we want an *absolute* measure as well. This absolute standard is supplied in University Examinations by dividing the candidates into classes.

Whether we adopt an alphabetical arrangement, or in order of merit in each class, the extent of the class must be determined by the examining body according to their idea of what it indicates. In the Universities there is an old traditionary idea of what is meant by the First, Second, and Third Classes respectively, and by Wranglers, Senior Optimes, and Junior Optimes. The difficulty of *drawing a line* is proverbial, and frequently this separation into classes causes much discussion. We find every shade of proficiency and ability, just as we find that plants pass by gradual changes from the lichens to the most perfect flowers; but just as at certain stages nature is most prolific of genera and species, so we find that near certain standards candidates lie thick together, and thus a first, second, and third class often mark roughly certain types of mind. Nevertheless the gra-

dation from one of these groups to another is continuous, and sometimes there is no considerable break between candidates near the place where the line, according to tradition, ought to be drawn.   In this case less
injustice is done by a system in order of merit than by an
alphabetical one, because the difference between being
last in the first class and first in the second is not so
great as that between a first class and a second class
degree when all those in each class are supposed to
be equal.   The more numerous the classes, the greater
will be the danger of a small difference in marks causing the difference of a class between two candidates.

If the distinctions drawn are unwarranted, if, for
instance, two or three marks make the difference of
a place, an arrangement in order of merit is not de-
fensible; but, even when it is warranted, objection is
taken to its use, as leading to over-anxiety, and "reading for a place."

Young people however need close gradations of success; if the steps are far apart they stagnate somewhere, they cannot love knowledge "for its own sake"
till they know what knowledge is.   We do not trust
entirely to duty or professional enthusiasm in the
case of grown-up people, but if we want our *employés*
to act with zeal and intelligence, we offer them opportunities for shewing intelligence and prospects of
advancement.   We must deal with young people in
the same way.

The spirit of contest goes all through life.   It is
found in the professions and in politics, and lies at
the bottom of all our recreations.   English boys
learn to love contest from our English games.   Happily they learn from them too that contest may be
quite free from jealousy and personal rivalry, and

they come to regard fair dealing as the air they breathe, that is, not as anything to be prized or praised, but as one of the ordinary conditions of existence. There are countries, and perhaps there are classes among ourselves, in which this ready spirit of give and take is not found, and then objection is felt, and, reasonably felt, to any close rivalry among students. Many University Examinations — our Mathematical Tripos at Cambridge, as at present constituted, for example — fulfil a double purpose. They are educational Examinations, and also Examinations in advanced knowledge. So far as they are educational, classification in order of merit is quite applicable, but so far as they represent learning, which they do as far as relates to the highest men, a less precise classification would be better. While receiving the higher knowledge men should be free from the disturbance produced by the idea of contest. If we divide the Examinations as I propose, we get rid of this difficulty. Our highest candidates *are* now and then pressed a little harder than is good for them, though a great deal that we hear on this point is exaggeration.

We now come to the objection that the closeness of our distinction causes over-anxiety and over-work. If we reckon work by the number of hours of application, we should say that the reading men of the present generation work infinitely less hard than those of the preceding one. Bishop Blomfield says, that he read twelve hours a day or more, while no one now reads more than eight or nine. It is not the highest men by any means who read the greatest number of hours, or who suffer most from over-work. We are in want of precise information as to the number of cases in which students suffer from over-work. I believe myself that though a few men are temporarily wearied at the end of term, no serious evil occurs. My impression is that young persons are more careful of themselves, and that they understand managing themselves better than they did. In College also they are under experienced eyes, and the first symptom of over-fag is observed.

It is, however, to be noted that brain-work depends on intensity as well as duration, and the work of our time demands great activity of mind. A great part of the labor in old time was mechanical. The references in Bishop Blomfield's time had to be made to the original works; now, the passages wanted are given in notes; proofs of Mathematical propositions were then dictated in lectures or copied from tutorial MS., while at present all that is wanted is found in the manuals. Mathematical processes are shorter, so that the student passes more rapidly from one conception to another: more thought is exercised in less time. Moreover, owing to the over-great extent of matter comprised in our University Schools, tutors are forced to go at a gallop to get through the subjects. Their teaching consists altogether in explaining difficulties: the student goes over the plain ground by himself. The tutor administers to him concentrated nourishment, divested of all which gives *bulk:* this is a strain on the mental digestion, and is terribly fagging both to pupil and tutor. In each lesson there are new conceptions to be conveyed, and every device of exposition and illustration is required. The remedy is two-fold: first to reduce the excessive range of the subjects; secondly, in a moderate degree to lengthen slightly, not indeed the formal University "terms," but the parts of them employed in instruction, by enforcing the beginning of residence in all the Colleges on a certain day, and making each term contain 60 clear days. People would be less exhausted by a few day's more work than they are by the tearing hurry of the present plan. *

Another cause of the exhaustion which we sometimes hear of, comes from the pupil having been, in sporting phraseology, "run off his legs," before he was fully grown. What with Scholarships and various other special Examinations, the schools are forced to let the education of a youth, considered in its largest sense, give place to his prospects of distinction. Thus boys have one faculty of their minds forced, at an over early age, into undue activity. I should be glad to get rid of this specializing in schools, and see young men come to the University fairly educated all round. At present we have a few well-trained candidates for Scholarships, and many dunces.

Evils may with particular temperaments follow from over-stimulation; such temperaments are not only

* The Long Vacation at Cambridge is the time when the greatest amount of healthy work is done, the idlers are away; about 500 or 600 genuine students, and 80 or 100 of those engaged in teaching and in maintaining discipline, occupy the place during July and August. The Medical Faculty too continues some of its lectures. The best work of the year is done in this season of quiet, and Cambridge is then truly "a seat of learning and a place of education." It has sometimes been suggested to interpose a compulsory term in the middle of the Long Vacation; that is to say, to oblige the idler men and the candidates for Ordinary Degrees to reside along with the studious ones. This would be very unwise. The Pass men would not benefit, for the term would be much what the end of the Easter Term now is, that is to say, it would be broken in upon by boat races and cricket matches, and worst of all by the constant intrusion of pleasure-seeking relatives and visitors: not only time but money would be spent in entertaining them. At present the backward Pass men often go to their old private tutors in the country for the summer (reading parties for such men are not to be recommended), and some of the better sort go and learn French or German on the Continent. Independent, continuous study or writing is now difficult enough; it is prevented not only by teaching, people must lay their account for this, but by the distraction caused by the administrative business carried on by Syndicates, and by the debates and agitation attendant on legislation, and College and University politics; and if the Vacation were turned into a prolongation of the "May term," the intellectual life of the University would be well nigh extinguished.

found among the ablest students, whose case is now before us, but, I believe, more commonly among the feebler men. Sometimes a Pass man reads himself, or rather worries himself, into a state of incapacity. With such men the evil is constitutional, and would probably display itself whenever a sudden call of any kind was made upon them. I see no reason for adapting an Examination system to persons thus morbidly affected, indeed I believe this over-anxious temperament spreads when it is too much attended to. There is also a class of young men who have intellectual tastes and sometimes also thoughtfulness, but who fall short in energy, and robustness, and fortitude of mind. They will occupy themselves pleasurably with study, but are wanting in the volition required for an effort. These are apt to cry out against competitions which require *production* with accuracy and completeness; but to be forced to aim at this is just what such persons want. They need a strong stimulus to brace them to an effort: they are of the type of the men who go through life with some reputation for cleverness, but who have nothing to shew in the way of work done at the end of it. It is one of the advantages of a competition, that it reveals to us something about the relative strength of will and moral courage of the candidates. Moreover it pitches the whole tone of a young man's character in a higher key, for him to have some achievement, or some feat of endurance and self-command, effected in early life, to turn back to. When he has proved himself equal to an occasion once, he is less likely to shrink from a call afterwards (see p. 26).

As to the arrangement, then, of the names of candidates in the lists resulting from Examinations, I conclude as follows:

When the Examinations are in the higher parts of learning, or when, as in Professional Examinations, the learner means to make use of the knowledge under review, the names in the classes should be in alphabetical order. The more classes the candidates are divided into, the more the Examination list will tell us about the acquirements of an individual; the more in fact the list will approximate to an order of merit.

In Natural and Moral Science, and when various subjects are included (see p. 366), no close determination of relative merit can be effected, so that, even though we should view our Examination as educational, we must be content with an alphabetical arrangement in numerous classes, or what comes nearly to the same thing, but is sometimes more convenient, with an arrangement in a few classes, each class being broken up into two or more brackets.

We now come to Examinations used to assist education. These we want to make available as means of selection, in order to avoid having our education warped, by youths being trained for competitions which are not framed in the interest of education. To effect this the results must be put into as close an order of merit as they can justly be. Moreover, for purely educational purposes, we require to supply motives of exertion to the student, so long, *but so long only*, as the student is of an age to be regarded as in a state of pupillage.

A list in order of merit supplies a continuous stimulant throughout. If a prize or a loss of prospects, dependent on a small difference, be of too much importance, this may produce a feverish action. In order to obviate this, emoluments should be of moderate value, and a *locus poenitentiae* afforded when possible. But the advantage of a continuous stimulus I hold to counterbalance the evils in most cases for the *young*. When a list is broken up into alphabetical classes, its action as a stimulus is intermittent, and it only operates *up to the standard* for admission to the first class. A student says, "I feel sure of a second class, and I know I cannot get a first." He then reads in a languid way, and the more so from *reaction*, because *until he felt sure* of his second class he was as much acted on by competition as though the classification were in order of merit. Hence, this plan causes alternate fits of excitement and languor. It is true that though classes are alphabetical, rumors get about. The successful man hears from some one that he is one of the "best first classes" in his year: but this kind of uncertain report is useless for selection, and is in all ways unwholesome. To prevent the higher men stagnating at the level of the bottom of the first class, some future competition, perhaps one for Fellowships, has to be brought into sight.

A third course is possible; it is to arrange the first class alphabetically or in two brackets, and the others in order of merit. This may be supported on the ground that with the higher men the Examination is a test of knowledge regarded as valuable in itself, and for the others a test of scholastic diligence. A *small* first class may be alphabetically arranged on the ground of the knowledge shewn being that of the *savant* in a certain degree: but it is very desirable that the lower classes should be arranged in order of merit as much as possible; for the students who fill these classes need all the stimulus that can be applied, and are not likely to be driven to over-reading. If the lower classes are alphabetically arranged they act as a mere pass Examination, and the aim of the students may then be to do as little as possible consistently with avoiding rejection. The third class in the Classical Tripos at Cambridge was at one time classed alphabetically, and the effect was very unsatisfactory.

One other point connected with close classification has to be mentioned. It is not thought fair to class one who has had four years of University study along with those who have had only three. This consideration had more force formerly than it has now, because tutors are found in many places who can bring a student forward as well as if he were at the University. There is still, however, some advantage got from long residence, so that a person might sometimes improve his degree by waiting for another year. This at Cambridge is not allowed, unless evidence is brought to shew that the student has been prevented from reading during this time by illness. He may then get permission to "degrade," as it is technically called. Here we have a singular instance of the importance attached to the obtaining places as compared with that of obtaining education, for the student is discouraged from reading what is best for him, and forced to take an ordinary degree, that he may not prejudice others. The rule was made early in this century. A more reasonable limit would be one of *age*, so that a person should not be allowed to compete *for a place* after a certain time of life.

At Oxford of course no such rule exists, as the alphabetical arrangement renders it unnecessary. The object of the rule might be very easily obtained without preventing those who have passed the proper age or standing from presenting themselves, or discouraging them from study. Their names might be appended to the *class* they gain, not put in any *place*, but alphabetically in a list at the end of the Wranglers or Senior Optimes, or whatever the appropriate class might be. I allow that it is not desirable to induce persons to *decline* Examinations at the last moment, but the penalty of getting *no place*, but only a *class*, with a mark indicating that they were superannuated for competition would meet the case.

The use of *viva voce* Examinations must not be altogether omitted, although they are spoken of at the end of Chapter IV. It is difficult to employ them on a large scale, because they are costly in time, and therefore in money.

In a *viva voce* Examination there ought to be not less than two Examiners present, and the Examination of each candidate in an important subject should last at least twenty minutes, but the number of candidates in almost all Examinations is now so large that the time required and the consequent expense of the Examination would be very considerable. The chief use of *viva voce* is to oblige the student to shew the state of his knowledge ; and it is more effective for finding out unsoundness and latent ignorance than for judging between the ablest men. When the candidates are examined with a view to some practical employment, the readiness and brightness of the candidate, brought out by *viva voce*, may properly go in his favor. We hear much of the allowances to be made for nervousness, but I have seldom known men of real knowledge or ability incapacitated by nervousness.

In pass Examinations *viva voce* is of great use ;

nothing so much defeats "cram." If unseen passages in classics cannot be given, *viva voce* should be more largely employed, but I fear its expensiveness will interfere with its coming into commoner use.

I will take this opportunity of remarking on the *expense of Examinations.* Those which are carried on in the Universities are defrayed by the Examinees themselves in the form of fees to the University, and, owing to the residence of Examiners in the University, this expense is comparatively small. When candidates have to go to a particular place for Examination the expense is great, and increases with the length of the Examination; hence the tendency to drop *viva voce,* and otherwise to shorten Examinations, which diminishes their trustworthiness. If 500 candidates attend a Government Examination in London, they may have to spend £10 each in the Examination fee, railway fare, lodging and maintenance. This amounts to a tax of £5000 a year on a certain class, paid for the sole purpose of enabling the patronage to be fairly dispensed: this is worth consideration. If Educational Examinations conducted at the schools could be turned to account, a considerable saving might be effected.

I need say but a few words on the marking and classing in Pass or Qualifying Examinations. It is usually necessary to insist on a pass in each subject separately, otherwise candidates may neglect some of the subjects. It is also desirable to exclude those who shew great "general debility" throughout. The best system seems to be to lay down a *minimum* in each subject, such as two-fifths of the full marks, and a higher standard, perhaps a half or three fifths, for the aggregate; a person would then fail altogether, who fell below the mark in a single subject, or who did not obtain the higher standard in his aggregate. Sometimes optional subjects are introduced in which the candidate is not obliged to pass, but which will yield him marks; these are sometimes allowed to reckon in his aggregate, so as to save him from failure, sometimes not so, but only to raise him in the Lists.

Pass Examination Lists, it may be observed, should be divided into Classes, in order to give scope for gaining a little credit. "Pass men" are keen for such distinctions, and we ought to take advantage of this. If we have an undivided alphabetical List the Candidates have no inducement to do more than is required for passing. Indeed, the man who narrowly escapes through, thinks he has done better for himself than other people, because he has attained what he wanted at less cost. Pass Examinations with a low standard are very injurious to education. When a notoriously weak man passes, his class-fellows lose respect for the Examination; and if reports circulate that A. or B. has been let through on answering a small portion of the paper, the standard of preparation immediately falls.

Pass Examinations have two leading objects: (1) to sift out incapacity; (2) to provide an educational course for persons of moderate ability: such persons are so numerous that their case demands great attention. Examinations which are preliminary to professional courses are supposed to aim at object (1), and also to ensure some sort of liberal education, but they are commonly too low to effect these purposes.

In a University course for an Ordinary Degree the chief object is mental discipline. Many youths on coming to College have little use of any faculties but the verbal memory; often they have great difficulty in concentrating attention, and much time is taken up in getting their brains into working order.

Subjects must therefore be chosen, not for their value as acquirements, but for their aptitude for forcing the pupil to do something else than learn by heart. The *form* of the subject, too, must be such that it can be given a portion at a time, and that the teacher can see whether the pupil has really done his part. Since we want to give *a habit*, the work will take *time;* for nearly the whole good got by a *Pass man* seems to come in his third year.

We want our subjects then to occupy a certain time, and we desire that they should be read steadily throughout this time, and not carried through by a rush at the last. This is notoriously very hard to effect. One difficulty is to oblige the student to read the whole of the book that is given. If he can get through with two-fifths of the marks he may think that he need only read half the book. If the subjects depend on consecutive reasoning, like Mathematics or Political Economy, our object may be effected by letting it be understood that the latter parts of the book will yield the most marks, for the student must read the earlier parts in order to understand the latter; but if the subject does not proceed by steps this cannot be done.

The German plan is to set only one question or passage; but the Pass students, though they may be twenty years old, are still at the Gymnasium, where they are forced to read the complete works : if youths were left to themselves, it is to be feared that they would read only "likely parts," and trust to fortune.

If we oblige students to pass separately in small portions of their work — each book, for instance, of Euclid, or of their classical author — we overwhelm them with worry, and drive them to private tutors, to *see that they know* their books "all round." Perhaps the best plan is, to have frequent Examinations with short subjects, and a more comprehensive one, gathering up the principal matters, at the end of the course. In fact, for the Pass men the criterion lies, not in their passing a particular Examination, but in their completing a *course*. The test is rather *moral* than intellectual, it is one of *conduct*, it turns on their having been able to get their work done by stated times when they were *left to themselves to do it*. The value of the B.A. depends on this last condition. A boy at home or at school can be put through all the Pass University Examinations, but is not a bit the more a University student — his tastes, propensities and will have not had room to grow. The essence of University life is free scope for individual development. The actual Examinations are of secondary importance, they are of use as shewing that the man has done what he had to do in one condition of life, and may therefore be expected to do it in another. A student at a tutor's may be forced through all the Examinations of a course *in a lump*, but this represents no education at all. All the sides of his mind but one are left blank. All his energies have been given to this special preparation. He may have learnt as well as he could have done at College, but he has *done nothing else*. His life has remained folded up, he has been absorbed in a master object, his time has been ruled by others; so when the germ at last breaks the husk, there is no knowing how it may turn out. With the University Pass man the Examinations are only among the *incidents* of three years of growing life; a nature of his own has burst out, he has chosen friends for himself; his character, good or bad, has taken shape, and people can now judge fairly what he is worth. Sometimes a student after some failures leaves the University and works up the subjects in the country with a tutor. He then passes: but this passing is of no real value. He has failed from *weakness* of character, and this weakness, for all we know, continues. For a man to order his own time, to resist temptations, to keep punctually to his College engagements, and pass all his Examinations, moderate as they are, at proper intervals throughout three years, when living in a state of great freedom, is something to his credit; but that he should have been able to get up a certain amount of matter with a tutor always at hand, and no temptation or conflicting interest near, shows only that he has some little power of acquiring.

APPENDIX A.

I THINK it will be useful to give some Extracts from that part of the Third Report of the Royal Commission on Scientific Instruction and the Advancement of Science which refers to Fellowships at the Universities, and I shall add a few notes. Some readers will require to be made acquainted with the principal differences in the circumstances under which Fellowships are acquired and held at Oxford and at Cambridge.

At Oxford the commonest mode of electing is to hold an open Examination, generally conducted by the College authorities or by Examiners engaged by them. In many cases it is made a necessary qualification for a candidate that he should have obtained a First Class in one of the Honour Schools.

At Cambridge there is an Examination at Trinity College, open to all members of the College and in certain cases open to the University. At other Colléges the University Examinations and Prizes are taken as tests of competency.

Each Society may, however, satisfy themselves as to the qualification of a person by his performances in science or literature, or by a special Examination if they think fit, as has been done for persons who have been ill at the time of the University Examinations. The desire to avoid jobbery has led the Colleges to cling rather closely to the published decisions of the University Examinations; but there is not, in any case that I know of, as Undergraduates sometimes suppose, a "hard and fast" line as to what constitutes a Fellowship Degree.

After stating these differences in the modes of election, the Commissioners observe as follows:

164. "This last remark leads us on to another important difference between the two Universities. At Oxford the Fellowships of each College are filled up in accordance with the results of a competitive Examination held by the College, but open (when the Fellowship is subject to no clerical restriction) to all members of the University who have passed the Examinations required for the degree of Bachelors of Arts, and in many cases open also to all Graduates of any University in the United Kingdom. At Cambridge, on the other hand, those Colleges which award their Fellowships according to the result of a Fellowship Examination, open the Examination, as a rule, only to members of the College, though the Statutes give power to the Governing Body, on any occasion when they think fit, to throw open the Examination to mem-

bers of the University. At the smaller Colleges it is generally understood that the electors look in the first instance to members of their own College; and in case there be no candidate of sufficient merit, or the needs of the College require a Fellow having some special qualifications not found among the otherwise eligible members of the College itself, they then 'go out of College,' as it is called, that is, elect to the Fellowship a member of some other College.

165. "At Oxford, where the Examinations for Degrees are not competitive, it would be difficult to suggest any mode of electing to Fellowships other than that by competitive Examination; but at Cambridge, where the names in the Honour lists are arranged in order of merit, there is something to be said on both sides with respect to the desirableness or otherwise of special Fellowship Examinations. On the one hand, the wider study which such a system demands, enlarges the foundation which lies at the base of a subsequent career of professional activity or original research, as the case may be; and means are afforded of remedying the result of accidental failure in a final examination, such as might arise from temporary illness or other similar cause. On the other hand, it is urged with great force that by the time a man has taken his degree, supposing him to have been industrious while an Undergraduate, he has had enough of study pursued with a view to the immediate production of his knowledge at a moment's notice; and that he should then be left free to pursue his studies in a more systematic and specialized manner, and his originality should be no longer cramped by preparation for an impending Examination. We attach great importance to this freedom from the immediate pressure of Examination at such a stage of the student's progress, and are disposed to regard the advantages, which may attend the holding of special Fellowship Examinations as too dearly purchased by its sacrifice. But whatever differences may exist in the system of election to Fellowships in the two Universities, we think it very desirable that in both of them alike original research should be encouraged by taking into account any evidence of power in this direction which a candidate for a Fellowship is able to give."

There is a difference in the rules at the two Universities with regard to the celibacy of Fellows. At Oxford, Fellows are not allowed to marry excepting when the Fellowship is attached to some important office. At Cambridge the restriction to celibacy has been abolished in four of the seventeen Colleges, and modified in some others. The Commissioners consider with reason that celibacy might be enforced on such of the Junior Fellows who from their offices must reside in College so as to be readily accessible to students and to preserve order. I should attach this obligation to the *office*, and not to the Fellowship.

At Oxford the Fellowships are commonly held until vacated by marriage or the acceptance of College preferment; and at Cambridge most of the clerical ones are so still, but the lay Fellowships are usually terminable. Fellowships may in some cases be held for an additional period as pensions for a term of College work.

I have given the above extract in this place, because some readers may first want to know how it is that persons come to be Fellows of

Colleges. I now give the general remarks on the subject from an earlier part of the Report.

139. "The following are the chief purposes to which in our judgment the Fellowships should be applied.

"In the first place a certain but not a very large proportion of the Fellowships will be always required, as at present, for the payment of the persons entrusted with the management of the College estates, and with the government and administration of the Colleges themselves.

"Secondly, a large number of the Fellowships is at present employed, and probably a still larger number ought hereafter to be employed, in connexion with the Instruction given in the Colleges.

"Thirdly, a smaller, but still a considerable number of Fellowships ought to be employed as Terminable Prize Fellowships.

"Fourthly, a certain number of Fellowships ought, as we have already said, to be united with Professorships in the University; the University Professor becoming *ex officio* a Fellow of the College and a member of its Governing Body.

"Lastly, it is, in our opinion, most important that a certain number of Fellowships should be appropriated to the Direct Promotion of Learning and Research in various directions. It has been objected to this proposal that the Fellowship system, as hitherto administered, has not shown any great tendency to encourage Original Research, either in the field of learning or in that of science; that, when an office is created simply and solely with the view of giving a man leisure and opportunity for original research, there is always the appearance, to say the least, of creating a sinecure; and that it is impossible, as Professor Jowett has said, to get a man for money who can make a discovery. But, though you cannot get a man for money to make a discovery, you may enable a man who has shown a special capacity for research to exert his powers; and we are of opinion that unless an effort is made to do this, one of the great purposes for which learned bodies, such as the Colleges, exist, may run the risk of being wholly lost sight of. Scientific discoveries rarely bring any direct profit to their authors, nor is it desirable that original investigation should be undertaken with a view to immediate pecuniary results. 'Research,' as Lord Salisbury has observed, 'is unremunerative: it is highly desirable for the community that it should be pursued, and, therefore, the community must be content that funds should be set aside to be given, without any immediate and calculable return in work, to those by whom the research is to be pursued.'

"It may be that properly qualified candidates for such scientific offices would not at first be numerous, but we believe that eventually a considerable number of Fellowships might be advantageously devoted to the encouragement of Original Research.

140. "We think that such Fellowships as might be expressly destined for the advancement of Science and Learning should only be conferred on men who by their successful labors have already given proof of their earnest desire, and of their ability to promote knowledge; and we believe that appointments, made with a due regard to this principle, would be abundantly justified by results. A man who has once acquired the habit of original scientific work, is very unlikely ever to lose it excepting through a total failure of his health and strength; and even if it

occasionally happened that a Fellowship awarded on the grounds of merit, as shown in original research, should only contribute to the comfort of the declining years of an eminent man of science, there are many persons who would feel that it could not have been better expended in any other way.

141. "We should not wish to attach any educational duties properly so called to a Fellowship awarded with a view of encouraging Original Research in Science. But for many reasons we should think it desirable that the holder of such a Fellowship should be expected to give an account, from time to time, in the form of public discourses, of the most recent researches in his own department of science.

142. "We now proceed to offer some suggestions with regard to one of the most difficult questions relating to the Fellowships, the Conditions of their Tenure. In doing so, we think it desirable to treat separately the cases of Fellowships held by those who aspire to make their way in the outer world, and by those who look to an University career.

143. "In the case of the former, or non-resident class, the tenure of the Fellowship should, as we have already said, be limited to a term of years; and we are disposed to think that a term of seven years would suffice for every useful purpose. In the case of such terminable Fellowships, held by non-residents; the restriction of celibacy which, originating doubtless in the celibacy of the Clergy, has been very generally retained as a means of leading to a more rapid succession, becomes unmeaning, and ought, we think, to be removed.

144. "The most important use of the latter, or resident class of Fellowships, is to enable the Universities to retain a large staff of able teachers and workers.

145. "From the evidence before us it appears that the Colleges find some difficulty in obtaining efficient tutors and lecturers. Professor Jowett observes, 'We have always a great difficulty about teachers. In fact, at Oxford the whole thing seems to require to be re-constituted; there is such a difficulty in keeping the best men there, and they stay for so short a time. If we are to keep men as teachers, we must get rid of the condition of celibacy.'

146. "There are other difficulties, which are not adverted to by Professor Jowett in these remarks, besides that occasioned by the restriction to celibacy. One of them is that in endeavoring to obtain teachers not only do the Colleges, to a certain extent, bid against one another, but each College bids against itself. A College offers a distinguished man, shortly after he has taken his degree, an income say of £250 a year as a Fellow, and of £250 a year additional as a Lecturer, so that, in fact, the College offers him £500 a year if he will stay and be a teacher, but at the same moment it offers him £250 a year even if he goes away. Under these circumstances we can hardly wonder that the inducements offered by tutorships and lectureships are not sufficient even in the first instance to command the services of the men whom it would be most desirable to retain; and the difficulty is greatly increased by the further fact that as the University system is at present organized the teaching offices in the Colleges do not offer any very inviting prospect of further advancement.

147. "A man who accepts a Fellowship and a Lectureship in a College will find that at the end of 20 years of service he is much less fit for the special work in which he has been engaged than he was when

he began it, and probably he will also find that he has not been in the meantime preparing himself for any other occupation for which he would be more suitable, and in which he might obtain larger emoluments. In former times, when the connection between Fellowships and the obligation to take Holy Orders was almost universal, the difficulty, which is here referred to did not arise. It was met by the system of College Livings. It was then the most natural thing in the world for a young clergyman to devote himself for nine or ten years to giving instruction in Classics and Theology, and if work of this kind was not continued too long, it was generally thought to form no bad preparation for the duties of a parish priest. But at the present time the Fellowships are very largely held by laymen, and there appears, for some reason, to be a growing disinclination on the part of the men who now engage in tuition in the Colleges to take Holy Orders. Thus the layman who becomes a College Tutor or Lecturer finds himself entirely cut off from every other profession, and dependent exclusively upon that of teaching, the great prizes of which are to be found in the Public Schools and not in the Colleges, inasmuch as the Professorships are too few in number to offer much prospect of promotion within the University, while the Headships are still to a greater extent restricted to clergymen. It is not surprising, under these circumstances, that there is a widespread feeling in the Universities that the tutorial system is falling into a state of disorganization. It is felt that the College Tutorships and Lectureships do no lead to any permanent positions in the end, although they are, perhaps, a little too highly paid at the beginning, if, at least, we regard the Fellowship as part payment for the work done. What is wanted is a graduated succession of offices, such as would make the business of a College Tutor a profession which an able and distinguished young man might embrace without imprudence.

148. "To a certain extent this want has been already supplied, in both Universities, by the increase which has recently taken place in the number and value of the Professorships. But, as we have already seen, these offices are still so few, and, in some cases, so poorly endowed as to offer little inducement to a man to look forward to an University career. Further, we do not think that an University office is in every case the most fitting reward for a man who has shown himself eminently useful in College work.

149. "We are, therefore, of opinion that it is to Offices within the Colleges that we must mainly look for inducements to able and useful men to devote themselves to College work. We think that one who has proved his success as an Educator, might fitly be elected to a Permanent (or, as we shall here call it, a Senior) Fellowship, which should be free from the restriction of celibacy, though subject, as a rule, to the condition of residence in the University and of readiness to take some part in the work of the College or the University.

150. "A Senior Fellowship would also (in accordance with the recommendation already made) be fitly conferred on the ground of Services rendered to Science or Learning by Original Research.

151. "The question remains, what should be the status of a resident Fellow who aspires to a Senior Fellowship?

152. "An advantage attending the old system of tenure undoubtedly is, that while it does not offer a man a permanent provision unless he looks forward to leading a life of celibacy, it yet permits him to apply

his mind to any course of study, free from all care as to his immediate future. We fear that the anxieties attending a short tenure would have the effect of discouraging men from engaging in Original Research; and even in the less uncertain career of Education, we fear that the prospect of election to a Senior Fellowship would be so uncertain that unless a considerably longer tenure were allowed to Probationary (or, as we will now call them, Junior) Fellows than would suffice for non-residents engaging in professions, the University would be drained of its best men.

153. "On the other hand, if there were no counterbalancing advantages in a non-resident Fellowship, we fear the effect might be to cause men to linger on at the University who would do better to engage at once in a profession. We think, therefore, it might be advisable for the individual Colleges to make such an adjustment between the advantages of the two kinds of Fellowships as should preserve a due balance in their attractiveness.

154. "The Junior Fellows might be expected to reside in College, and thereby aid in preserving the discipline of the place. Accordingly, the retention of a Junior Fellowship might in the discretion of the College be subject to the restriction of celibacy.

155. "While it is only right to give a Junior Fellow ample time for exhibiting his capacity for an University career, it seems highly desirable to allow a Fellow who had preferred the junior to the non-resident tenure, but who afterwards found that he was not suited for University Work or Original Investigation, and had small chance of promotion, to engage without delay in some promotion independent of the University. We should, therefore, allow a Junior Fellow the option of stepping on to the non-resident tenure, in which case the same proportion of the whole time of tenure of a non-resident might be allowed to him as remained to him of his time of tenure as a junior. The option of a newly-elected Fellow to be placed on the non-resident tenure, or of a junior to transfer himself to the non-resident class, should be limited by the restriction that there be at least a certain number of juniors, so as to preserve a sufficient staff of Fellows resident in College.

156. "The questions relating to the tenure of Fellowships, which we have now discussed, have been incidentally brought under our notice in various parts of the evidence which we have taken. These questions are also raised in a Memorial submitted to the First Lord of the Treasury, by a large number of influential resident members of the University of Cambridge, a copy of which has been forwarded to us, and will be found in the Appendix to this Report.

157. "We are convinced that the future interests of Scientific Study and Research at the two Universities must of necessity be greatly affected by any changes that may be made in the tenure of the Fellowships, and, consequently, in the Constitution of the Governing Bodies of the Colleges. But as we have not taken a complete body of evidence on this subject, and as we consider that any attempt to do so would lead us into inquiries beyond the scope of our Commission, we shall abstain from offering any detailed recommendations with regard to these important questions. We desire, however, to express our conviction that if the Colleges are to become, to a greater degree than in times past, the homes of men distinguished for Original Research in Science, provision must be made for attaching such men in a permanent manner

to the College Foundations, and for rendering them permanent members of the Governing Bodies.

158. "The following proposals appear to us to sum up the results of the preceding discussion. To adapt them to the case of some of the smaller foundations, important modifications would be required; and, even in the case of the larger Colleges, we should wish them to be regarded only in the light of suggestions, which we feel to be worthy of attention, but at the same time to be by no means free from objection.

"(1) That there should be three classes of Fellows, which we have distinguished as Senior, Junior, and Non-resident.

"(2) That the Senior Fellowships should be permanent, and free from the restriction of celibacy, but subject, as a general rule, to the condition of residence in the University and readiness to take some part in the work of the College or University.

"(3) That the elections to the Seniority should, in ordinary cases, be made from the class of Juniors, but should not be limited to that class.

"(4) That the Junior Fellowships should be tenable for, say fourteen years, and should be subject to such restrictions as to residence in College and duties as may appear desirable to the several Colleges.

"(5) That the Non-resident Fellowships should be tenable for about half that time, free from all restrictions.

"(6) That a person elected to an Ordinary (as distinguished from a Senior) Fellowship should have the option of being placed on the junior or non-resident tenure, and that a Junior Fellow should at any time be at liberty to place himself on the non-resident tenure (but not conversely), with a proportionate allowance for the unexpired portion of his time of holding his Fellowship as Junior Fellow; provided that the number of Junior Fellows be not suffered to sink below a certain minimum.

159. "The effect of these proposals would be to constitute in each College a seniority of a very permanent kind, because its members would hold their places for life, and would be free from the restriction of celibacy. Whatever share in the government of the College it might be thought proper to assign tö the holders of the terminable Junior Fellowships, it is evident that the influence of such a permanent seniority would be very great, and that the prosperity of the College would depend in great measure on its constitution. According to the above proposals (taken in connection with the recommendations we have already made), the seniority in each College would consist (i) of University Professors officially attached to the College; (ii) of persons elected for eminent services to Learning or Science; (iii) of men who had given some of the best years of their lives to the service of the College, and had proved their fitness for College work. It would be for the Universities and the Colleges to consider whether a body so constituted would be in all respects suitable for the important functions it would have to discharge. In particular, it would be worthy of careful consideration whether such a seniority should be allowed to appoint its own members by co-optation, or whether the whole body of Fellows should elect, or whether the filling up of vacancies should be vested in some authority external to the College; or, lastly, whether some course intermediate between these several modes of procedure should be adopted."

The suggestions (in Sec. 139) agree in the main with my own views, but I would make a clearer distinction between the Fellowship which gives a voice in the government of the College and the mere *prize* Fellowship, which I have called a "Studentship." The holder of a Studentship might of course be employed as a Lecturer by the authority at the head of the educational department. This might be the Master of the College or a Council, but he should be simply engaged as a stipendiary. The higher officers of the College occupied in conducting education or maintaining discipline should, I conceive, be *ex officio* members of the Governing Body.

I am not sanguine of a harvest of great achievements from the " endowment of research;" but the University, by encouraging undertakings which only want assiduity and intelligence, by setting afoot, for instance, the framing of Books of Reference in various departments of learning — a point in which we are much worse provided than Germany — or by issuing carefully-executed editions of erudite works, might keep together a body of literary men by paying for results with only moderate retaining pensions. An inducement to exertion in some special direction must be held out, or some definite employment must be provided. A person who has no motive for exertion may, no doubt, study for his own pleasure, but this is another thing from prosecuting work that the world will be the better for.

The question of remuneration has become a most important one. When Fellows of Colleges were clergymen, there were few careers open to them, and the current pay of clerical work afforded a standard for that of College work; but now a young man of high degree looks to the large prizes to be obtained in active life as depicted by youthful hopes.

The question now, is not "What is a sufficient return for so much work?" but "On what terms can we secure the services of the men we want?" First-class ability of all kinds is in good demand, and some varieties of it fetch higher prices than others. The maintaining of discipline, for instance, is unpleasant, and it requires energy, conscientiousness, promptitude of decision, kindliness and judgment; but those who possess these qualities allied with high cultivation are suited for many high positions. Their possessor soon finds his value. Even if he would himself prefer staying at the University, he may feel it imperative on him to attend to the wishes and interests of his family. There will be more difficulty in keeping the Universities well provided with a disciplinal and administrative staff equal to their increasing needs, than in attaching to them men of literary or scientific pursuits.

But not only have Colleges now to go into the open market to obtain Lecturers, but they really, as is said in section 146, raise the market against themselves; for by giving large annuities, free from duties to young men, they enable them to take pleasant positions of moderate profit which they would not otherwise have accepted. Many Fellows of Colleges take *school* work, and it is sometimes urged that exceptional privileges should be allowed to those who do so, as being engaged in education. But the funds of an establishment must first be applied to the purposes of that establishment. If they may be put to any uses that are beneficial, they may be dissipated by being, thereby, spread over a very large area. If a Fellow of a College is not a better man for the purpose of assistant master than the school could otherwise get for the pay it gives, then education does not benefit by his taking the place; and if he is better, the persons who benefit are the parents of the boys. Now these persons in the case of the public schools, to which these remarks chiefly apply, are the most opulent class of the country.

The remarks of Sect. 147 are most just; the concluding sentences point out a cause of discontent. Since the Fellowship is a fixed sum, College Lecturers are at starting rich compared with their contemporaries, but the ultimate prospect is insufficient. The question of retiring pensions will be a very serious one. The change from a clerical to a lay body has been very costly. The College livings, which took off the College Tutors in middle life, answered the purpose of retirements, but now they answer this purpose only in a few cases. College Tutors who find themselves fathers of families will not retire when they have ceased to be effective, unless handsome retirements are provided. The same difficulty exists in the case of Professors in all Universities, and also in the Government Public Offices, and I think that the scale of retiring allowances in use in these last may be found serviceable as a guide.

The difficulty will be to find *capital*, as the Colleges have no ready money, while Examination Halls, Scientific Workshops, and above all, buildings for the reception of more students are much needed. Cambridge at present is over-full. The prices of lodgings are too high. Students coming up on short notice in October are forced to go into undesirable quarters, and are glad to get a room at all. The lodging-house keepers have the upper hand of the Tutors. This is a great trouble and a very ancient one. Hostels, we find, were set up in the earliest days to avoid the *extortion of the townspeople*. Probably the townspeople got no more than a fair return for what they gave. In every town there must be some spare accommodation, there are interstices, as it were, which can be occupied without much cost. While this lasts, lodgings are cheap in a University town; but afterwards houses are built, not because the fixed town population wants more room, but on purpose for lodgings. People come to the place to make a living by keeping lodging-houses. Then we have a sudden rise in price, because the whole rent of the house is to be made out of the lodgings, and we have also to pay *wages of superintendence;* the landlords have to be maintained, in great part at least, by the profits. At Cambridge the superintendence is difficult; many tradesmen are giving up lodgers as not being worth the trouble; restrictions must be imposed in order to see that students keep reasonable hours, and sanitary regulations as to water supply, &c. are now being enforced under the charge of an Inspector appointed on purpose. All this costs money; an ! as the lodgings are not occupied more than seven months—for in the Long Vacation all the students come in to the Colleges—and ground is limited, there turns will not be good enough to induce more building, unless, the rents be very high. The Licensing Board attempts to prevent the rents being immoderate, and, as a fact, insufficent building of lodgings, compared to our necessities, takes place. Many Colleges have still room to build, some are engaged in building, and large Hostels may be erected on a joint-stock principle; but without extensive building the increase of our numbers must soon stop. The large proportion of students in lodgings is beginning to be found a serious inconvenience. Considerable additions are wanted also for the Halls and Lecture-rooms of the Colleges, and, if the College system is to be maintained in efficiency, College funds should be devoted to these needs before creating any Professorships which are not absolutely needed.

This difficulty about lodgings is not confined to England: Berlin, from the high price of lodgings, has lost a large number of its students who have gone to Leipzig for cheapness.

(Sect. 158.) I think that the two classess of Fellows here spoken of would cause complications. I would have it made quite clear whether a man gets his pay as a prize or for work done. Much difficulty comes from the two being confused.

No person, whether be be called a Student or Junior Fellow, should be in a position to consider that he had *rights* to any tutorial office, or that he was aggrieved by being passed over. The supreme educational authority should be as free in engaging its officers as is the Head Master of a school. The superior officers, Tutors, Deans, and Bursars, should be *ex officio* Fellows, and therefore members of the Governing Body, but they should lay down this position with their office, unless they were transferred into non-official Fellowships, see p. 321. But a pensioned official would not, as a rule, remain a Fellow, according to my view.

The Seniority described in section 159 would consist too exclusively of men advanced in life to constitute by itself a good Governing Body. The object should be to preserve a due proportion of old and young. The admission of the College officers into this " Seniority " and the removal of those who accepted retirements would keep it on a level with the general body of the University in point of the standing of its members.

APPENDIX B.

ON FELLOWSHIPS AS "LADDERS."

THE action of Fellowships as "ladders" enabling young men to enter on various careers hardly comes under the notice of the Scientific Commission. This side of the question has, however, a great interest for some classes of the community. Mr. Henry Sidgwick, of Trinity College, Cambridge, deals with this topic in a very able article, headed "Idle Fellowships," in the *Contemporary Review* of April, 1876. I must refer my readers especially to the statistics there given as to the lines of life followed by the non-resident Fellows of Colleges. Mr. Sidgwick points out conclusively that Society gets no return for subsidizing the Masters of School Boarding-Houses, School Inspectors, or those who are engaged in other practical vocations. The Bar, he observes, is the Profession, in which such "Ladders" are supposed to operate most advantageously. A few cases in which striking service is rendered catch the eye of the public, but Mr. Sidgwick is not inclined to believe that the great men who are instanced, would have remained in obscurity if a Fellowship had not come to their aid; that by College help, men, not of marked forensic ability, should get called to the Bar, Mr. Sidgwick rightly regards as a doubtful good to themselves and to the Profession. He allows that it is desirable to have the best ability of the country to choose from in selecting the Judges of the Highest Courts and the Law-Officers of the Crown. Mr. Sidgwick thinks that it is rather the business of the corporations who have the supervision of the Bar, to draw first-rate talent to their Profession by offering some provision at starting to those who have shewn evidence of superior powers.

The connection of the English Bar, however, with the Universities is supported by a strong sentiment, and this sentiment can give an account of itself. It is a distinguishing feature of English Society, that men in high positions are so often persons of great general cultivation. Provision might be made whereby a College, with the consent of the Visitor or of a large majority of the body, could extend the tenure of a Studentship where they saw unusual promise of professional success, or even, at particular Colleges, such promise might, in a marked case, be admitted as a ground of election to one of the Terminable Fellowships spoken of in p. 321.

Mr. Sidgwick pronounces against all Prize emoluments except those which go to maintain the Student during his course. I agree with the general tenor of his remarks so far as they apply to the prospect of an immediate return in money for the highest kinds of study; these ought to have some charm of their own, and are degraded by being viewed as directly marketable commodities. But some criterion must be found for deciding whether these attainments are possessed, because the fitness of persons for certain posts depends on these attainments; the kind of Examination spoken of in p. 140, which would be far less competitive and less mechanical than those now in use, might serve the purpose. Those who did well might obtain Fellowships, not as rewards for what they had done in Examinations, but as places given them because they are proved competent to perform the duties. But though in this way the higher literary and scientific culture may lead to employment enough to provide for its genuine votaries, yet this is not the case with that kind of study which results only in what I have called *student knowledge*, see pp. 185–189. and it will be rarely that young men of 21 or 22 can attain much more. I do not, then, see my way to dispensing with some compensation to young men for the prolonged *education drill*, as Mr. Sidgwick calls it, which is necessary both for laying in the requisite scientific apparatus and for fitting the mind for thorough and accurate investigation. The want of this is often apparent even in men of great ability, whose learning has come late. Parents, especially those of the class whose attention is now being drawn to the Universities, and also youths themselves, are impatient of this preparation. A youth entering an office at 17, may find himself in the receipt of £120 to £180 a-year when he is 22. I find that men taking a business view of the matter expect some chance of direct advantage, equivalent to this income, to follow from the prolongation of study.

It may, then, be necessary to award, not Prize *Fellowships*, but Prize *Studentships*, as rewards for proficiency in the educational parts of the course, which I have proposed to separate, whenever it is possible, from the higher study intended for those meaning to pursue learning as an occupation for life, pp. 299, 300. In the case of those who proceed to these higher subsequent studies, the Studentships would actually support the learner during his prolonged course, for others they would serve as "Ladders," but they would be *short* ones, and less costly than Fellowships; they might require a little lengthening to afford access to the Bar, but would lend effectual assistance for admission to many callings. The expense of entering Professions in England is far greater than in Germany. It costs a large sum to "article" a youth to a

Solicitor or a Civil Engineer, and a heavy stamp-duty is levied in many cases: this seems to me an objectionable form of tax. To remove such artificial barrier is a legitimate form of giving assistance to promising youths, and unless such a removal be effected by external aid, the "Ladder" system which connects the lower with the upper strata, stops short of the tableland, on the top of the cliff, and only lands the climber on a narrow strip.

Considering the competition of Government appointments obtainable by Examination, of openings in business, of colonial enterprise, and the need for something like Fellowships which has been felt in Germany, where scientific and literary appointments are ten times as many as in England, and where the patience of young men in waiting for a post contrasts strongly with the hurry to be making money which prevails around us; I do not think it advisable at present, at any rate, to throw aside *all* rewards and trust to the love of learning and the respect for culture for keeping up the standard of our Schools and Universities. It may be observed that it will be almost impossible for any modification of Prize rewards to be made, unless by some central authority empowered to deal with both Universities and with the Colleges in each, for such modifications must be made on some general system. Our experience shews that the number of promising students at the different places of education is nearly proportional to what each has to give. If this is affected the distribution of such students will also be changed. No state in Europe could disarm by itself, and each would keep a keen eye on the peace establishments retained by its neighbors. Something may recall this to our minds when reductions in Fellowships and "Open Scholarships" in the several Colleges of the two Universities come under discussion.

APPENDIX C.

NOTES ON PROFESSORIAL TEACHING.

THE working of what is called the Professorial system may soon attract attention, and I therefore append some rough notes which I had made with a view to a chapter on Public Teaching in relation to Examinations. (See Preface, p. vii).

The Professorial system, as it is called, comprises a variety of different modes of teaching which have only this in common, that the teachers have the title of Professors. It is difficult to determine in what the essence of the system lies. According to one of many attempts that have been made to lay hold of such a *differentia*, it consists in the "teaching by the great authorities" in the various subjects.

As a matter of fact it can hardly be said that those who have the title of Professor are always superior in knowledge to other teachers who have it not. Neither are there many Universities in which the chief part of this teaching is carried on by the great authorities: it would be a waste of power if it were so; indeed if the time of such persons were spent in teaching, they would cease to be the great authorities in their departments. In Germany, the Privatdocenten do much of the lecturing, and still more of the closer kind of instruction; some of these are waiting to take the places of Professors.

That the great luminaries should have a voice in the public teaching is quite clear. They should exercise some control as to the mode in which a subject is presented, and take care that the latest views or discoveries are duly represented; but whether they should themselves be the teachers is a question. The duties of research and of instruction are each enough to occupy all a man's thoughts and interests. The *savant*, to keep abreast of his subject, must read all the new works, and look at numberless memoirs and scientific papers. His business is *avant tout* with science; that of the teacher is with his pupils, he must be familiar with the ways in which young people's minds act, and the difficulties in getting the kind of action wanted; he must understand how to keep interests alive, and must mistrust professions of comprehension. The *savant* and teacher are now and then, but only rarely, combined.

As science extends, and education becomes more directed to the forming of habits of mind, the more requisite will it be to separate the functions of *savant* and of teacher. Lecturing, in the sense of delivering a discourse *ex cathedra*, differs from teaching in this, that it only contains one of the two essential elements of instruction : these are, (1) to put before the pupil what it is desired he should know; (2) to see that he has rightly got hold of what has been given him. It is for want of this second element that what is called the Professorial system, when the teaching is not catechetical, has commonly broken down whenever the knowledge has had to be tested by Examination or in any other way.

The non-catechetical *ex cathedra* discourse has advantages for particular purposes; it partakes of the nature of preaching, and when a new view of a science is started, it is an effective means of kindling enthusiasm; it introduces the personal element more effectively than a book, and a great Lecturer may produce a considerable sensation; but then he must possess a combination of qualities which is likely to get rarer every day. He must be first-rate in knowledge of the matter he deals with; he must put himself in relation with his audience, and must understand what difficulties they are likely to find, a point in which the *savant* is often deficient; finally, he must be a good elocutionist. When a branch of learning has passed the Rhetorical stage, and its principles are accepted and contained in books, then the Professor must either dictate a *new* book or see that the pupils know existing ones, or take an intermediate course—commenting, amending, and questioning. Only the first plan can be adopted in what I have called the *ex cathedra* discourse, in contrast to the *catechetical* lecture in which the pupils are questioned, and which is only a higher form of *class-teaching*. I am not here speaking of *experimental* Lectures.

Mathematical Lecturers, when there were no books, dictated MS. to their pupils, and German students now take down word for word some of these Lectures, meaning to "put it all in" to the "Programm" or Dissertation which they will one day have to write. Such dictation is not *teaching* at all, and is superseded by the multiplication of books.

The *ex cathedra* Professorial Lecture, which is like the reading of a Dissertation, is common in Germany. Any number of persons can listen to it, while for a catechetical Lecture the class must be limited. In the Scotch Universities, the Lectures of the Professors are often catechetical, and are much like those that are given in the Colleges of the English Universities, and in the *Seminarium* of the German Universities, which is an establishment within the University for those who want to be prepared for the Examination for the *Diploma docendi*. The second function, *that of seeing that the pupil knows what has been given him*, is sometimes performed abroad by a *répétiteur*, who examines the class in what it has received from the Professor's lips a day or two before. A catechetical Lecturer is in part his own *répétiteur*; but Examinations, from time to time, will be required to supplement his questioning. A hardworking student may do this work for himself; he may rewrite his notes fully, and examine himself in what he has heard. Some persons find the listening to a lecture and taking notes extremely exhausting: those who have been used to learn from books feel this especially. The straining to catch the point, the distress when an important word is missed, and the twofold action of the mind in attending and abridging at the same time, is to them very distressing. Listening to what is called a popular lecture, without having to give an account of it afterwards, is pleasant enough.

At lectures in which experiments, or specimens, or objects of Art, are exhibited, the student's attention is kept alive by what he sees or does, and he gets from the lecture the illustrations which he could not get in any other way. In Natural and Experimental Science, lecturing must always be the principal mode of teaching; and where the necessary apparatus is costly, or particular skill is required for experimenting, the teaching will be monopolized by the Professor. In this way certain branches of learning will be *localised* in Universities. The student should not be merely *passive:* this is avoided where the Professor translates a book, also in Lectures *broken by discussions*, a useful form for small classes.

The student wants, however, not only persons who shall communicate *portions* of knowledge, and afford the requisite appliances, but he wants *continuous* direction in the way of study, and is much supported by feeling that some interest is taken in him. The weak point of German teaching, as was remarked to me by a Professor, is, that there is no one to direct a student as to what Lectures he had best attend; no one to see that he knows what he has been told; and above all, no one to act as his mentor, or who is called on to care for him personally in any degree; he is at one time attending one Lecturer, at another time, another; neither of them knows his name, or what course of study he is pursuing. Our College system can supply this; the Domestic element may form a valuable supplement to the teaching given in the courses conducted by Professors and Intercollegiate Lecturers. These classes of teachers now work together, and furnish satisfactory courses of teaching of a high order. Each College should, however, provide a teacher to take *general charge* of the progress of its pupils in each particular branch, whose business it should be to understand their mental constitution, to advise them, and ascertain how they get on. The Pass men, of course, must be wholly in the hands of the College, for with them everything depends on personal influence and on their feeling that the teacher has an interest in them: moreover, he must be accessible, so that they may readily bring their difficulties to him.

The Science Commission recommend that all the Professors should lecture, but they cannot provide for there being anybody to listen to them. Some might find themselves without an audience, and yet they might do good work without lecturing. If a Professor were to call together the Lecturers in his branch of study once or twice a term, and inform them of anything of importance done in his branch of learning, or of any improvements in modes of teaching his subject, or of the views he wishes to see enforced, he would do good work. The actual teachers are too much taken up in the drudgery of their daily business to look far abroad: it is only in the Vacations that they can carry on their own reading, and even then many have pupils or Examinations to attend to, so that a system exclusively in their hands would be apt to run on in the same lines. Here the man of matured learning, whith leisure secured for study, should step in.

It should be understood, when a Professor is appointed, whether he is intended for teaching, or for superintendence of studies and research. It would be well to have different names for the different offices. If he be intended to be a teacher, his income should depend, in some degree, on his fees. Where we wish a man's mental interest to be, there his pecuniary interest should lie also. The Professors and all endowed Lecturers would, I conclude, agreeably to the recommendation of the Cambridge Syndicate, be prohibited from taking private pupils; otherwise the endowment might become a mere subsidy to a private tutor. If research is really desired, some inducement must be held out to the Fellows and Professors to pursue it. The University might be enabled to grant a very limited number of Professorships Extraordinary or University Fellowships, as, in fact, good service Pensions, accompanied by an Honorary Degree. The prospect of these would have an effect. The Colleges have, in a measure, performed this function of late by awarding Fellowships to distinguished Professors.

There has been, lately, a movement with respect to the Candidates for the Further Examination for the Indian Civil Service. It is thought desirable, for the sake of social advantages, that they should resort to a University, and there has been talk of making Professors of Indian History and Indian Law for their benefit, but few Candidates will attend Lectures of a high order. They must, under heavy penalties, pass an Examination in London in certain languages, and portions of Law, History, and Political Economy, from *specified books* every six months; and if they have time to spare they will spend it in learning the additional Oriental languages, which bring them a higher position on the List which governs their Seniority in the Service. What they want, then, is not extra means of information, but some one to see that they know what they are set to learn; this was done by those who prepared them in London, and they will not accept anything less immediately suited to their wants. So we may set up a whole staff of Professors in the University, but if one or two tutors make themselves thoroughly acquainted with the requirements of the Examination, and supply just what is needed, the greater part of the teaching will fall into their hands.

When a system of Examination is *given*, it contains implicitly, rolled up in itself, the system of instruction that belongs to it. The case just mentioned illustrates this truth, for the Examination in question is most precisely laid down, and a corresponding system of instruction has established itself.

No doubt the Candidates will find all they require provided for them at both Universities, whether the teachers be called Professors or not. Many, indeed, have already done so in the course of the last twenty years; and if the number of those who resort to the Universities be increased by the recent regulations, arrangements for their instruction will be more easily made. I have touched on this point in the Preface, p. vi.